Grammar Dimensions

Book One   **Second Edition**

Form, Meaning, and Use

Grammar Dimensions

BOOK ONE   SECOND EDITION

Form, Meaning, and Use

Diane Larsen-Freeman
Series Director

Victoria Badalamenti   Carolyn Henner Stanchina
LaGuardia Community College   Queens College
City University of New York

Listening Activities in this text were developed by the editorial team
at Heinle & Heinle Publishers.

Heinle & Heinle Publishers

I(T)P An International Thomson Publishing Company

Pacific Grove • Albany • Bonn • Boston • Cincinnati • Detroit • London
Madrid • Melbourne • Mexico City • New York • Paris
San Francisco • Tokyo • Toronto • Washington

The publication of *Grammar Dimensions Book One*, Second Edition, was directed by members of the Newbury House ESL/EFL Team at Heinle & Heinle:

Erik Gundersen, Editorial Director
Bruno R. Paul, Market Development Director
Kristin M. Thalheimer, Production Services Coordinator
Nancy Mann Jordan, Developmental Editor
Stanley J. Galek, Vice President and Publisher

Also participating in the publication of this program were:

Project Manager/Desktop Pagination: Thompson Steele Production Services
Production Editor: Maryellen Eschmann Killeen
Manufacturing Coordinator: Mary Beth Hennebury
Associate Editor: Ken Pratt
Associate Market Development Director: Mary Sutton
Photo/Video Specialist: Jonathan Stark
Media Services Coordinator: Jerry Christopher
Interior Designer: Greta Sibley
Illustrators: Lyle Miller and Walter King
Photo Coordinator: Philippe Heckly
Cover Designer: Gina Petti, Rotunda Design
Cover Photo: Rowena Otremba, The Fringe

Heinle & Heinle Publishers is a division of International Thomson Publishing, Inc.

Manufactured in the United States of America

Library of Congress Cataloging-in-Publication Data

Badalamenti, Victoria.
        Grammar dimensions: Form, meaning, and use / Victoria Badalamenti, Carolyn Henner Stanchina; Diane Larsen-Freeman, series director.
            p.   cm.
        Includes index.
        ISBN 0-8384-6582-X
        1. English language—Textbooks for foreign speakers. 2. English language—Grammar—Problems, exercises, etc. I. Henner Stanchina, Carolyn. II. Larsen-Freeman, Diane. III. Title.
        PE 1128, B233   1997
        428.2'4—dc21   96-48584
                                                                              CIP

ISBN 0-8384-6582-X

    10   9   8   7   6   5   4   3

A Special Thanks

The series director, authors, and publisher would like to thank the following individuals who offered many helpful insights and suggestions for change throughout the development of *Grammar Dimensions, Second Edition.*

Jane Berger
Solano Community College, California

Mary Bottega
San Jose State University

Mary Brooks
Eastern Washington University

Christina Broucqsault
California State Polytechnic University

José Carmona
Hudson Community College

Susan Carnell
University of Texas at Arlington

Susana Christie
San Diego State University

Diana Christopher
Georgetown University

Gwendolyn Cooper
Rutgers University

Sue Cozzarelli
EF International, San Diego

Catherine Crystal
Laney College, California

Kevin Cross
University of San Francisco

Julie Damron
Interlink at Valparaiso University, Indiana

Glen Deckert
Eastern Michigan University

Eric Dwyer
University of Texas at Austin

Ann Eubank
Jefferson Community College

Alice Fine
UCLA Extension

Alicia Going
The English Language Study Center, Oregon

Molly Gould
University of Delaware

Maren M. Hargis
San Diego Mesa College

Mary Herbert
University of California, Davis Extension

Jane Hilbert
ELS Language Center, Florida International University

Eli Hinkel
Xavier University

Kathy Hitchcox
International English Institute, Fresno

Joyce Hutchings
Georgetown University

Heather Jeddy
Northern Virginia Community College

Judi Keen
University of California, Davis, and Sacramento City College

Karli Kelber
American Language Institute,
New York University

Anne Kornfeld
LaGuardia Community College

Kay Longmire
Interlink at Valparaiso University, Indiana

Robin Longshaw
Rhode Island School of Design

Bernadette McGlynn
ELS Language Center,
St. Joseph's University

Billy McGowan
Aspect International, Boston

Margaret Mehran
Queens College

Richard Moore
University of Washington

Karen Moreno
Teikyo Post University, Connecticut

Gino Muzzetti
Santa Rosa Junior College, California

Mary Nance-Tager
LaGuardia Community College,
City University of New York

Karen O'Neill
San Jose State University

Mary O'Neal
Northern Virginia Community College

Nancy Pagliara
Northern Virginia Community College

Keith Pharis
Southern Illinois University

Amy Parker
ELS Language Center, San Francisco

Margene Petersen
ELS Language Center, Philadelphia

Nancy Pfingstag
University of North Carolina, Charlotte

Sally Prieto
Grand Rapids Community College

India Plough
Michigan State University

Mostafa Rahbar
University of Tennessee at Knoxville

Dudley Reynolds
Indiana University

Ann Salzman
University of Illinois at Urbana-Champaign

Jennifer Schmidt
San Francisco State University

Cynthia Schuemann
Miami-Dade Community College

Jennifer Schultz
Golden Gate University, California

Mary Beth Selbo
Wright College, City Colleges of Chicago

Stephen Sheeran
Bishop's University, Lenoxville, Quebec

Kathy Sherak
San Francisco State University

Keith Smith
ELS Language Center, San Francisco

Helen Solorzano
Northeastern University

Contents

DIRECT AND INDIRECT OBJECTS,
UNIT 13   ### OBJECT PRONOUNS

187

CAN, KNOW HOW TO,
UNIT 14   ### BE ABLE TO, AND/BUT/SO/OR

205

UNIT 15   ### PRESENT PROGRESSIVE TENSE

219

REFLEXIVE PRONOUNS,
UNIT 19   RECIPROCAL PRONOUN, EACH OTHER

293

UNIT 20   FUTURE TIME
Will and Be Going To; May and Might   303

UNIT 21   PHRASAL VERBS

325

APPENDICES

From the Series Director

To the Teacher

ABOUT THE SERIES

Grammar Dimensions, Second Edition is a comprehensive and dynamic, four-level series designed to introduce English-as-a-second or foreign language students to the form, meaning, and use of English grammatical structures with a communicative orientation. The series has been designed to meet the needs of students from the beginning to advanced levels and includes the following:

- *Grammar Dimensions, Book 1* ....beginning/high beginning
- *Grammar Dimensions, Book 2* ....intermediate
- *Grammar Dimensions, Book 3* ....high intermediate
- *Grammar Dimensions, Book 4* ....advanced

The textbooks are supplemented by workbooks, cassettes, instructor's manuals with tests, and a CD-ROM entitled *Grammar* 3D.

THE STORY OF GRAMMAR DIMENSIONS

Everywhere I went teachers would ask me, "What is the role of grammar in a communicative approach?" These teachers recognized the importance of teaching grammar, but they associated grammar with form and communication with meaning, and thus could not see how the two easily fit together.

Grammar Dimensions was created to help teachers and students appreciate the fact that grammar is not just about form. While grammar does indeed involve form, in order to communicate, language users also need to know what the forms mean and when to use them appropriately. In fact, it is sometimes learning the meaning or appropriate use of a particular grammar structure that represents the greatest long-term learning challenge for students, not learning to form it. For instance, learning when it is appropriate to use the present perfect tense instead of the past tense, or being able to use two-word or phrasal verbs meaningfully represent formidable learning challenges for ESL students.

The three dimensions of form, meaning and use can be depicted in a pie chart with their interrelationship illustrated by the three arrows:

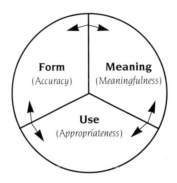

Helping students learn to use grammatical structures accurately, meaningfully, and appropriately is the fundamental goal of *Grammar Dimensions*. It is a goal consistent with the goal of helping students to communicate meaningfully in English, and one that recognizes the undeniable interdependence of grammar and communication.

ABOUT THE BOOKS

The books have been designed to allow teachers to tailor their syllabi for different groups of students. Some teachers have told us that they prefer to teach the units in a different order from that of the book. Teachers should feel free to do so or only to teach part of one unit and then return to do another part at a later time. Since the acquisition process is not a linear one (students do not completely master one structure before moving on to tackle another), teachers can construct syllabi which permit a recycling of material that causes their students difficulty. Of course, some teachers and students would rather use the book more conventionally, as well, by working their way through the units chronologically.

To allow for this possibility, some thought has been given to the sequencing of units within a book. The units have been ordered following different principles depending upon the level of the book. In Book 1, where students are introduced (or reintroduced in the case of false beginners) to basic sentence and subsentence grammatical structures and grammatical forms associated with semantic notions such as time and place, the units have been sequenced following conventional linguistic grading, building from one structure to the next. In Book 2, basic sentence and subsentence grammatical structures are dealt with once again. In addition, Book 2 also introduces language forms that support certain social functions such as making requests and seeking permission. At this level, units that share certain features have been clustered together. No more than three or four units are clustered at one time, however, in order to provide for some variety of focus. Although the four skills are dealt with in all of the books, the listening and speaking skills are especially prominent in Books 1 and 2.

Clustering 2-3 units that address related topics has been done for levels three and four as well. Book 3 deals with grammatical structures that ESL/EFL students often find challenging, such as the use of infinitives and gerunds. It also employs a discourse orientation when dealing with structures such as verb tenses and articles. Students learn how to use grammar structures accurately within contexts above the level of the single sentence. Book 4 deals with grammatical forms that are especially needed for academic and technical writing. It reveals to students the subtleties of certain grammatical structures and how they contribute to cohesion in discourse. Both books highlight the reading and writing skills and target structures for which students at these levels can benefit from special guidance in order to avoid their learning plateauing and their errors fossilizing.

ABOUT THE UNITS

Within a unit, the grammar structure is introduced to students within a communicative orientation. First, students have an opportunity to produce the target grammatical structures in a meaningful opening task. Thus, the grammar is contextualized and students are introduced to its meaning and use prior to any treatment of its form. Next, a series of alternating focus boxes and exercises presents students with the relevant form, meaning, and use facts concerning the target structure and provides practice with each. Finally, communication activities conclude each unit where students can more freely express themselves using the target grammar for communicative purposes. The following elaborates on this format.

Opening Task

In addition to providing a context for the meaningful use of the target grammar structures, the opening task serves several other purposes:

1. The tasks are motivating. Teachers tell us that students find the problem solving enjoyable and somewhat challenging.

2. Moreover, doing the task should activate the knowledge that students do have and help them recognize the need to learn the target structures they have not yet acquired.

3. Students' performance provides teachers with useful diagnostic information about where students' particular learning challenges lie. Thus, teachers can select material within a unit that has the most relevance for their students' learning needs.

Knowing their students' learning challenges helps teachers use their limited time more effectively. For instance, it may be the case that the students already know the target structure, in which case the unit may be skipped. It might also be that only the meaning or use of a particular structure is causing most students difficulty, in which case the focus boxes that deal with form issues can be ignored. Teachers are encouraged to see the book as a resource from which they can select units or parts of units that best meet their students' needs. (See the Instructor's Manual for tips on how to do this.)

Focus Boxes

The facts concerning the target structures are displayed in boxes clearly identified by the dimension(s) they address—form, meaning, or use. Each rule or explanation is preceded by examples. The examples, rules, and explanations are all arrayed in chart form for easy reference. Because the learning challenge presented by the three dimensions of language is not equal for all structures (for instance, some structures present more of a form-based challenge; for others the challenge is learning what the structures mean or when or why to use them), the number and foci of boxes differ from one unit to another.

Exercises

It is important to point out that it is not sufficient for students to know the rules or facts concerning these three dimensions. Thus, in *Grammar Dimensions*, we strive to have students develop the skill of "grammaring"—the ability to use structures accurately, meaningfully, and appropriately. To this end, the exercises are varied, thematically coherent, but purposeful. Often, students are asked to do something personally meaningful (e.g., students might be asked to register some opinion or to explain why they chose the answer that they did).

Activities

Located at the end of each unit, the communicative activities (purple pages) are designed to help students realize the communicative value of the grammar they are learning. As a complement to the meaningful task that opened the unit, grammar and communication are again practiced in tandem. Teachers, or students, may select from the ones offered those that they feel will be most enjoyable and beneficial.

NEW FEATURES IN THE SECOND EDITION

Teachers who have taught with *Grammar Dimensions* will note that the basic philosophy and approach to teaching grammar have not changed from the first edition. We believe they are still sound linguistically and pedagogically, and users of the first edition have confirmed this. However, our series users have also requested several new features, and modifications of others, and we have carefully woven these into this second edition:

1. One new feature that series users will notice is the incorporation of listening. Each unit has at least one activity in which students are asked to listen to a taped segment and respond in some way that involves the target structures.

2. A second new feature is the inclusion of a quiz after every unit to help teachers assess what students have learned from the unit. These 15-minute quizzes are available for duplication from the Instructor's Manuals.

3. Another change we have implemented is to streamline the grammar explanations and make them more user-friendly. You will notice that grammar terms are consistently labeled in the most straightforward and common manner. Also, note that, in each focus box, examples are consistently outlined on the left and explanations on the right to enhance clarity.

4. In response to user feedback, we have limited the texts to 25 units each. As was mentioned above, the material is meant to be used selectively, not comprehensively; still, some users preferred that the books have fewer units to begin with, and we agree that a reduced scope of grammatical topics in each book will help both teachers and students focus more successfully on their greatest learning challenges.

5. To honor the multiplicity of learning styles in the classroom and to capitalize on the dynamism of emerging technologies, we have developed a CD-ROM component called *Grammar* 3D to complement the *Grammar Dimensions* print materials. A wealth of exciting exercises and activities in *Grammar* 3D review and expand upon the lessons presented in the textbooks.

In all these ways, it is our hope that this series will provide teachers with the means to create, along with their students, learning opportunities that are tailored to students' needs, are enjoyable, and will maximize everyone's learning.

Diane Larsen-Freeman
School for International Training

OTHER COMPONENTS

In addition to the student text, each level of *Grammar Dimensions* includes the following components:

Audio Cassette

The audio cassette contains the listenings from the communicative activities (purple pages) in the student text.

An icon 🎧 indicates which activities use the audio cassette.

Workbook

The Workbook provides additional exercises for each grammar point presented in the student text. Many of the workbook exercises are specially designed to help students prepare for the TOEFL® (Test of English as a Foreign Language).

Instructor's Manual

The Instructor's Manual contains:

- an introduction to philosophical background of the series
- general teaching guidelines
- unit-by-unit teaching notes
- student text answer key
- workbook answer key
- tapescript
- tests for each unit
- test answer key

CD-ROM

Grammar 3D is an ideal supplement to *Grammar Dimensions*. It provides comprehensive instruction and practice in 34 of the key grammar structures found in the text series.

Grammar 3D is appropriate for high-beginning to advanced students, and allows students to progress at their own pace. Students can access each grammar category at 3 or 4 levels of difficulty. They can then move to a lower level if they need basic review, or to a higher level for additional challenge.

An instructional "help page" allows students to access grammar explanations before they begin an exercise, or at any place within an exercise. Instruction is also provided through feedback that helps students understand their errors and guides them toward correct answers.

An icon indicates which focus boxes are supported by exercises in *Grammar* 3D.

To the Student

All grammar structures have a form, a meaning, and a use. We can show this with a pie chart:

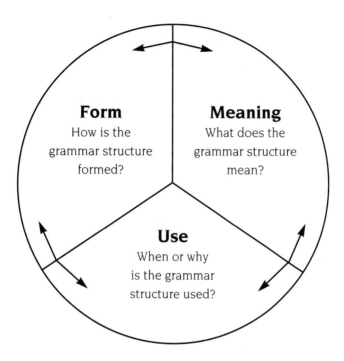

Often you will find that you know the answer to one or more of these questions, but not to all of them, for a particular grammar structure. This book has been written to help you learn answers to these questions for the major grammar structures of English. More importantly, it gives you practice with the answers so that you can develop your ability to use English grammar structures accurately, meaningfully, and appropriately.

At the beginning of each unit, you will be asked to work on an opening task. The task will introduce you to the grammar structures to be studied in the unit. However, it is not important at this point that you think about grammar. You should just do the task as well as you can.

In the next section of the unit are focus boxes and exercises. You will see that the boxes are labeled with FORM, MEANING, USE, or a combination of these, corresponding to the three parts of the pie chart. In each focus box is information that answers one or more of the questions in the pie. Along with the focus box are exercises that should help you put into practice what you have studied.

The last section of each unit contains communicative activities. Hopefully, you will enjoy doing these and at the same time receive further practice using the grammar structures in meaningful ways.

By working on the opening task, studying the focus boxes, doing the exercises, and engaging in the activities, you will develop greater knowledge of English grammar and skill in using it. I also believe you will enjoy the learning experience along the way.

Diane Larsen-Freeman
School for International Training

Acknowledgments

Series Director Acknowledgments

This edition would not have come about if it had not been for the enthusiastic response of teachers and students using the first edition. I am very grateful for the reception *Grammar Dimensions* has been given. By the same token, I want to give special thanks to those users who accepted our invitation to let us know how to better meet their needs with this second edition.

I am grateful for all the authors' efforts as well. To be a teacher, and at the same time a writer, is a difficult balance to achieve. So is being an innovative creator of materials, and yet, a team player. They have met these challenges exceedingly well in my opinion.

Then, too, the Heinle & Heinle team has been impressive. I am grateful for the leadership exercised first by Dave Lee, and later by Erik Gundersen. I also appreciate all the support from Ken Mattsson, Ken Pratt, Kristin Thalheimer, John McHugh, Bruno Paul, and Mary Sutton. Deserving special mention are Jean Bernard Johnston, and above all, Nancy Jordan, who never lost the vision while they attended to the detail with good humor and professionalism.

I have also benefited from the counsel of Marianne Celce-Murcia, consultant for this project, and my friend.

Finally, I wish to thank my family members, Elliott, Brent, and Gavin, for not once asking the (negative yes-no) question that must have occurred to them countless times: "Haven't you finished yet?"

Author Acknowledgments

This book is dedicated to Joel, Melanie, and Michele, who stood steadfastly by, tolerating all the moods and missed moments, as we reeled through this revision process. Their stamina was a great source of strength. This book also stands as an affirmation of the power of friendship.

We are deeply grateful to Diane Larsen-Freeman for her patient guidance and supportive ear.

We wish to extend our sincere thanks to the women at Thompson Steele Production Services, especially Marcia Croyle who, in the crunch, gave so generously of her time.

We also wish to thank both our ESL students at the City University of New York, and our Methods students at Queens College and The New School For Social Research, for their insights.

Finally, we credit Nancy Mann Jordan for her personal vision and uncompromising efforts in bringing this project to fruition.

UNIT

1

The Verb Be
Affirmative Statements, Subject Pronouns

Introductions

STEP ❶ Match the introductions to the pictures.

a. **4**

3 b.

c. **2**

d. **1**

1. "Hello. My name is Monique. I'm French. I'm from Paris."

2. "I'm Chen. I'm Chinese. I'm from Beijing."

3. "I'm Fernando and this is Isabel. We are married. We are Colombian. We're from Bogota."

4. "Hi. I'm Genya. I'm Russian. I'm from Moscow."

STEP ❷ Look at Monique's information card. Then complete the information card about yourself. Introduce yourself to the class.

Information Card

Name: *Monique Delande*
Country: *France*
City: *Paris*
Nationality: *French*
Age: *28 years old*
Married/Divorced/Single: *single*

Information Card

Name: *Julio Cesar Carrillo*
Country: *Guadalaja Jal.*
City: *Vancuber*
Nationality: *Mexicano*
Age: *23*
Married/Divorced/Single: *Single*

My name is *Julio* .

I am from *Mexico* .

I'm *live in vancouver*

I'm *29* years old:

I'm *Sigle* .

Be: Affirmative Statements

SUBJECT	VERB Be		
Monique She Paris	is	single. from Paris. in France.	singular
Fernando and Isabel They	are	Colombian. married.	plural

EXERCISE 1

Go back to the Opening Task on page 1. Underline all the singular subjects (one) and the verb *be*. Circle all plural subjects (more than one) and the verb *be*.

EXAMPLE: <u>My name is</u> Monique.

(We are) married.

EXERCISE 2

Fill in the blanks with the verb *be* or a name.

1. Genya _is_____ from Russia.

2. Isabel ____ _IS_____ twenty-four years old.

3. ~~They~~ ~~Are~~ ____ is from the People's Republic of China.

4. Monique _____ _IS_____ twenty-eight years old.

5. ~~They~~ ~~ارe we~~ are married.

6. Chen _____ _IS_____ twenty-five years old.

7. Genya _____ _IS_____ divorced.

8. Fernando and Isabel _____ _Are_____ Colombian.

9. Monique _____ _IS_____ from France.

10. Moscow _____ _IS_____ in Russia.

Fill in the blanks with *is* or *are* and the continents or regions.

Continents/Regions

Europe	Africa	The Caribbean
Central America	North America	South America
Asia	The Middle East	

1. Japan _is_____ in _Asia_____ .

2. The Dominican Republic _the Caribe_____ in _Centio Auesica_ .

3. Senegal and Nigeria _Euloca_____ in _Asia_____ .

4. Honduras and El Salvador _Norte. Amsia_ in _____ .

5. Peru and Ecuador _Euioca_____ in _Asia_____ .

6. Bangladesh _____ in _____ .

7. Israel _Themede_____ in _Cemtro Amfica_ .

8. Canada _Norte America_ in _South Ams_____ .

9. Italy and Greece _____ in _____ .

Now write two sentences of your own.

10. _____

11. _____

Subject Pronouns with Be

SUBJECT PRONOUN	VERB Be	
I	am	single.
You	are	married.
He She It	is	Brazilian.
We You They	are	from Korea.

Note: Use subject pronouns only after you know the subject.
Chen is Chinese. He is from Beijing.

EXERCISE 4

Read the dialogues. Fill in the blanks with a subject pronoun.

EXAMPLE: _We_ are from the Dominican Republic.

1. A: We are from Wellington.

   B: ___We___ are from
   New Zealand. How interesting!

2. A: He is Finnish.

   B: Yes, ___He___ is from
   Helsinki.

3. A: They are from Argentina.

   B: I know. _They_ are students in our class.

4. A: _She_ is from Berlin.

   B: Oh, she is German.

5. A: _We_ are Nigerian.

   B: You are far from home!

6. A: _I_ am from Florence.

   B: Oh, you are Italian.

EXERCISE 5

The subject pronouns in the sentences below are not correct. Circle the incorrect pronouns and write the correct sentences in the blanks.

1. Miyuki and Seung are from Asia. (You) are Asian. _They are Asian._

2. John is thirty years old. She is from Cyprus. _____

3. You and Hamid are Algerian. They are from Algiers. _____

4. Port-au-Prince is in Haiti. She is the capital city. _____

5. Clemente and I are from Rome. They are Italian. _____

6. Pedro and Miguel are from Puebla. You are Mexican. _____

7. Ayelet and Amir are from Tel Aviv. We are Israeli. _____

Information Gap. Here are two lists of students in an English-as-a-Second-Language (ESL) class. Work with a partner. You look at List A and make a statement about student number 1 on your list. Your partner looks at List B on the next page and makes a second statement about student number 1 with a subject pronoun.

EXAMPLE: You say: Mario is from Ecuador.

Your partner says: He is Ecuadoran.

List A

Men	Country	Nationality
1. Mario	Ecuador	
2. Mohammed		Moroccan
3. Hideki and Yoshi	Japan	
4. Leonardo		Dominican
5. Oumar	Senegal	
Women		
6. Lilik		Indonesian
7. Krystyna	Poland	
8. Liisa and Katja		Finnish
9. Belen	Spain	
10. Margarita and Dalia		Brazilian

List B

Men	Country	Nationality
1. Mario		Ecuadoran
2. Mohammed	Morocco	
3. Hideki and Yoshi		Japanese
4. Leonardo	The Dominican Republic	
5. Oumar		Senegalese
Women		
6. Lilik	Indonesia	
7. Krystyna		Polish
8. Liisa and Katja	Finland	
9. Belen		Spanish
10. Margarita and Dalia	Brazil	

EXERCISE 7

Make ten summary statements about the students in the ESL class in Exercise 6. Use the continents/regions.

EXAMPLES: Africa

Two students are from Africa. One is from Morocco and one is from Senegal.

1. Africa

_____

2. Asia

_____

3. Europe

_____

4. Central America

_____

5. South America

_____

FOCUS 3 ▷▷▷▷▷▷▷▷▷▷▷▷▷▷▷▷▷▷▷▷▷▷ FORM

Contraction with *Be*

SUBJECT PRONOUN + *Be*		*Be* CONTRACTIONS	
I am		I'm	
You are		You're	
He is		He's	
She is	American.	She's	from the United States
It is		It's	
We are		We're	
You are		You're	
They are		They're	

EXERCISE 8

Think about the people and places in this unit. Match the people and places on the left with a letter on the right. Make two statements aloud. Use the name in the first statement and the subject pronoun and *Be* contraction in the second statement.

EXAMPLE: Genya is Russian. She's divorced.

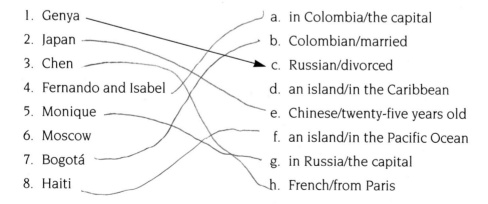

1. Genya
2. Japan
3. Chen
4. Fernando and Isabel
5. Monique
6. Moscow
7. Bogotá
8. Haiti

a. in Colombia/the capital
b. Colombian/married
c. Russian/divorced
d. an island/in the Caribbean
e. Chinese/twenty-five years old
f. an island/in the Pacific Ocean
g. in Russia/the capital
h. French/from Paris

Draw a line from the famous people on the left to the country they come from on the right. Fill in the nationality column on the right. Then tell the class what you know about the people.

EXAMPLE: Madonna is from the United States. She's American.

She's a pop music star.

Famous People	Country	Nationality
1. Madonna	France	1. _American_
2. Sophia Loren	South Africa	2. _____
3. Arnold Schwarzenegger	The United States	3. _____
4. The Rolling Stones	Great Britain	4. _____
5. Steffi Graff	Austria	5. _____
6. Michael Jordan	Germany	6. _____
7. Luciano Pavarotti	Brazil	7. _____
8. Catherine Deneuve	Italy	8. _____
9. Pele		9. _____
10. Nelson Mandela		10. _____

Introductions and Greetings

Introductions

EXAMPLES		EXPLANATIONS
(a) Hello. My name's Mario Ortiz. I'm from the Philippines		
(b) Hi! I'm Jennifer Brown. I'm from Florida. Please call me Jenny.		Introducing yourself
(c) Susan: Hello, John. This is Mario Ortiz. He's from the Philippines. John: Hi, Mario. Nice to meet you. Mario: Nice to meet you too, John.		Introducing another person
(d) Jeff: Hi, my name is Jeff Jones. I'm from California. What is your name? Alicia: Alicia Torres. Jeff: Where are you from, Alicia? Alicia: I'm from Chile. Jeff: Oh, really? Nice to meet you.		Meeting someone for the first time

Greetings

EXAMPLES	EXPLANATIONS
(e) Ms. Chen: Good morning, Mr. Brown. Mr. Brown: Good morning, Ms. Chen. How are you today? Ms. Chen: I'm fine, thank you. How are you? **(f)** Bill: Hello, Lautaro. How's everything? Lautaro: Fine thanks, Bill. And how are you? **(g)** Jake: Hi, Yoshi. How are you doing? Yoshi: O.K., Jake. How about you? Jake: Not bad.	Greetings can be formal or informal (very friendly). Formal ↑ ↓ Informal
(h) Hello, Ms. Smith. **(i)** NOT: Hello, Ms. Susan Smith. Hello, Ms. Susan.	Use a title (*Mr.*, *Ms.*, *Ms.*, *Dr.*, *Professor*) with a family name (last name), not with the full name, not with the first name.

EXERCISE 10

Introduce the person next to you to the class.

EXAMPLE: This is Yoshi. He's from Japan.

Fill in the blanks in the conversation.

EXAMPLE: Susan: I'm Susan Wilson from New York.

Jim: <u>Nice to meet you,</u> Susan. <u>My name is</u> Jim. <u>I'm</u> from California.

1. **Fred:** Hello. I'm Fred.

   Phillippe: <u>Luis</u>, Fred. <u>Jesss</u> Phillippe.

2. **Lilik:** Hi! I'm Lilik. _____?

   Demos: My name's Demos.

   Lilik: _____?

   Demos: Greece. _____?

   Lilik: I'm from Indonesia.

3. **Michael:** Hi, Gregg. _____ Jane.

   Gregg: Hello, Jane. _____?

   Jane: Fine, thanks. _____?

   Gregg: Great!

Activities

Make a list of all the students in your class. Make a list of the countries they come from and their nationalities.

Names	Countries	Nationalities
_____	_____	_____
_____	_____	_____
_____	_____	_____
_____	_____	_____
_____	_____	_____

ACTIVITY 2

Write summary statements about the students in your class with the information from Activity 1.

EXAMPLE: Two students are Colombian.

Six students are from Asia.

ACTIVITY 3

On a piece of paper write three sentences about yourself. Do not write your name on the paper. Give the paper to your teacher. Your teacher reads each paper and the class guesses who the person is.

EXAMPLE: I am twenty-two years old. I'm from North Africa. I'm Algerian.

ACTIVITY 4

Work with a partner. Write information about yourself on a piece of paper. Exchange papers with your partner. Introduce your partner to the class.

EXAMPLE: This is Maria Gomez. She is from Mexico City. She is twenty-five years old. She is married.

ACTIVITY 5

Role-play with a partner.

1. You are a student and you greet your professor in school.

2. You greet your classmate.

ACTIVITY 6

Listen and decide. Three different people greet Mr. Maxwell Forbes, a bank manager, at a job interview. In two of the conversations, the greetings are wrong. Who gets the job? Circle the person who gets the job.

1. Mr. Blake   2. Ms. Robbins   3. Kevin Dobbs

The Verb Be

Yes/No Questions, Be + Adjective, Negative Statements

Asking Personal Questions

Here are some advertisements from the newspaper. Match the questions below to the correct advertisers on the next page.

A. Are you single? Are you lonely? Are you ready to meet someone?
Call 1-800-555-LOVE

B. Is English hard for you? Are verbs difficult? Are you unhappy about your pronunciation?
Enroll now! Call 555-4433

C. Are you sad? Are you nervous? Are you worried?
Call 555-HELP

D. Are you overweight? Are you out of shape? Is your body weak? Call now! 555-SLIM

Dr. Friend, Psychiatrist <u>C</u>

The Lonely Hearts Dating Service <u>A</u>

New Body Health Club <u>D</u>

The Cool School of English <u>B</u>

Be: Yes/No Questions and Short Answers

YES/NO QUESTIONS		SHORT ANSWERS		
		AFFIRMATIVE	**NEGATIVE**	**CONTRACTIONS**
(a) Am I overweight?		you are.		you aren't. you're not.
(b) Are you nervous?		I am.		I'm not.
(c) Is he/she lonely?		he/she is.		he/she isn't. he's/she's not.
(d) Is English difficult?	Yes,	it is.	No,	it isn't. it's not.
(e) Are we out of shape?		you are.		you aren't. you're not.
(f) Are you single?		we are.		we aren't. we're not.
(g) Are verbs difficult?		they are.		they aren't. they're not.

EXERCISE 1

Ask your partner *yes/no* questions from the Opening Task on pages 15–16. Use short answers and contractions.

EXAMPLE: You: Are you single?

Your Partner: Yes, I am. OR No, I'm not.

EXERCISE 2

Read the conversations. Fill in the blanks with *yes/no* questions or short answers.

1. **A:** Hello, this is the New Body Health Club.

   B: Hello, _____ Ar ͨ _____ you open on Sunday?

The Verb Be   **17**

A: Yes, _They_ _and_. We're open from seven in the morning until ten at night.

2. **Mitch:** Hello, my name is Mitch Brown. _Are_ you Karen Jones?

   Karen: Yes, _nice too me yous_.

   Mitch: I got your telephone number from the Lonely Hearts Dating Service. How are you, Karen?

   Karen: Fine, thanks. And you?

   Mitch: Not bad, thanks. _____ _____ free tonight?

   Karen: No, I'm sorry, _____ _____. How about tomorrow?

   Mitch: Great!

3. **A:** Hello, is this Dr. Friend's office?

   B: Yes, _____ _____.

   A: _____ Dr. Friend busy? I need to speak to him.

   B: Just a minute, please.

4. **Secretary:** Cool School of English. May I help you?

   Hui Chen: Yes, I'd like some information about your classes, please.

   Secretary: Of course.

   Hui Chen: _____ the classes big?

   Secretary: No, _____ _____. We have only ten people in a class.

   Hui Chen: _____ the teachers good?

   Secretary: Yes, _____ _____. All the teachers are excellent.

   Hui Chen: _____ the tuition expensive?

   Secretary: No, _____ _____. It's only $800 for ten weeks.

   Hui Chen: O.K. Thank you very much.

   Secretary: You're welcome. Goodbye.

FOCUS 2 ≫≫≫≫≫≫≫≫≫≫≫≫≫≫≫≫≫≫≫ **FORM**

Be + Adjective

EXAMPLES	EXPLANATIONS
(a) Dr. Friend is **busy.** **(b)** The health club is **open.** **(c)** Verbs are **difficult.**	An adjective describes a person, place, or thing. Adjectives can come after the verb *be*.
(d) They are **excellent.** **(e)** NOT: They are excellents.	Do not put "s" on the adjective when the subject is plural (more than one).
(f) The classes are **very good.**	*Very* makes the adjective stronger. *Very* comes before an adjective.

EXERCISE 3

Go back to the Opening Task on page 15 and circle all the adjectives.

EXAMPLE: Are you (single)? Are you (lonely)?

EXERCISE 4

Work with a partner. Ask your partner questions about the pictures. Use the adjectives in parentheses. Your partner finds the opposites of each adjective from the box at the bottom of the next page and answers your questions.

Is he young?
No, he isn't.
He's old.

Example: (young)

1. (sad)

2. (weak)

3. (thin)

4. (rich)

5. (neat)

6. (short)

7. (serious)

8. (calm)

9. (healthy)

10. (energetic)

Opposites

funny	sick	lazy	happy	poor	nervous
old	strong	overweight	tall	messy	

Mark Heller is single and lonely. He wants a girlfriend. He puts this advertisement in the newspaper. Fill in the blanks with *am* or *are*. Use contractions where possible.

1) <u>I'm</u> 28 years old. (2) I _____ 6'2" tall. (3) I _____ single. (4) I _____ handsome and athletic. (5) I _____ romantic. (6) I _____ (negative) shy. (7) _____ you under 30? (8) _____ you tall? (9) _____ you outgoing? (10) _____ you ready for marriage? Then call me: (718) 555-7954.

Information gap. Three women answer Mark's advertisement. Work with a partner. You look at Chart A and your partner looks at Chart B on page E-1. Ask each other *yes/no* questions to find the information that you do not have in your chart. Then put a check in the correct place.

EXAMPLE: You: Is Shelley tall?

Your Partner: No, she isn't.

You: Is she average height?

Your Partner: Yes, she is.

Chart A

Name: Age:	Cindy 22	Shelley 27	Gloria 30
1. Height tall			
average height			✔
short	✔		
2. Weight thin			
average weight			✔
overweight		✔	

3. Personality	Cindy	Shelley	Gloria
shy			
friendly	✔		✔
quiet			
talkative	✔		✔
neat			
messy	✔		
funny	✔		
serious			
nervous	✔		
calm			✔

EXERCISE 7

Ask a partner questions with the adjectives below.

young	funny	tall	strong	serious	healthy
energetic	calm	neat	lazy	messy	rich

EXAMPLE: You: Are you tall?

Your Partner: Yes, I am. OR No, I'm not.

EXERCISE 8

Write five statements about what you **like** about your partner.

EXAMPLE: My partner is funny. He's energetic.

_____

_____

_____

_____

_____

FOCUS 3

Be: Negative Statements and Contractions

NEGATIVE STATEMENT	CONTRACTION OF SUBJECT + Be	CONTRACTION OF Be + NOT
I am not shy.	I'm not shy.	*
You are not old.	You're not old.	You aren't old.
He She It } is not ready.	He's She's It's } not ready.	He She It } isn't ready.
We You They } are not nervous.	We're You 're They're } not nervous.	We You They } aren't nervous.

Note: The contraction of *be* followed by *not* (*he's not*) makes a negative statement stronger than a negative contraction (*he isn't*).

Read the statements below each ID (Identification) card. If the information is correct, say "That's right." If the information is not correct, make a negative statement with a *be* contraction + *not* and a correct affirmative statement.

EXAMPLE: 1. His last name is Yu-ho.

His last name's not Yu-ho.

It's Oh.

Last Name:	*Oh*
First Name:	*Yu-ho*
Country:	*Taiwan*
Nationality:	*Taiwanese*
Age:	23
Marital Status:	*single*

1. His last name is Yu-ho.
2. He is Korean.
3. He's twenty-five.
4. He's single.

Last Name:	*Ryperman*
First Name:	*Aline*
Country:	*Holland*
Nationality:	*Dutch*
Age:	32
Marital Status:	*married*

5. Her first name is Alice.
6. She is Dutch.
7. She's from Germany.
8. She's fifty-two.

Last Name:	*Mafegna*
First Name:	*Abiy*
Country:	*Ethiopia*
Nationality:	*Ethiopian*
Age:	30
Marital Status:	*single*

9. His first name is Mafegna.
10. He's Indian.
11. He's thirty.
12. He's married.

Last Name:	*Shram*
First Name:	*Jehad*
Country:	*Lebanon*
Nationality:	*Lebanese*
Age:	27
Marital Status:	*single*

13. Jehad is Jordanian.
14. He is twenty-nine.
15. He's single.

Complete each dialogue with an affirmative or a negative statement and an adjective from the list below.

Adjectives:					
delicious	smart	ugly	beautiful	selfish	mean

1. **Ann:** I'm short. I (a) _____ fat.
   I (b) _____ ugly.

   Marilyn: No, you (c) _____ .
   You (d) _____ , Ann!

2. **Woman:** This dinner is terrible! I'm sorry.

   Guest: No, it (a) _____ .
   It's (b) _____ !

3. **Mike:** I (a) _____ nervous about this test. I (b) _____ stupid, Sam!

   Sam: No, you (c) _____ , Mike.
   You (d) _____ ! Your average is 98!

4. **Sally:** You know Jill, I'm in love with Jack. He (a) _____ kind and generous.

   Jill: Kind and generous??? No, he (b) _____ .

   He (c) _____ .

5. **Salesperson:** That dress is perfect on you.

   Customer: Perfect? Oh no, it (a) _____ .
   It (b) _____ .

Activities

Work with a partner. Make true statements with the subjects and adjectives below. Use the affirmative or negative form of the verb *be*. The pair with the most correct sentences wins.

EXAMPLE: The President is not tall.

Subject	Be	Adjective
My country		happy
I		single
My classmate		tall
The President		delicious
The United States		old
My friends		beautiful
My father		smart
English		big
Roses		important
		expensive

STEP ❶ Check all the adjectives that describe you.

Adjective	Column A: You	Column B: Your Partner
shy		
quiet		
talkative		
romantic		
practical		
athletic		
lazy		
healthy		
funny		
friendly		
messy		
serious		

STEP ❷ Ask your partner *yes/no* questions with the adjectives in the box. Check the adjectives in Column B.

> **EXAMPLE: You ask:** Are you shy?
>
> **Your partner answers:** Yes, I am. OR No, I'm not.

STEP ❸ Write three ways you and your partner are similar and three ways you are different.

> **EXAMPLE:** Similar   Different
>
> 1. _We are athletic._   1. _My partner is romantic_
>   _I'm practical._
>
> 2. _We are healthy._   2. _He's serious. I'm funny._
>
> _____   _____
>
> _____   _____
>
> _____   _____

ACTIVITY 3

Write your own personal advertisement for the newspaper or write one for a friend who is single.

> **EXAMPLE:** My name is (1) _____.
>
> I'm (2) _____ (nationality).
>
> I'm (3) _____ years old.
>
> I'm (4) _____ (adjective).
>
> I'm (5) _____ (adjective).
>
> And I'm (6) _____ (adjective).
>
> Are you (7) _____ (adjective)?
>
> Are you (8) _____ (adjective)?
>
> PLEASE CALL ME!

ACTIVITY 4

Look at your answers to Exercise 6. Who is the best woman for Mark? Discuss your answers.

ACTIVITY 5

STEP ❶ Consuela is at the Cool School of English to register for classes. Listen to the conversation and look at the questions below. Check Yes or No.

	Yes	No
1. Is Consuela a new student?		
2. Is Consuela an intermediate-level student?		
3. Is Consuela interested in morning classes?		

STEP ❷ With a partner, ask and answer the questions. If the answer is no, make a true statement.

STEP ❸ Role-play the conversation.

The Verb Be
Wh-Question Words, Prepositions of Location

Test Your World Knowledge

STEP ❶ Match the questions with the answers.

Questions

1. What's the Amazon?

2. Where is the Kremlin?

3. Who is the head of the
   Catholic Church?

4. How is the weather in Argentina in
   June?

5. Where are the Himalayas?

6. When is Thanksgiving in the United
   States?

7. It's 9 A.M.* in California. What time
   is it in New York?

8. How old are the Pyramids in Egypt?

9. What are the names of the seven
   continents?

10. Why is July 4th special in the
    United States?

Answers

a. the Pope

b. It's a river.

c. It's 12:00 noon.

d. about 4,700 years old

e. in Moscow

f. It's cold.

g. North America, South America,
   Africa, Asia, Australia, Europe, and
   Antarctica

h. because it is Independence Day

i. the last Thursday in November

j. in India, Nepal, and Tibet

*A.M.: in the morning

STEP ❷ Make up two questions of your own. Ask your classmates the questions.

Wh-Question Words with Be

Wh-question words are: *what, where, who, when, how, what time, how old,* and *why.*
Use Wh-question words to ask for specific information.

QUESTION WORD	Be	SUBJECT	ANSWER	MEANING
What	is 's	the Amazon?	a river	THING
Where	are	the Himalayas?	in India, Nepal, or Tibet	PLACE
Who	is 's	the head of the Catholic Church?	the Pope	PEOPLE
How	is 's	the weather in Argentina in June?	It's cold.	CONDITIONS
When	is 's	Thanksgiving in the United States?	the last Thursday in November	TIME
What time	is	it in New York?	It's 12:00.	TIME ON A CLOCK
How old	are	the Pyramids in Egypt?	about 4,700 years old	AGE
Why	is 's	July 4th special in the United States?	because it is Independence Day	REASON

56-11-77 95 56

2   35

Fill in the blanks with one of these *wh*-question words: *what, where, how, how old, what time,* and *why.*

Questions   **Answers**

1. __How old_____ is the Great   about 2,200 years old
   Wall of China?

2. _____ are the   Victoria Badalamenti and
   authors of *Grammar Dimensions,*   Carolyn Henner Stanchina.
   Book I?

3. _____ is Morocco?   in Africa

4. _____ is the weather   It's hot.
   in the summer in Washington,
   D.C.?

5. _____ is the capital   Brussels.
   of Belgium?

6. _____ is the first day   June 21st.
   of summer?

7. It's 10 A.M.* in Boston.   It's 4:00 P.M.*
   _____ is it in Paris?

8. _____ is Indepen-   July 14th.
   dence Day in France?

9. _____ are you in   to learn English
   this class?

10. _____ are the Nile   rivers
    and the Mississippi?

*A.M. = morning
*P.M. = afternoon, evening, night

Match the question in Column A to the answer in Column B. Write the letter in the blank on the left.

	Column A	**Column B**
_d_	1. What's your name?	a. October 17th.
_____	2. Where are you from?	b. I'm Turkish.
_____	3. Where is Istanbul?	c. To study English.
_____	4. What's your nationality?	d. Mehmet.
_____	5. How old are you?	e. It's in Turkey.
_____	6. When's your birthday?	f. Twenty-five.
_____	7. Why are you here?	g. Fine, thanks.
_____	8. How are you?	h. Istanbul.

Write questions with *wh*-question words for these answers.

1. _What time is it?_ _____?

It's 10:15 right now.

2. _____?

It's Monday.

3. _____?

My name is Berta.

4. _____?

I'm twenty-five years old.

5. _____?

My birthday is July 15th.

6. _____?

I'm Mexican.

7. _____?

My hometown is Mexico City.

8. _____?

My family is in Mexico City.

9. _____?

The weather in Mexico City is hot.

10. _____?

I am here to study English.

Work with a partner. Ask your partner the same questions for Exercise 2 above.

EXERCISE 4

Write five questions about students in the class with the question word *Who*. Then ask your partner the questions.

EXAMPLE: Who is from Asia?

Who is twenty-five years old?

Who is tall?

FOCUS 2 >>>>>>>>>>>>>>>>>>>>>>>>> USE

How to Ask Questions about English

When you need to ask about a word in English, you say:

(a) **What** is the meaning of *crowded*?

(b) **What** is the spelling of *crowded*?

(c) **What** is the pronunciation of *c-r-o-w-d-e-d*?

EXERCISE 5

Read the paragraph below about Vancouver. Underline the words you don't know or can't pronounce. Ask your teacher or classmates questions.

EXAMPLE: What is the meaning of <u>crowded</u>?

Vancouver is a city in Canada. It's on the Pacific coast. The city is magnificent. It is clean and open. It isn't <u>crowded</u>. Almost three-quarters of the population are of British ancestry. Other ethnic groups are the Chinese, French, Japanese, and East Indians. As a result, the food in Vancouver is varied and delicious. It is a wonderful place for a vacation.

Using It to Talk about the Weather

QUESTIONS	ANSWERS		
	It's sunny **It's** hot		summer.
How's the weather in New York?	**It's** cold **It's** snowy	in the	winter.
	It's cloudy **It's** rainy		spring.
	It's windy **It's** cool		fall.
What's the temperature today?	**It's** 77 degrees Fahrenheit/25 degrees Celsius.		

Work with a partner. You look at Map A and your partner looks at Map B (on page E-2). You have some information about the weather in the different cities in Map A. Your partner has other information in Map B. Ask each other questions to find out the missing information.

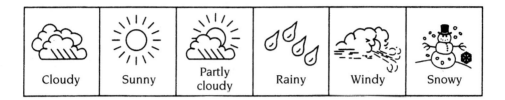

| Cloudy | Sunny | Partly cloudy | Rainy | Windy | Snowy |

MAP A

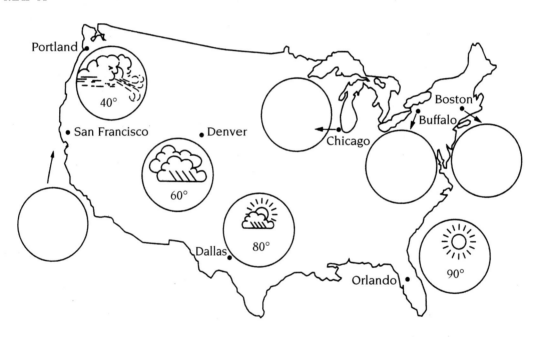

EXAMPLE: **You:** How's the weather in San Francisco today?

Your Partner: It's sunny.

You: What's the temperature?

Your Partner: It's 65 degrees.

Using *It* to Talk about Time

WHAT TIME IS IT?

3:00	**It's** three o'clock. **It's** three.	
3:05	**It's** five after three.	
3:15	**It's** three-fifteen. **It's** a quarter past three. **It's** a quarter after three.	
3:30	**It's** three-thirty. **It's** half past three.	
3:45	**It's** three forty-five. **It's** a quarter to four.	

3:50   **It's** three-fifty.
              It's ten to four.

12:00   **It's** twelve o'clock.
              It's noon.
              It's midnight.

EXERCISE 7

Work with a partner. You say the time one way. Your partner says the time a different way.

EXAMPLE: 6:30

It's six thirty.

It's half past six.

1. 8:15	2. 5:20	3. 7:35	4. 9:45	5. 11:30
6. 1:55	7. 3:10	8. 2:40	9. 4:10	

Look at the map of the time zones in the United States. Ask and answer the questions.

1. It's 7:00 A.M. in San Francisco. What time is it in New York? _____.

2. It's 10:45 P.M. in Miami. What time is it in Salt Lake City? _____.

3. It's 6:50 P.M. in Minneapolis. What time is it in New Orleans? _____.

4. It's 10:30 P.M. in Santa Fe. What time is it in Chicago? _____.

5. It's 2:15 A.M. in Los Angeles. What time is it in Boston? _____.

6. It's 9:10 A.M. in Dallas. What time is it in Portland? _____.

7. It's 10:20 A.M. in Atlanta. What time is it in Denver? _____.

8. It's 10:05 A.M. in Seattle. What time is it in Atlanta? _____.

Now make five questions of your own for your partner to answer.

Prepositions of Location

Prepositions of location tell where something is.

COMMON PREPOSITIONS OF LOCATION

The ball is **in** the box.	The ball is **on** the box.	The ball is **above** the box.
The ball is **next to** the box.	The ball is **in back of** the box.	The ball is **under** the box.
The ball is **near** the box. It isn't next to the box.	The ball is **behind** the box.	The ball is **opposite** the box.
The ball is **between** the two boxes.	The ball is **in front of** the box.	

SUBJECT +	Be +	PREPOSITIONAL PHRASE (PREPOSITION + NOUN)
Prague	is	**in** the Czech Republic.
It	's	**on** the Vultava River.
The hotel	is	**near** the Vultava River.

Sally and her family are in Prague, in the Czech Republic. Read the postcard and circle the prepositions of location.

Hi everybody. Here we are in Prague, the capital city of the Czech Republic. It is a beautiful city in Central Europe. I am between Ken and Jirka, our Czech friend. In this photo, we are at a cafe next to the Charles Bridge. Michele is behind me—she's camera shy! And right opposite the cafe is a souvenir shop. Prague is very popular in the summer. Many tourists come here to visit. The couple next to us is from Italy. They love Prague too!

Information Gap. You cannot find items 1–6 in Picture A. Your partner cannot find items 7–12 in Picture B on page E-3. Ask each other questions with *where*.

EXAMPLE: **Student A asks:** Where are my slippers?

Student B says: They're under the sofa.

PICTURE A

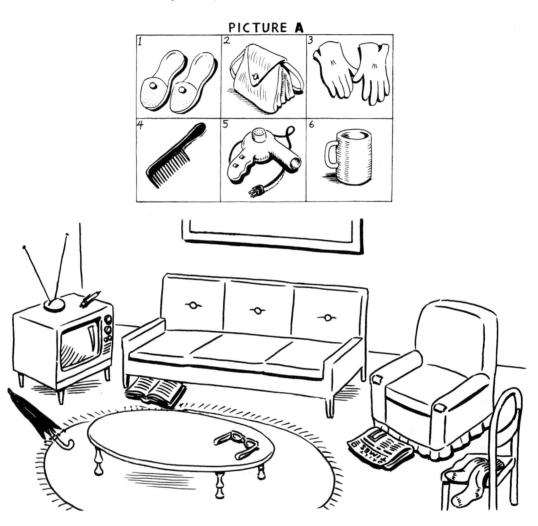

This is a map of your neighborhood. The names of the places are missing. Read the sentences and fill in the names of the places on the map.

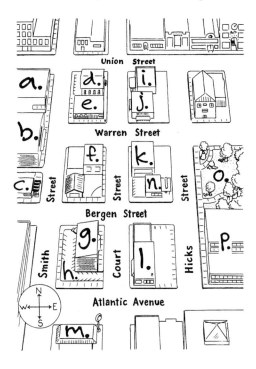

1. The park is on the corner of Hicks and Warren Street.
2. The hospital is next to the park.
3. The bank is on the southwest corner of Court Street and Union.
4. The drugstore is next to the bank.
5. The liquor store is across the street from the drug store on Court Street.
6. The video store is near the liquor store.
7. The movie theater is on the west side of Court Street between Bergen and Atlantic.
8. The parking lot is behind the movie theater.
9. The bakery is across the street from the movie theater.
10. The gas station is on the corner of Hicks and Bergen.
11. The hardware store is on the southeast corner of Court Street and Warren.
12. The bookstore is opposite the hardware store.
13. The newsstand is on the corner of Bergen and Smith Streets.
14. The pet store is on the southwest corner of Union Street and Smith Street.
15. The supermarket is between the pet store and the newsstand on Smith Street.
16. The diner is on Atlantic Avenue.

The Verb Be   **43**

Activities

TEST YOUR KNOWLEDGE GAME

Get into two teams.

STEP ❶ Team 1 chooses a category and an amount of money. Team 2 asks a question with *what* or *where*. If Team 1 answers correctly, they get the money.

STEP ❷ Team 2 chooses a category and an amount of money. Team 1 asks a question with *what* or *where*. If Team 2 answers correctly, they get the money. The team with the most money at the end wins.

EXAMPLES: Step 1.

Team 1: Monuments for $30.

Team 2: Where is the Colosseum?

Team 1: It's in Rome, Italy.

Categories					
Amount $$$	**Monuments**	**Capitals**	**Countries**	**Continents**	**Rivers, Mountains, Deserts**
Question	Where is/ are	What's the capital of	Where's	Where's	Where is/ are
$10	The Eiffel Tower	Afghanistan	Managua	Canada	The Sahara Desert
$20	The Great Wall	Greece	Nagasaki	Chile	The Rocky Mountains
$30	The Colosseum	Israel	Budapest	India	The Amazon River
$40	The Pyramids	Peru	Capetown	Egypt	Mt. Everest
$50	The Taj Mahal	Turkey	Zurich	Portugal	The Nile River

Ask a classmate about his or her hometown. Ask questions with *is/are* . . . or *wh-*question words.

EXAMPLE: You: Where are you from?   **Your Partner:** Acapulco.

Where's Acapulco?   It's in Mexico.

How is the weather?   It's hot in the summer and mild in the winter.

Are the people friendly?   Yes, they are.

The words in the box will help you:

Weather	People	Other
hot	happy	expensive
warm	friendly	cheap
mild	hard-working	small
cold	cold	big
sunny	religious	crowded
dry	outgoing	delicious
humid	quiet	safe
rainy	rich	dangerous
cloudy	poor	clean

ACTIVITY 3

Write about your partner's hometown.

EXAMPLE: My classmate is from Mexico City. Mexico City is the capital of Mexico. Mexico City is big. It is crowded. It is hot in the summer. People are friendly. The food is delicious.

ACTIVITY 4

Draw a map of your hometown or the place where you live now. Describe your map to your partner. Then write down the description, using prepositions.

EXAMPLES: This is my house. It's on Main Street. The drugstore is on the corner of Main and 1st Avenue. The supermarket is opposite the drugstore.

ACTIVITY 5

Listen to the telephone conversation between a student and a secretary at a college. Fill in the following places on the campus map:

- Parking B,
- Administration Building
- library
- bookstore

- English as a Second Language Department
- auditorium
- cafeteria

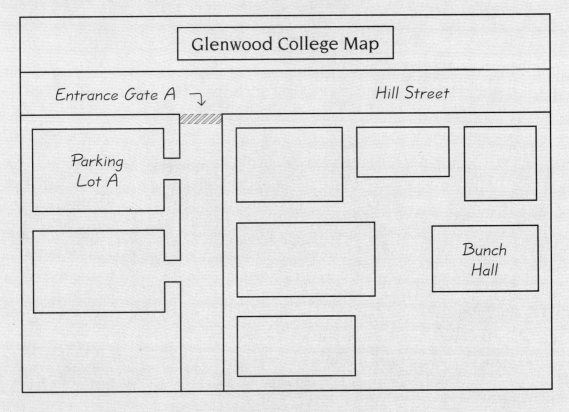

UNIT

4

Nouns

Count and Noncount Nouns, Be + Adjective + Noun

OPENING TASK

Categories

STEP ❶ Write each word in the box in one of the three circles below.

milk	dresses	cash
dollars	bread	a shoe
a shirt	cents	an egg

Category

1. Food

3. Money

2. Clothing

STEP ❷ Look at the same words in different groups. What are the categories? Write a name for each category.

Category

1. _____

a shirt
a shoe
an egg

3. _____

milk
bread
cash

2. _____

dollars
cents
dresses

FOCUS 1 >>>>>>>>>>>>>>>>> FORM/MEANING

Count Nouns and Noncount Nouns

Cash

Coins

We can see things as whole or as things we can count. We use noncount nouns like *cash* when we see a thing as whole. We use count nouns like *coins* when we refer to things we can count.

EXAMPLES	EXPLANATIONS
Count Nouns	**Things we can count**
SINGULAR PLURAL a dress dresses an egg eggs	Count nouns take *a/an* in the singular. They take *-s* or *-es* in the plural.
Noncount Nouns	**Things we don't count**
money cash clothing	Noncount nouns have one form. They are not singular or plural.

EXERCISE 1

Look at the list of words from the Opening Task. Check count or noncount.

	Count Noun	**Noncount Noun**
food		
milk		
egg		
bread		
clothing		
dresses		
shirt		

	Count Noun	Noncount Noun
shoe		
money		
dollars		
cents		
cash		

A/An with Singular Count Nouns

A	AN
a house **a** movie **a** uniform*	**an** orange **an** egg **an** hour*
Use *a* before a word beginning with a consonant or a consonant sound. *uniform* begins with a vowel but has the consonant sound of "y" as in *you*.	Use *an* before a word beginning with a vowel (a, e, i, o, u) or a vowel sound. *hour* begins with a consonant but the "h" is silent.

EXERCISE 2

List the words below under the correct categories. Then, read your lists to your partner with *a* or *an*.

earring	bed	watch	necklace
dormitory	table	apple	house
orange	apartment	ring	desk
armchair	banana	pear	hotel

Fruit	Furniture	Jewelry	Housing
an orange			

For each picture write a sentence to show the person's occupation. Use *a/an*.

EXAMPLES:

He's a waiter.

She's an athlete.

1. actor

_____

2. secretary

_____

3. dentist

4. cashier

5. flight attendant

6. doctor

7. nurse

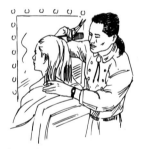

8. hairdresser

9. engineer

10. accountant

Test your knowledge. Work with a partner. You read the question on the left. Your partner finds the answer on the right and reads it using *a/an*.

EXAMPLE: **You:** What's Poland?

   Your Partner: (m) It's a country.

1. What's Poland?	a. It's _____ continent.
2. What is Thanksgiving?	b. It's _____ car.
3. What is the Atlantic?	c. It's _____ hour
4. What is Puerto Rico?	d. It's _____ clock.
5. What's the Sahara?	e. It's _____ river.
6. What is Africa?	f. It's _____ island.
7. What's New York?	g. It's _____ holiday in the United States and Canada.
8. What's the Concorde?	h. It's _____ museum.
9. What's Big Ben?	i. It's _____ university.
10. What is the Louvre?	j. It's _____ ocean.
11. What is Harvard?	k. It's _____ city.
12. What's sixty minutes?	l. It's _____ airplane.
13. What's a Mercedes?	m. It's _____ country.
14. What's the Amazon?	n. It's _____ desert.

FOCUS 3 >>>>>>>>>>>>>>>>>>>>>>>>>>> **FORM**

Spelling of Regular Plural Count Nouns

SINGULAR	PLURAL	EXPLANATIONS
(a) a car a book	two cars three books	To make the plural form of most count nouns, add -s.
(b) a boy a radio	four boys two radios	Nouns that end in: vowel + *y* vowel + *o* Plural form: add -s.
(c) a class a sandwich a dish a box	two classes two sandwiches two dishes three boxes	Nouns that end in: *ss* *ch* *sh* *x* Plural form: add -es.
(d) a potato a tomato	six potatoes four tomatoes	Nouns that end in: consonant + *o* Plural form: add -es.
(e) a baby a city	babies cities	Nouns that end in: consonant + *y* Plural form: change *y* to *i*, add -es.
(f) a thief a life	two thieves three lives	Nouns that end in: *f* or *fe* Plural form: change *f* to *v*, add -es. Exceptions: *chief—chiefs* *chef—chefs*

Write the plural form of the words below.

1. party   _parties_
2. shoe   _____
3. fox   _____
4. dictionary   _____
5. week   _____
6. glass   _____

7. wife   _____
8. watch   _____
9. leaf   _____
10. lady   _____
11. month   _____
12. key   _____

Complete the sentences with the plural of one of the nouns below.

city	story	holiday	university	state
mountain	country	continent	company	ocean

1. Thanksgiving and Christmas are _holidays_____.
2. The Atlantic and the Pacific are _____.
3. Africa and Asia are _____.
4. Harvard and Yale are _____.
5. IBM and Sony are _____.
6. "Cinderella" and "Beauty and the Beast" are _____.
7. The Alps are _____.
8. Colombia and Venezuela are _____ in South America.
9. Colorado and Vermont are _____ in the United States.
10. Vienna and Oslo are two _____ in Europe.

Regular Plural Nouns: Pronunciation of Final -s, and -es

EXAMPLES	EXPLANATIONS
(a) books, students, groups months, desks, cats	**/S/** Final -s is pronounced /s/ after voiceless sounds.*
(b) beds, rooms, lives years, days, dogs	**/Z/** Final -s is pronounced /z/ after voiced sounds.**
(c) classes, faces exercises, sizes dishes, wishes sandwiches, watches colleges, pages	**/ɪZ/** Final -es is pronounced /ɪz/ after "s" sounds "z" sounds "sh" sounds "ch" sounds "ge/dge" sounds. This adds an extra syllable to the noun. *Voiceless sounds: /p/t/f/k/th. **Voiced sounds: /b/d/g/v/m/n/l/r/ and vowels.

Make the words below plural. Then, write each word in the correct pronunciation group. Read each group aloud.

✔ book	radio	dress	house	ticket	rule
thing	horse	head	list	bus	cup
car	train	boat	church	peach	hat

/S/	/Z/	/IZ/
books		

EXERCISE 8

Look at the list of common measurements. Make the measurement on the right plural. Then read the statements aloud using the verb *equals*.

EXAMPLE: 98.6 degrees Fahrenheit = 37 degree_s_ Celsius.

98.6 degrees Fahrenheit equals 37 degrees Celsius.

1. one foot = 12 inch ____
2. one pound = 16 ounce ____
3. one minute = 60 second ____
4. one hour = 60 minute ____
5. one day = 24 hour ____
6. one year = 365 day ____
7. one quart = 2 pint ____
8. one gallon = 4 quart ____
9. one inch = 2 1/2 centimeter ____
10. one kilo = 2.2 pound ____

EXERCISE 9

Rhymes. Make the nouns in italics plural. Then, read the rhymes aloud.

1. On Education

Word ____, *sentence* ____, *exercise* ____, *rule* ____,

Dictionary ____, *textbook* ____, *page* ____, *school* ____,

Classroom ____, *teacher* ____, *student* ____, –all *jewel* ____

Of education, these are the *tool* ____

2. On Age

Day ____, *week* ____, *month* ____, *year* ____.

Getting old? Please, no *tear* ____!!!

3. On Imports

The *shoe*____ are Brazilian,

The *glove*____ are Italian,

The *chef*____ are from France;

from South America—the salsa dance.

The *toy*____ are Chinese,

The *camera*____ are Japanese:

Tell me, what's American, please?

FOCUS 5 >>>>>>>>>>>>>>>>>>>>>>>>>> FORM

Irregular Plural Nouns

EXAMPLES		EXPLANATIONS
(a) child man woman foot tooth mouse	children men women feet teeth mice	Some nouns change spelling in the plural.
(b) a deer a sheep a fish	two deer three sheep four fish	Some nouns do not change in the plural.
(c) scissors pajamas glasses shorts clothes pants		Some nouns are always plural. They have no singular form.

Fill in the blanks with an irregular plural noun.

1. Big Bird is eight ___feet_____ tall.

2. Mickey Mouse and Minnie are famous _____.

3. Actresses are _____ and actors are _____.

4. *Bambi* is a movie about _____.

5. Famous _____ in Hollywood are rich.

6. Bugs Bunny has two big front _____.

7. *Sesame Street* is a television show for _____.

8. _____ of all ages like Disney movies.

FOCUS 6 >>>>>>>>>>>>>>>>>>>>>>>>>>>> **FORM**

Count and Noncount Nouns

COUNT NOUNS	NONCOUNT NOUNS
Can take *a/an* or *one* in the singular. **(a)** It's a job. **(b)** My vacation is for one week.	Cannot take *a/an* or *one* in the singular. **(c)** It's work.
Can take *-s* or *-es* in the plural. **(d)** They are earrings. **(e)** They're watches.	Cannot take *-s* or *-es*. **(f)** It's jewelry.
Can take a singular or plural verb. **(g)** It is a table. **(h)** They are chairs.	Always take a singular verb. **(i)** Furniture is expensive.

Some Common Noncount Nouns

food	bread	rice	sugar	bacon
fruit	cheese	fish	salt	water
coffee	tea	milk	traffic	transportation
hair	clothing	jewelry	money	furniture
love	advice	help	crime	news
work	homework	information	luck	electricity
music	mail	luggage	garbage	pollution

EXERCISE 11

Check count or noncount for each underlined noun.

	COUNT	NONCOUNT
1. <u>Money</u> is important.		
2. A <u>dollar</u> is useful.		
3. Grammar <u>exercises</u> are fun.		
4. <u>Homework</u> is interesting.		
5. <u>Fruit</u> is healthy.		
6. <u>Apples</u> are my favorite fruit.		
7. Here is my <u>suitcase</u>.		
8. Good <u>luggage</u> is expensive.		
9. <u>Mail</u> from home is important to an international student.		
10. <u>Stamps</u> are cheap.		

EXERCISE 12

Work with a partner. Use the words below to ask questions about the country your partner comes from.

EXAMPLE: hamburgers/popular/in . . .?

Are hamburgers popular in Russia?

Yes, they are.

No, they aren't.

1. pizza/popular/in . . .?
2. fruit/cheap/in . . .?
3. cars/big/in . . .?
4. electricity/cheap/in . . .?
5. American music/popular/in . . .?

6. housing/expensive/in . . .?
7. families/big/in . . .?
8. taxes/high/in . . .?
9. public transportation/good/in . . .?
10. American movies/popular/in . . .?

Now make three questions on your own.

FOCUS 7 >>>>>>>>>>>>>>>>>>>> FORM/USE

How Much Is/How Much Are . . .?

EXAMPLES	EXPLANATIONS
(a) Singular: How much is a television set in China? **(b) Plural:** How much are newspapers in Russia? **(c) Noncount:** How much is gas in Italy?	To ask about prices use: **How much is . . .?** **How much are . . .?**

EXERCISE 13

Work with a partner. Ask your partner questions about prices in the country he or she is from, using *How much is/are . . .?* Your partner gives the answer in United States dollars.

EXAMPLE: jeans/in . . .?

How much are jeans in Turkey?

Answer: Jeans are about 50 dollars.

1. a bus ticket/in . . .?
2. a compact disc/in . . .?
3. bread/in . . .?
4. sneakers/in . . .?
5. a movie ticket/in . . .?

6. an apartment/in . . .?
7. bananas/in . . .?
8. a hamburger/in . . .?
9. chocolate/in . . .?
10. a local telephone call/in . . .?

Be + Adjective + Noun

EXAMPLES	EXPLANATIONS
(a) Harvard and Yale are **private** universities.	An adjective can come before the noun.
(b) They are **excellent** colleges.	Do not put -s on the adjective when the noun is plural.
(c) It's **a** large university. **(d)** English is **a** universal language.	Use *a* before an adjective with a consonant or a consonant sound.
(e) He's **an** "A" student. **(f)** She's **an** honor student.	Use *an* before an adjective with a vowel sound.
(g) Psychology is a **very** interesting subject.	Put *very* before the adjective to make the adjective stronger.

EXERCISE 14

Make sentences using *be* + adjective + *very* + noun. Choose an adjective from the list. You can use an adjective more than once.

exciting	violent	tall	expensive	dangerous	
crowded	popular	talented	useful	interesting	famous

1. The Twin Towers are very tall _____ buildings in New York City.

2. Disneyworld is a very popular _____ place in Florida.

3. Luciano Pavarotti _____ singer.

4. *Rambo* and *The Terminator* _____ movies.

5. A Mercedes _____ car.

6. Teaching _____ profession.

7. Baseball _____ sport in the United States and Japan.

8. Sao Paolo _____ city.

9. Eleanor Roosevelt and Jacqueline Kennedy Onassis _____ women in American history.

10. Computers _____ tools.

Activities

CATEGORIZING GAME.

STEP ❶ Get into two teams. Write the words in the box in the correct categories below.

STEP ❷ Then, next to each word, write C for count nouns and NC for noncount nouns.

STEP ❸ Each correct answer is one point. The team with the most points wins.

shirts	ears	coffee	shoes	feet	tea
toothpaste	underwear	lemonade	soap	coat	rice
cheese	shampoo	bread	jacket	eyes	head
hair	toothbrush	juice	beans	milk	pizza
soda	hairbrush	hamburger	socks	towels	arm

Things to Wear

shirts C

_____

_____

_____

_____

_____

Things to Eat

_____

_____

_____

_____

_____

Things to Drink

_____

_____

_____

_____

_____

Things in the Bathroom

_____

_____

_____

_____

_____

Parts of the Body

_____

_____

_____

_____

_____

ACTIVITY 2

Plan a party for the class. Get into groups. Each group plans what they are going to bring to the party under the following categories.

Food   Drink   Entertainment

Compare your plans with the other groups'. Which group has the best plan?

ACTIVITY 3

Say three or four things about a famous person. The class will guess his or her name.

EXAMPLE: She's an actress. She's French. She's blonde. She's beautiful.

Who is she?

Class guesses: Catherine Deneuve.

ACTIVITY 4

Tell your classmates what you have for:

Breakfast	Lunch	Dinner	Snack
coffee			
cereal			
orange juice			

ACTIVITY 5

STEP ❶ Listen to what kind of pizza the woman orders.

STEP ❷ Check (✔) what the woman wants on the pizza.
Then mark C for count nouns and NC for noncount nouns.

❑ cheese _____   ❑ pepperoni _____

❑ tomatoes _____   ❑ mushrooms _____

❑ olives   _____   ❑ anchovies _____

❑ peppers _____   ❑ onions   _____

STEP ❸ Ask a classmate about his or her favorite pizza.

STEP ❹ Role play. Telephone the pizza store with your order.

UNIT

5

The Verb *Have*

*Affirmative and Negative
Statements, Questions and
Short Answers, Some/Any*

OPENING TASK

Modern and Traditional Lifestyles

Look at the photographs of two Inuit women in North Canada. Check (✔) and say the things Mary has. Check and say the things Nilaulaq and her husband have.

**Mary
(at right)**

**Nilaulaq
(below)**

	Mary	Nilaulaq (Nila) and Her Husband, Napachee
1. a house		
2. an Inuit name		
3. Inuit clothing		
4. dogs		
5. furniture		
6. electricity		
7. fresh fish		
8. a bed		

In the photographs, who has a traditional lifestyle? Who has a modern lifestyle? Say why.

1. _____ a traditional lifestyle.

2. _____ a modern lifestyle.

Have and *Has*: Affirmative Statements

The verb *to have* means to own or possess.

SUBJECT	VERB	
I You	have	
He She It Mary	has	a house.
We You They (Nila & Napachee)	have	

Fill in the blanks about Nilaulaq and Mary with *have* or *has*. Read the sentences aloud.

A. Nilaulaq __has__ an Inuit name. She _____ a husband. He_____ an Inuit name too. They _____ two children. They _____ two dogs. Nilaulaq says, "I _____ a beautiful family."

B. Mary _____ wallpaper in her house. Mary _____ a clock. She _____ photographs and a map. She _____ furniture. She _____ canned food.

C. Modern Inuit people live in towns. The towns _____ stores. Modern Inuit people _____ money. They _____ jobs.

Have: Negative Statements and Contractions

SUBJECT	DO/DOES	BASE FORM OF VERB	
I You We They Nilaulaq and her husband	do not (don't)	have	a telephone.
He She It Nilaulaq	does not (doesn't)		

EXERCISE 2

Make the words below into sentences with *has/have* or *doesn't have/don't have*.

Traditional families are big.

1. They/many children.

2. They also/grandmothers and grandfathers living with them.

3. In a traditional family, only the father/a job.

4. The mother/a job.

5. The children/a babysitter.

Modern families are different.

6. Sometimes they/two people.

7. Sometimes they/one or two children.

8. Sometimes, they/children.

Now make four sentences of your own about modern families.

9. _____

10. _____

11. _____

12. _____

Have: Yes/No Questions and Short Answers

DO/DOES	SUBJECT	HAVE	
Do	I you we they Nilaulaq and Napachee	**have**	a telephone?
Does	he she it Mary		

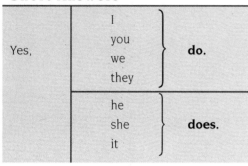

Affirmative Short Answers				Negative Short Answers			
Yes,	I you we they	}	**do.**	No,	I you we they	}	**do not.** (don't)
	he she it	}	**does.**		he she it	}	**does not.** (doesn't)

EXERCISE 3

Find Someone Who

Ask your classmates if they have the things on the left. Write the names of the students who say "yes."

EXAMPLE: Do you have a telephone?

Yes, I do. OR No, I don't.

Things   **Students' Names**

1. a cordless telephone   _____

2. pets   _____

3. a car   _____

4. children   _____

5. relatives in this country   _____

6. a job   _____

7. English-speaking friends   _____

8. a bicycle   _____

9. a driver's license   _____

10. a video cassette recorder (VCR)   _____

Work with a partner. Take turns asking and answering questions. Make questions about the Inuit people in the Task. Use short answers.

EXAMPLE: You: Does Mary have a house?

Your Partner: Yes, she does.

1. Nilaulaq/children
2. Mary/bed
3. Napachee/boat.
4. Nila/wallpaper in her house

5. Nilaulaq/furniture
6. Mary/an Inuit name
7. Nilaulaq/a television set
8. Mary/canned food

EXERCISE 5

Read about the Amish people. Then work with a partner. Take turns asking and answering questions. Give short answers.

The Amish are a special group of Americans. There are about 85,000 Amish people in the United States. They have their own language. They also have a simple way of life.

The Amish are farmers, but they don't have machines on their farms. They have horses. They do not have electricity or telephones in their homes.

The Amish are called "the plain people." They wear dark clothing. The men all have beards and wear hats. The women wear long dresses and hats.

Amish children have one-room schoolhouses. They have Amish teachers. They have no school after the eighth grade.

EXAMPLE: An Amish man/car?

       You: Does an Amish man have a car?

       Your Partner: No, he doesn't.

1. Amish people/a simple life?   _____?
         _____.

2. Amish women/jewelry?   _____?
         _____.

3. Amish home/electricity?   _____?
         _____.

4. An Amish farmer/horses?   _____?
         _____.

5. An Amish home/telephone?   _____?
         _____.

6. Amish people/their own language?   _____?
         _____.

7. An Amish child/computer?   _____?
         _____.

8. Amish people/colorful clothing?   _____?
         _____.

9. An Amish home/television?   _____?
         _____.

10. Amish children/special teachers?   _____?
         _____.

11. Amish children/school after eighth grade?   _____?
         _____.

12. Amish people/a modern lifestyle?   _____?
         _____.

Some/Any

EXAMPLES		EXPLANATIONS
STATEMENT	**(a)** The children have **some** books. **(b)** They have **some** money.	Use *some* in a statement.
NEGATIVE	**(c)** They don't have **any** books. **(d)** She doesn't have **any** money.	Use *any* in a negative sentence.
QUESTION	**(e)** Do they have **any** books? **(f)** Does she have **any** money?	Use *any* in a question.
(g) They don't have **any** books. (plural count noun) **(h)** He doesn't have **any** money. (noncount noun)		Use *any* with plural count nouns and noncount nouns.

EXERCISE 6

Complete the rhyme with *some* or *any*.

I don't have (1) _any_____ time today

I have (2) _____ problems to solve.

I have (3) _____ bills to pay

Do you have (4) _____ time to play?

I have (5) _____ places to go

I have (6) _____ people to see

Do you have (7) _____ advice for me?

Yes, I do: "Slow down!"

Fill in *some* or *any* in the sentences below. Say if the sentence is true or not true. If it is not true, change the verb and change some/any. Then say what you think . . . is it good or bad? Why?

EXAMPLE: An Amish person has <u>some</u> friends.   True

Amish people have <u>some</u> music.   Not true. Amish people don't have any music.

I think this is good/bad . . .

1. The Amish people don't have _____ cars.

2. Amish homes have _____ books.

3. An Amish woman has _____ jewelry.

4. An Amish woman doesn't have _____ make-up.

5. The Amish have _____ special schools.

6. Amish schools have _____ computers.

7. An Amish child doesn't have _____ school after eighth grade.

8. An Amish farmer has _____ machines.

9. Amish people have _____ colorful clothing.

10. Amish children don't have _____ American toys.

FOCUS 5 ⊳⊳⊳⊳⊳⊳⊳⊳⊳⊳⊳⊳⊳⊳⊳⊳⊳⊳⊳⊳⊳⊳⊳⊳⊳ **USE**

Asking for Something Politely

Use *Do you have . . .?* to ask for something politely.

EXAMPLES	EXPLANATIONS

Use:
    (a) Do you have an eraser?
Answer
    (b) Yes, I do. OR Sure.
	• to ask for something politely.

Use:
    (c) Excuse me, do you have the time?
Answer
    (d) No, I don't. OR Sorry, I don't.
	• to stop a person and ask for something.

EXERCISE 8

Ask for something politely. Use *a/an/any* and the nouns below the pictures.

EXAMPLE: (pen)

Do you have a pen?

Yes, I do. OR

Sorry, no I don't.

1. (coffee)

3. (milk)

2. (match)

4. (stamps)

5. (change)

7. (sugar)

6. (eraser)

Using *Have* to Describe People

He **has** short hair.
He **has** a mustache.

HAIR COLOR	HAIR LENGTH	HAIR TYPE	OTHER	EYE COLOR
dark	long	straight	a mustache	black
light	short	wavy	a beard	brown
black	medium-length	curly	bangs	blue
brown				green
red				gray
blond				
gray				
white				

Look at the photographs of Mary and Nilaulaq and of the Amish. Fill in the blanks with *be* or *have* and the correct nouns.

1. John Lapp is Amish.

    He _is_____ married.

    He _____ long _____.

    He _____ a long _____.

2. Nilaulaq _____ an Inuit name.

    She _____ long black _____.

    She _____ a nice smile.

3. Daniel _____ a young Amish boy.

    He _____ long blond hair.

    He _____ bangs.

4. Mary _____ a modern Inuit woman.

    Mary _____ a round face.

    She _____ dark hair.

Correct the mistakes in the sentences.

1. He have a car.   *has*

2. She have not a house.

3. He no have a TV set.

4. He doesn't is rich.

5. She doesn't has children.

6. Does he has a sister?

7. Does she is an Inuit?

8. Excuse me, have you change?

Activities
ACTIVITY 1

WHO IS HE OR SHE?

Describe one of your classmates. Do not write the person's name. Read your written description to the class. Your classmates guess who it is.

EXAMPLE: This student is tall. He has short black hair. He has brown eyes. He has a mustache. Who is he?

ACTIVITY 2

Think of a person or people you know with traditional lifestyles. Write about these people. Write about what they look like. Tell how their lives are different. Tell what they have and what they don't have. Then make an oral presentation to the class.

ACTIVITY 3

Go to the library and take out a book about the Inuit or the Amish. Write down five new things you have learned about what they have and don't have.

ACTIVITY 4

What American things do people in your country have today? Is it good or bad to have these things? Discuss this with a partner.

EXAMPLE: In my country today, we have fast-food restaurants. This is bad/good because . . .

ACTIVITY 5

 STEP ❶ Listen to this news report. Then fill in the blanks with information from the news report.

In Zorlik—*Not Any*	On the American airplanes—*Some*
_____	_____
_____	_____
_____	_____

STEP ❷ Tell the class about a place in the world where things are bad. Use *some* and *any*.

EXAMPLE: In Zaire, many children don't have any food to eat.

UNIT

6

This/That/These/Those
Possessives

OPENING TASK

Wally the Waiter

Wally the waiter is new at his job.

STEP ❶ Ask your partner questions about the names of all the foods on Wally's tray.

STEP ❷ Read the conversation

Wally: Uh, excuse me, whose steak is this?

Charles: It's not ours.

Wally: Oh, I'm sorry. Is this your soup?

Charles: Yes, it is.

Wally: Then this bread is yours too . . . and what about these french fries?

Jim: No, the french fries aren't ours.

Wally: This salad?

Jim: That's mine.

Wally: And the pizza?

Charles: That's his pizza.

Wally: Is the hamburger for this table?

Charles: No, it isn't. But those strawberries are.

Wally: I'm very sorry. Today is my first day on this job. I'm a little confused.

Jim: No problem. But those are our sodas too, please.

Wally: Sure, thanks again for your patience!

STEP ❸ Try to help Wally remember whose foods these are. You ask questions. Your partner answers.

Foods	Charles	Jim	Someone Else
a. sodas	❑	❑	❑
b. hamburger	❑	❑	❑
c. french fries	❑	❑	❑
d. strawberries	❑	❑	❑
e. salad	❑	❑	❑
f. steak	❑	❑	❑
g. soup	❑	❑	❑
h. pizza	❑	❑	❑
i. bread	❑	❑	❑

This, These, That, Those

NEAR SPEAKER	FAR FROM SPEAKER
SINGULAR	
(a) This is a hamburger. **(b) This** hamburger is good.	**(c) That** is a steak. **(d) That** steak is delicious.
PLURAL	
(e) These are baked potatoes. **(f) These** baked potatoes are hot.	**(g) Those** are french fries. **(h) Those** french fries are salty.
NONCOUNT	
(i) This is Italian bread. **(j) This** Italian bread is round.	**(k) That** is French bread. **(l) That** French bread is long.

EXERCISE 1

Go back to the Opening Task on page 80. Find at least five sentences with *this*, *these*, *that*, and *those*. Write them below.

1. _____ .

2. _____ .

3. _____ .

4. _____ .

5. _____ .

EXERCISE 2

Are the things in the pictures singular, plural, or noncount? Are the things near or far from the speaker? Fill in the blanks with *this/that/these/those* and the correct form of the verb *be*.

1. __That__ __is__
   a sweater.

2. _____ _____
   high-heeled shoes.

3. _____ _____
   a belt.

4. _____ _____
   shorts.

5. _____ _____
   a dress.

6. _____ _____
   sunglasses.

7. _____ _____
   jewelry.

8. _____ _____
   a skirt.

9. _____ _____
   blouses.

10. _____ _____
    women's clothing.

Asking What Things Are

QUESTION	ANSWER
(a) What's **this**? **that**	**Singular** **It's a** sandwich. **It's an** egg.
(b) What are **these**? **those**	**Plural** **They are** french fries. **They're** cookies.
(c) What's **this** dish? **that** dish?	**Noncount** **It's** soup.

This is Maria's first American party. She doesn't know about American food. She asks her American friend, Chris, about the food on the table.

Ask questions with *what*. Then fill in the subject, verb, and *a/an* where necessary. Then match each sentence to the picture.

Letter in the Picture

1. ___What's this? It's a___ _____	hamburger.	_d_
2. _____	hot dog.	_____
3. _____	french fries	_____
4. _____	ketchup.	_____
5. _____	pizza.	_____
6. _____	sandwich.	_____
7. _____	doughnuts.	_____
8. _____	cookies.	_____
9. _____	muffin.	_____
10. _____	ice cream.	_____

Possessive Nouns

EXAMPLES	EXPLANATIONS
(a) The boy has a dog. The **boy's dog** is small. **(b)** Carol has a magazine. **Carol's magazine** is on the table.	Add an apostrophe (') and -s to a singular noun.
(c) The boss has an office. The **boss's office** is big. The **boss' office** is big. **(d)** Charles has a sister. **Charles's** sister is twenty-six. **Charles'** sister is twenty-six.	Add an apostrophe (') and -s or just an apostrophe (')to singular nouns and names that end in -s.
(e) The waiters have trays. The **waiters' trays** are heavy.	Add only an apostrophe (') at the end of a plural noun.
(f) The **children's school** is near here. **(g)** **Women's clothing** is cheap here.	Add apostrophe (') -s to irregular plural nouns.
(h) Paul and **Mary's dog** is friendly. **(i)** My mother-in-**law's cookies** are delicious.	For two or more subjects or a subject with hyphens (-_, add '-s at the end of last noun.

EXERCISE 4

Complete these sentences about Madeline the movie star and her family. Fill in the blanks with the possessive nouns in parentheses.

1. (The movie star) _____ life is very exciting.

2. (Madeline) _____ clothes are expensive.

3. (friends) Her _____ homes are big.

4. (brother) Her _____ wife is a lawyer.

5. (husband) Her _____ name is Mark.

6. (husband) Her _____ mother is very nice.

7. (parents) His _____ home is near the ocean.

8. (sister) His _____ hobby is motorcycling.

9. (children) Their _____ lives are busy.

10. (grandparents) Her _____ car is very large.

EXERCISE 5

This is Charles's family tree. Read the sentences. Write each person's relationship to Charles under the name in the box.

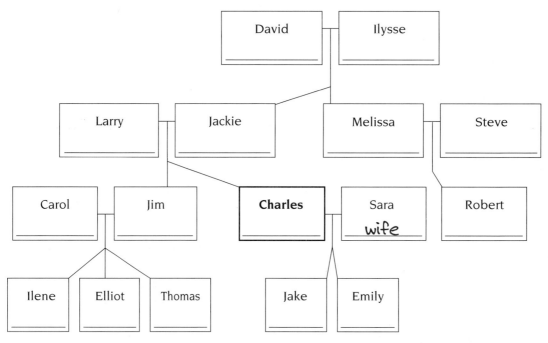

1. Sara is Charles's wife.

2. Emily is Charles's daughter.

3. Jake is Charles's son.

4. Jim is Charles's brother.

5. Carol is Charles's sister-in-law.

6. Elliot and Thomas are Charles's nephews.

7. Ilene is Charles's niece.

8. Melissa is Charles's aunt.

9. Steve is Charles's uncle.

10. Robert is Charles's cousin.

11. Jackie is Charles's mother.

12. Larry is Charles's father.

13. David is Charles's grandfather.

14. Ilysse is Charles's grandmother.

Write the correct possessive nouns in the blanks. Say each sentence aloud.

EXAMPLE: Sara is __Charles's__ wife.

1. Charles is _____ brother.

2. David is _____ father.

3. Emily is _____ sister.

4. Jim is _____ husband.

5. Melissa is _____ daughter.

6. Elliot is _____ cousin.

7. Jim is _____ uncle.

8. Jake is _____ nephew.

9. Carol is _____ sister-in-law.

10. Ilysse is _____ mother-in-law.

Look carefully at the apostrophes in the sentences below. How many people are there in each sentence? How many dogs? Check *one* or *more than one* for each sentence.

	How many people?		How many dogs?	
	One	More than one	One	More than one
1. My daughter's dog is big.	✔		✔	
2. My daughters' dogs are big.				
3. My son's dog is big.				
4. My sons' dogs are big.				
5. My sons' dog is big.				
6. My son's dogs are big.				
7. My children's dog is big.				
8. My children's dogs are big.				

FOCUS 4 ➤➤➤➤➤➤➤➤➤➤➤➤➤➤➤➤➤➤➤➤ FORM

Possessive Adjectives, Pronouns

POSSESSIVE ADJECTIVES		POSSESSIVE PRONOUNS	
My	car is new.	The car is	**mine.**
Your	house is beautiful.	The house is	**yours.**
His	dog is old.	The dog is	**his.**
Its	fur is white.	(*Its* cannot be a possessive pronoun.)	
Her	jewelry is expensive.	The jewelry is	**hers.**
Our	children are cute.	The children are	**ours.**
Their	television is big.	The television is	**theirs.**

NOTE: Do not confuse a possessive adjective (*its*) with the contraction of *it* + *is* (*it's*).

Use possessive determiners with parts of the body.

My hair is black..

Your eyes are blue.

EXERCISE 8

Describe a person in the class to your partner without saying his or her name. Your partner guesses who he or she is.

EXAMPLE: You say: Her hair is black. Her eyes are blue. Her skin is dark.

Your partner says: Is it Luisa?

EXERCISE 9

Fill in each blank with a possessive word (a possessive adjective or a possessive pronoun). Then look at the two dogs. Whose dog is A? Whose dog is B?

Many people have pets. (1) _____Their_____ pets are very important to them.

Charles's family loves pets. (2) _____ children have a dog. Emily says the

dog is (3) _____, Jake says the dog is (4) _____.

(5) _____ dog is small. (6) _____ legs are short,

(7) _____ ears are long. It's cute.

Charles's parents have a dog too. They introduce their dog: "This is

(8) _____ dog. (9) _____ name is Buck. He's strong.

(10) _____ nose is flat. (11) _____ fur is short. We love

Buck. He's part of (12) _____ family."

A. It's _____ dog.　　　　　　B. It's _____ dog.

Questions with *Whose*

Use *whose* to ask who owns or possesses something.

WHOSE	NOUN	VERB		ANSWERS
Whose	dog	is	this?	It's Carol's dog. It's her dog. It's hers. Carol's.
Whose	glasses	are	these?	They're Jim's glasses. They're his glasses. They're his. Jim's.

Who's and Whose

EXAMPLES	EXPLANATIONS
(a) **Who's** she? My sister. (b) **Whose** car is that? Mine.	Do not confuse *who's* and *whose*. *Who's* and *whose* have the same pronunciation. *Who's* = *who is*. *Whose* asks about who owns something.

EXERCISE 10

Ask questions with *whose* to find out who owns each object. Answer in two ways as in the example.

EXAMPLE: Whose hammer is it?

It's Jackie's hammer. It's hers.

A. John is a hairdresser.

B. Jackie is a . carpenter

C. Jim is a . secretary

D. Pierre and Daniel are cooks.

1. spoon

2. pencil sharpener

3. shampoo

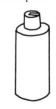

4. screwdriver

5. computer

6. comb

7. hammer

8. hairbrush

9. sauce pan

10. scissors

11. envelope

12. can opener

13. ladder

14. nails

15. frying pan

16. paperclip

EXERCISE 11

Correct the mistakes in the following sentences.

1. This is Jim magazine
2. Charles is married. Sara is her wife.
3. That computer is her's.
4. Is Jim the brother of Charles?
5. Who's son-in-law is Charles?
6. Charles and Sara have two children. Jake and Emily are theirs children.
7. What's that name's man?
8. The Larry's dog is small.
9. Whose hungry?
10. This dogs are cute.
11. A: Is this the dog's food?
    B: Yes, that's its.
12. The teacher has chalk on the face.

Activities

STEP ❶ Draw your family tree.

STEP ❷ Ask a classmate about his or her family tree. Draw your classmate's family tree. Then write five sentences about your classmate's family.

ACTIVITY 2

The teacher asks each student to put a personal object into a bag. One student picks an object and asks, "Whose is this?" The class guesses who the owner is. If the class is not correct, the owner says, "It's mine."

ACTIVITY 3

STEP ❶ Bring something to class that is special from your country or another country you know (something you eat, something you wear, something people use, etc.). Tell the class about the special thing.

> **EXAMPLE:** This is a special dress. It's for a wedding.

STEP ❷ Choose one of the objects from the class. Write about it.

ACTIVITY 4

Bring in a menu from an American restaurant. Ask questions about the foods on the menu. Role-play a dialogue between a confused waiter (like Wally) and two customers in a restaurant.

ACTIVITY 5

STEP ❶ Listen to the conversation. What are the people talking about?

STEP ❷ Listen again. In the chart, write *this/that/these* or *those* next to each thing. Then check (√) if each thing is *near* or *far from* the speaker.

This/that/these/those?		Near	Far from
1. these	chairs	√	
2.	table		
3.	lamp		
4.	pictures		
5.	statue		
6.	sofa		

UNIT

There Is/There Are
A/An versus The

Whose Apartment Is This?

Read the statements on the next page. Then circle the type of person you think lives in this apartment. Give reasons for your choice.

1. The person   is   a man/a woman.
2. The person   has   a baby/doesn't have a baby.
3. The person   has   a pet/doesn't have a pet.
4. The person   is   athletic/not athletic.
5. The person   drinks   coffee/doesn't drink coffee.
6. The person   is   well-educated/not well-educated.
7. The person   loves   music/doesn't love music.
8. The person   is   on a diet/not on a diet.

What are your reasons?

FOCUS 1 >>>>>>>>>>>>>>>> MEANING/USE

There + Be

EXAMPLES	EXPLANATIONS
	Use *there + be*:
(a) **There are** a lot of things in the apartment.	• to show something or somebody exists.
(b) **There is** a cat under the bed.	• to show something or somebody's location.
(c) **There is** a mouse in the house. NOT: A mouse is in the house.	• when you talk about something or somebody for the first time.
(d) **There are** two men in the picture. **They are** not happy.	Do not confuse *there are* and *they are*.

EXERCISE 1

Circle (a) or (b) for the correct sentence.

EXAMPLE: (a)   Two men are in this picture.

(b)   There are two men in this picture.

1. An angry restaurant customer says,
   (a) "Waiter, a fly is in my soup."
   (b) "Waiter, there's a fly in my soup."

2. The waiter answers,

   (a) "Sorry, sir. There's more soup in the kitchen."

   (b) "Sorry, sir. More soup is in the kitchen."

3. The customer gets the bill. He says,

   (a) "Waiter, a mistake is on the bill."

   (b) "Waiter, there's a mistake on the bill."

 **FOCUS 2** FORM

There Is/There Are

The form of the *be* verb depends on the noun phrase that follows it.

THERE + BE	NOUN PHRASE		EXPLANATIONS
(a) There is	an angry man	at the table.	singular count noun
(b) There are	two people	in the restaurant.	plural count noun
(c) There is	soup	in his dish.	noncount noun
(d) There is	a dining room, kitchen, and restroom	in this restaurant.	When there is more than one noun, *be* agrees with the first noun.

Contractions: *There is = There's.*

EXERCISE 2

Go back to the Opening Task on page 93. Write sentences about the picture with *there is/are* and the words below.

EXAMPLE: one bed in the apartment

   There's one bed in the apartment.

1. a tennis racquet in the closet

2. high-heeled shoes in the closet

3. women's clothing in the closet

4. sneakers in the closet

5. a coat in the closet

6. CDs on the shelf

7. a CD player on the shelf

8. books on the shelf

9. women's jewelry in the box on the table

10. coffee in the coffee pot

11. a big cake on the counter

12. an exercise bicycle in the apartment

13. an expensive rug on the floor

14. two pillows on the bed

EXERCISE 3

STEP ❶ Get into groups. Choose one student to read the following sentences. Listen to the description and draw the picture.

STEP ❷ Compare your drawings.

1. There's a table in the center of the room.

2. There are two chairs at the table—one at each end.

3. There's a tablecloth on the table.

4. There's a plate on each end of the table. On one plate, there's a steak and potatoes.

5. The other plate is empty. There's only a napkin.

6. Next to the empty plate, there's an empty glass.

7. Next to the plate with food, there's a half-full glass.

8. There's a bottle of water on the right side of the table. The bottle is half full.

9. There is a vase in the center of the table.

10. There are eight flowers on the floor next to the table.

STEP ❸ Choose the best title for your picture.

A. A Wonderful Dinner

B. Disappointed Again!

C. Always Eat Your Vegetables

There Isn't/There Aren't/
There's No/There Are No

THERE	BE		TYPE OF NOUN
There	isn't	a vase on the table.	singular count noun
There	aren't	any children in this restaurant.	plural count noun
There	isn't	any water on the table.	noncount noun

THERE	BE	NO	
There	is		vase on the table
There	are	no	children in the restaurant.
There	's		water on the table.

EXERCISE 4

Go back to the Opening Task on page 93. Make sentences with *there is/are, there isn't/there aren't*, or *there's no/there are no* with the words below.

EXAMPLE: There isn't an armchair in the apartment.

OR There's no armchair in the apartment.

1. television set
2. rug
3. men's clothing
4. computer
5. window
6. desk
7. books
8. toys
9. exercise bicycle
10. plants
11. coffee pot
12. ties

EXERCISE 5

Use the information in the chart on the next page about the city Utopia. Write sentences with *there is/are, there isn't/there aren't*, or *there's no/there are no*.

EXAMPLE: In Utopia, there aren't any guns.

In Utopia, there are no guns.

THE CITY OF UTOPIA

	Yes	No		Yes	No
1. guns		X	6. universities	X	
2. public transportation	X		7. noise		X
3. crime		X	8. jobs	X	
4. museums	X		9. parks	X	
5. traffic problems		X	10. poor people		X

Read the politician's speech about the city of Utopia. Fill in the blanks with *there is/are, there isn't/there aren't*, or *there's no/there are no.*

Good evening, Ladies and Gentlemen. I am the Mayor of Utopia. I am here tonight to talk about our wonderful city.

Today, (1) __there are__ 50,000 people in our city. We are all happy.
(2) _____ problems in our city.

(3) _____ jobs for all our people. (4) _____ good schools for the children. (5) _____ nice houses for all our families. The houses are comfortable. They aren't expensive.

(6) _____ homeless people on our streets. Our streets are safe.
(7) _____ crime here. (8) _____ drugs. Our streets are clean. (9) _____ garbage on the streets. (10) _____ pollution.

(11) _____ many museums, theaters, and parks in our city.
(12) _____ entertainment for everyone. (13) _____ good and cheap public transportation for everyone.

(14) _____ many reasons why Utopia is a great city!
(15) _____ a good quality of life here in Utopia. And don't forget:
(16) _____ an election this year. I want to be your Mayor for four more years. Are you happy in Utopia? Then (17) _____ only one thing to do: VOTE FOR ME, your Mayor Lucas Lime, on November sixth!

Yes/No Questions with *There Is/There Are*

YES/NO QUESTIONS	SHORT ANSWERS	TYPE OF NOUN
(a) Is there a computer in the room?	Yes, there is. No, there isn't.	singular count noun
(b) Are there any books on the shelves?	Yes, there are. No, there aren't.	plural count noun
(c) Is there any jewelry in the box?	Yes, there is. No there isn't.	noncount noun

EXERCISE 7

Complete the questions for each picture.

1. __Are there_____ any messages for me?

3. _____ any food in here, Mom?

2. _____ a doctor in the house?

4. _____ a post office near here?

5. _____ any tickets available for the 10:00 show?

6. _____ any room for me?

7. _____ any instructions in the box?

8. _____ any mail for me?

9. _____ any small sizes?

10. _____ a seat for me?

Test your knowledge. Ask your partner *yes/no* questions with Is *there/Are there* and the words below.

EXAMPLE: eggs in an eggplant?

Are there any eggs in an eggplant?

No, there aren't.

1. rain in a desert
2. two billion people in China
3. fifty-two states in the United States
4. earthquakes in Japan

5. billions of stars in the sky
6. life on the moon
7. trees at the North Pole
8. cure for the common cold

FOCUS 5 ➤➤➤➤➤➤➤➤➤➤➤➤➤➤➤➤➤➤➤➤➤➤➤ **USE**

Choosing A/An or The

A/An and *the* are articles. *A/An* are indefinite articles (see Unit 4). *The* is the definite article.

A/AN	THE
Use only with singular count nouns. **(a)** Susan has **a** bicycle.	Use with all nouns. **(b)** **The** bicycle is new. (singular) **(c)** **The** books are on the shelf. (plural) **(d)** **The** jewelry is in the box. (noncount)
Use to talk about a person or thing for the first time. **(e)** Susan has **a** necklace.	Use the second time you talk about a person or thing. **(f)** Susan has a necklace. **The** necklace is beautiful.
Use to classify people, animals, and things. **(g)** She is **a** businesswoman. It's **a** restaurant.	Use when both speakers know which noun they are talking about. **(h)** When's **the** party? It's at 8:00.
	Use when the noun is the only one. **(i)** **The** sun is hot.

Look at the pictures. Fill in the blanks with *a/an* or *the*.

1. **Nurse:** It's (a) _____ girl!
   Congratulations, Mr. Spade.

2. **Passenger:** Boy, it's hot. Do you have
   (a) _____ air conditioner in this car?

   Driver: Yes, but (b) _____ air conditioner doesn't work. Sorry about that!

3. **Husband:** What's in (a) _____ box?

   Wife: I have (b) _____ surprise for you.

   Husband: What's (c) _____ surprise?

   Wife: Open it!

4. **Man:** Do you have (a) _____ room for
   tonight?

   Clerk: Sorry, sir. (b) _____ motel is full
   tonight.

5. **Husband:** Do you have (a) _____ key or do I?

   Wife: I think (b) _____ key's in the car.

6. **Receptionist:** Take your feet off (a) _____ table, please young man!

7. **Woman:** Who is it?

   Mailman: It's (a) _____ mailman, Ms. Wallace. Here's your mail.

   Woman: Thanks, Mr. Brown. Have a good day!

EXERCISE 10

Read the paragraph. Fill in *a/an* or *the*. Then answer the question: *Who is Susan's brother-in-law?* (Refer to Unit 6.)

Susan owns (1) _____ restaurant. (2) _____ restaurant is very small. It has (3) _____ cook, (4) _____ cashier, and (5) _____ waiter. Susan is (6) _____ boss. Susan has (7) _____ excellent cook in (8) _____ kitchen: her mother! Susan has (9) _____ sister. Her sister is (10) _____ cashier in

(11) _____ restaurant. Her sister's husband is (12) _____ waiter.
Susan's sister is (13) _____ good cashier, but her brother-in-law is not
(14) _____ very good waiter. He doesn't have (15) _____ good
memory and is always confused. This is (16) _____ big problem for Susan.

EXERCISE 11

Correct the mistakes in the following sentences.

1. It's a picture on a wall.
2. There are a bathroom, a kitchen, and a living room in my house.
3. There have three bedrooms and two bathrooms in the apartment.
4. Is a good restaurant in my neighborhood.
5. There aren't milk in the refrigerator.
6. In my picture, have one woman and two men.
7. Are homeless people in your city?
8. Is there a jewelry in Susan's apartment?
9. Susan owns a restaurant.
   Really? Where is a restaurant?
10. Are there any museums in your town?
    Yes, they are.
11. Excuse me, is there the men's room in this restaurant?
12. Do you have any children?
    Yes, I have the daughter.
13. Are there pollution in your city?
14. There no are women in the restaurant.
15. There are no any poor people in Utopia.

Activities

FIND THE DIFFERENCES

Work with a partner or a group. Look at the two pictures. What is different in Picture B? Write as many sentences as you can with *There is/isn't*, or *There are/aren't* in ten minutes. The person with the most correct sentences wins.

EXAMPLE: In Picture B, there is a cat.

Picture A

Picture B

ACTIVITY 2

Find out about your partner's neighborhood.

STEP ❶ Ask questions with *Is there . . . ? Are there . . . ?* Check Yes or No in the Chart.

EXAMPLE: A: Is there a hospital in your neighborhood?

B: Yes, there is. No, there isn't.

	Yes	No
supermarkets		
movie theaters		
bookstore		
hospital		
bank		
fast-food restaurants		
gas station		
post office		
public library		
schools		
crime		
coffee shop		
trees		
public transportation		

STEP ❷ Tell the class or group about your classmate's neighborhood.

ACTIVITY 3

STEP ❶ Use the categories below to find out about your classmates. Fill in the blanks with numbers of students.

Total number of classmates _____

Sex: Male _____   Female _____

Physical Characteristics: Dark eyes _____   Blue/Green eyes _____

Women with short hair _____   Women with long hair _____

Nationalities: _____

Personalities: Shy _____   Outgoing _____

Marital Status: Married _____   Single _____

Add your own categories.

STEP ❷ Write sentences about your classmates.

EXAMPLE: There are ten Mexicans, two Chinese, three Koreans, one Vietnamese, and one Brazilian in my class.

ACTIVITY 4

Think of a place that's important to you, write a short description of this place.

ACTIVITY 5

Write a letter to the mayor of your city. Write about the problems in your city or neighborhood.

EXAMPLE: Dear Mayor,

I live in _____. There are many problems in my

neighborhood. . . .

ACTIVITY 6

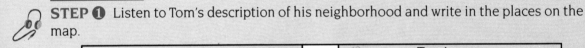

STEP ❶ Listen to Tom's description of his neighborhood and write in the places on the map.

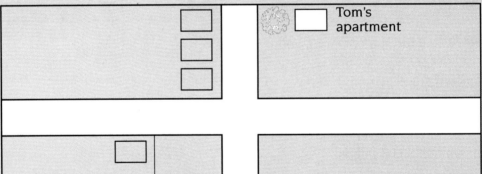

Tom's apartment

STEP ❷ Work with a partner. Ask about these places in Tom's neighborhood:

1. police station
2. supermarket
3. banks
4. gas station
5. laundromat
6. mini-market
7. library
8. schools

EXAMPLE: Is there a police station?

No, there isn't.

8

Simple Present Tense

Affirmative and Negative
Statements, Time Expressions:
In/On/At, Like/Need/Want

Looking at Healthy and Unhealthy Habits

STEP ❶ Read about Fran Tick and Janice Lowe.

Fran Tick and Janice Lowe are friends and roommates. Fran is a doctor. She takes care of people, and she loves her job. She starts work at 6:30 A.M. and finishes at 7:30 P.M. She visits her patients in the hospital every morning. Then she hurries to her office to see other patients. She often skips meals, but she eats fruit during the day.

Janice is an accountant. She works in an office from nine to five. She's not very busy, so she often eats snacks like potato chips, cake and candy at work. After work, she plays tennis. Then she goes home and prepares a light dinner.

Fran comes home at 8:00 and eats dinner with Janice. They talk, listen to music together and relax. Then Fran goes to the gym. Janice watches television. Before bed, Janice and Fran feel hungry. They enjoy some ice cream or milk and cookies. They go to sleep at midnight.

STEP ❷ Complete the chart about Fran and Janice's healthy and unhealthy habits.

	Healthy	Unhealthy
Fran	She loves her job	She starts work at 6:30 a.m. and finishes at 7:30 p.m.
Janice		
Fran and Janice		

STEP ❸ Who is healthier? Whose life is more stressful? Why?

Talking about Habits and Routines

EXAMPLES	EXPLANATION
(a) Fran and Janice **listen** to music together. **(b)** Fran **goes** to the gym every evening.	Use the simple present tense to talk about habits or things that happen again and again.

EXERCISE 1

Go back to the Opening Task. Underline all the simple present tense verbs that tell about Fran and Janice's habits and routines.

EXAMPLE: They <u>live</u> together.

Simple Present Tense: Affirmative Statements

SUBJECT	VERB
I You* We They	work.
He She It	work**s**.

*Both singular and plural.

Circle the correct form of the verb.

1. Fran is a doctor. She (take/takes) care of sick people.

2. Janice is an accountant. She (work/works) in an office.

3. Fran (love/loves) her job.

4. Fran (start/starts) work at 6:30 A.M.

5. Janice (eat/eats) snacks like potato chips, cake, and candy at work.

6. Janice (prepare/prepares) a light dinner every night.

7. Fran and Janice (exercise/exercises) every day.

8. Janice (play/plays) tennis after work.

9. Fran (go/goes) to the gym.

10. They (relax/relaxes) together after dinner.

11. They (enjoy/enjoys) ice cream or milk and cookies.

12. They (go/goes) to sleep late.

Match the occupations with what they do.

1. A doctor   a. repairs cars

2. Construction workers   b. protect people

3. A mechanic   c. answers the telephone

4. Air traffic controllers   d. takes care of sick people

5. A receptionist   e. build houses

6. Taxi drivers   f. direct airplanes

7. Police officers   g. works in emergencies

8. A fire fighter   h. take passengers to different places

Which of these jobs are the most stressful? Explain why.

Third Person Singular: Spelling and Pronunciation

BASE FORM OF VERB	SPELLING	PRONUNCIATION
1. The final sound of the verb is "voiceless" (for example: p/t/f/k/s/th): **sleep**	Add -s. He **sleeps** eight hours every night.	 /s/
2. The final sound of the verb is "voiced" (for example: b/d/v/g/l/m/n/r or a vowel): **prepare**	Add -s. He **prepares** dinner.	 /z/
3. The verb ends in **sh, ch, x, z,** or **ss:** **watch**	Add -es. He **watches** TV.	 /IZ/
4. The verb ends in a consonant + **y:** **hurry**	Change y to i and add -es. She **hurries** home.	 /z/
5. The verb ends in a vowel + **y:** **play**	Add -s. He **plays** tennis on Saturday.	 /z/
6. Irregular Forms: **have** **go** **do**	 Jane **has** a job. She **goes** to work every day. Fred **does** the dishes.	 /z/

The pictures of Lazy Louie and his wife Hannah are not in the correct order. Number the pictures in the correct order. Then write the number of the picture next to the sentences below.

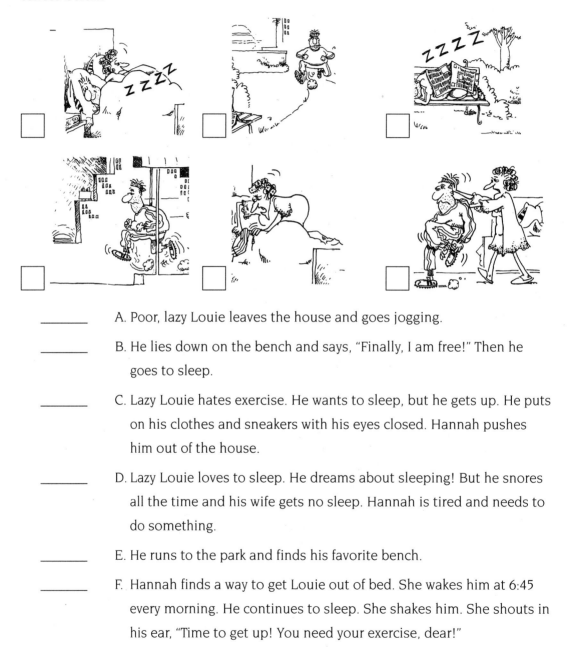

_____ A. Poor, lazy Louie leaves the house and goes jogging.

_____ B. He lies down on the bench and says, "Finally, I am free!" Then he goes to sleep.

_____ C. Lazy Louie hates exercise. He wants to sleep, but he gets up. He puts on his clothes and sneakers with his eyes closed. Hannah pushes him out of the house.

_____ D. Lazy Louie loves to sleep. He dreams about sleeping! But he snores all the time and his wife gets no sleep. Hannah is tired and needs to do something.

_____ E. He runs to the park and finds his favorite bench.

_____ F. Hannah finds a way to get Louie out of bed. She wakes him at 6:45 every morning. He continues to sleep. She shakes him. She shouts in his ear, "Time to get up! You need your exercise, dear!"

Here is a list of third-person singular verbs from the story about Lazy Louie. Check the sound you hear at the end of the verb. Then read the verbs aloud.

Verb	/S/	/Z/	/ɪZ/
1. loves			
2. wakes			
3. pushes			
4. leaves			
5. lies			
6. hates			
7. puts			
8. dreams			
9. snores			
10. needs			
11. goes			
12. finds			
13. says			
14. continues			
15. shakes			
16. shouts			
17. gets			
18. wants			
19. runs			

Sit in a circle. The first person in the circle starts to tell the story of Louie and Hannah and the next continues, and so on all around the circle.

FOCUS 4 >>>>>>>>>>>>>>>>>>>>>> MEANING

Frequency and Time Expressions

EXAMPLES	EXPLANATIONS
every morning/afternoon/evening/night every day/week/year every summer/winter/spring/fall all the time once a week twice a month three times a year	Frequency expressions tell how often we do something.

in + the morning
      the afternoon
      the evening
in + June
      1939
      the summer
at + 7:30
      night
      noon
on + Wednesday(s)
      March 17
      the weekend
	Time expressions tell when we do something.

EXERCISE 7

Fill in the blanks with a frequency or time expression.

Fred and Jane get up (1) _____ seven (2) _____ day of the week, but not (3) _____ weekends. (4) _____ Saturday, they get up (5) _____ nine and play tennis (6) _____ the morning. (7) _____ the afternoon, they go shopping.

(8) _____ the evening, they go out with friends. They go to bed

(9) _____ midnight. (10) _____ Sunday, they get up

(11) _____ ten and have breakfast (12) _____ noon. They

stay home and read (13) _____ Sunday.

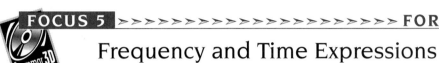 **FORM**

FOCUS 5

Frequency and Time Expressions

EXAMPLES	EXPLANATIONS
(a) They cook dinner **every night.** **(b)** She gets up at 7:00 **every morning.**	Frequency and time expressions usually come at the end of a sentence.
(c) They cook dinner **every night at 7:00.** **(d)** They cook dinner **at seven every night.**	When there is both a frequency and a time expression in one sentence, the frequency expression can come before or after the time expression.
(e) **Once a week,** they go out to eat. **(f)** **On weekends,** they stay in.	Frequency and time expressions can sometimes come at the beginning of a sentence. Use a comma (,) after the expressions at the beginning of a sentence.
(g) I work **on Saturdays.** **(h)** I work **Saturdays.**	With days and dates, *on* is not necessary.

EXERCISE 8

Make true statements about yourself using the time and frequency expressions below and the simple present tense.

EXAMPLE: once a week

> **You say:** I go to the library once a week.

1. once a week
2. every weekend

3. twice a week
4. on my birthday

5. once a year

6. at 7:30 in the morning

7. on Friday nights

8. in August

9. in the summer

10. all the time

11. on December 31

12. at 6:00

EXERCISE 9

Look at Wendy's weekly schedule. Then fill in the blanks in the exercise with the simple present tense or a frequency or time expression.

	Monday	Tuesday	Wednesday	Thursday	Friday
7:00	wake up				
7:30	eat breakfast at home				go out for breakfast
9:30	teach French	go jogging	teach French	do aerobics	teach French
12:00	eat lunch at school	eat lunch at home	eat lunch at school	eat lunch at home	attend meetings
3:00	play tennis	prepare lessons	play tennis	go food shopping	clean apartment
6:00	meet a friend for dinner	go to cooking class	go to the movies	take dancing lessons	go out with friends
8:00	do the laundry	talk on the phone	read a novel	prepare lessons	
10:30	go to bed early				
12:00					go to bed

1. Wendy _goes food shopping_____ on Thursday afternoon.

2. Wendy cleans her apartment _on Friday afternoon_____.

3. Wendy_____ every day at 7:00.

4. She eats breakfast at home _____.

5. Once a week, on Friday mornings, she _____.

6. She_____ three times a week.

7. She does aerobics _____.

8. She eats lunch at school _____.

9. She attends meetings _____.

10. _____ she eats lunch at home.

11. She goes to cooking class _____.

12. She reads _____.

13. On Friday evening, she _____.

14. She goes to bed early _____.

15. She _____ at midnight on Friday.

16. She does the laundry _____.

17. She _____ at 8:00 on Thursday night.

Now make two more statements about Wendy's schedule.

18. _____.

19. _____.

FOCUS 6 ▸▸▸▸▸▸▸▸▸▸▸▸▸▸▸▸▸▸▸▸▸▸▸ FORM

Simple Present: Negative Statements

SUBJECT	DO/DOES NOT	BASE FORM OF VERB
I You* We They Jim and Peter	do not don't	work.
He She It Mary	does not doesn't	

*Both singular and plural.

Do you have a healthy life? Check (✔)Yes or No.

	Yes	No
1. I smoke.	＿＿＿	＿＿＿
2. I exercise every day.	＿＿＿	＿＿＿
3. I drink six or more cans of soda every day.	＿＿＿	＿＿＿
4. I eat fruit and vegetables.	＿＿＿	＿＿＿
5. I eat fast food every day.	＿＿＿	＿＿＿
6. I live a quiet life.	＿＿＿	＿＿＿
7. I go to bed late.	＿＿＿	＿＿＿
8. I skip meals.	＿＿＿	＿＿＿
9. I feel tired every day.	＿＿＿	＿＿＿
10. I eat red meat every day.	＿＿＿	＿＿＿
11. I cook fresh food at home.	＿＿＿	＿＿＿
12. I find time to relax.	＿＿＿	＿＿＿
13. I overeat.	＿＿＿	＿＿＿
14. I worry all the time.	＿＿＿	＿＿＿

Now look at your partner's Yes and No checks. Does he or she have a healthy life? Tell the class why your partner has a healthy or unhealthy life.

EXAMPLE: My partner has a very healthy life. He doesn't smoke. He exercises every day.

FOCUS 7 >>>>>>>>>>>>>>>>>>>>>>>>>> **USE**

Talking about Things that Are Always True

EXAMPLES	EXPLANATION
(a) The sun **rises** in the East. **(b)** A healthy person **enjoys** life. **(c)** A healthy person **doesn't use** drugs.	Use the simple present to make statements about things that always happen or things that are always true.

Use the simple present affirmative or negative to complete the definitions of the new words below.

1. Workaholics (love) _love_____ to work all the time.

2. Vegetarians (eat) _____ meat.

3. Couch potatoes (sit) _____ in front of the TV all the time.

4. An alcoholic (drink) _____ a lot of wine, beer, or liquor every day.

5. A pacifist (like) _____ war.

6. An insomniac (sleep) _____ at night.

7. A stressed person (worry) _____ a lot.

8. A health-conscious person (care) _____ about his or her health.

9. Environmentalists (like) _____ pollution.

Fill in the blanks. Use the simple present affirmative or negative of the verbs in parentheses.

Today, many Americans are under stress. They (move) (1) __move__ at a
fast pace. They (work) (2) _____ all the time. They often (work)
(3) _____ overtime. An average worker (have) (4) _____
too much work and (have) (5) _____ enough time to finish it. Many
Americans (take) (6) _____ vacations. Time is important, but people
(have) (7) _____ time for themselves or their families.

Why are Americans so busy all the time? One reason is modern technology. Modern
technology (keep) (8) _____ us busy and (give) (9) _____
us stress. Technology (help) (10) _____ us relax. We (wear)
(11) _____ beepers. We (use) (12) _____ fax machines to
send messages fast. We (take) (13) _____ time to rest. Even on Sundays,
many stores (stay) (14) _____ open and people (go shopping)
(15) _____. Today, stress is one of the top reasons why Americans (get)
(16) _____ sick.

FOCUS 8 >>>>>>>>>>>>>> FORM/MEANING
Like, Want, Need

EXAMPLES	EXPLANATIONS
I { **like** / **want** / **need** } coffee.	Subject + Verb + Noun
I { **like** / **want** / **need** } to drink coffee.	Subject + Verb + Infinitive
(a) I love animals. I **want** a cat. **(b)** I love Bill. I **want** to marry him.	*Want* expresses desire.
(c) I have a headache. I **need** some medicine. **(d)** You don't look well. You **need** to see a doctor.	*Need* expresses something that is necessary.

What do these people need? Write one sentence with *need* + noun and another sentence with *want* + infinitive. Use the nouns and verbs in the box.

EXAMPLE:

He needs some flour

He wants to bake some cookies

Nouns	Verbs
cup of coffee	write down a message
hammer	hang a picture
a quarter	fix a broken cup
peace and quiet	paint a room
pen	wake up
glue	go to sleep
a can of paint	make a telephone call

1.

   _____

   _____

2.

   _____

   _____

3.

_____

_____

4.

_____

_____

5.

_____

_____

6.

_____

_____

7.

_____

_____

Correct the mistakes in the following sentences.

1. She is smile every day.
2. He every day takes a walk.
3. He finish his dinner every night.
4. He don't cook dinner on Sundays.
5. We are study in the library on Saturdays.
6. She don't work on Tuesdays.
7. English classes begin at September.
8. She need a pen to write
9. He want to make a sandwich
10. Wendy plays tennis on 3:00.

Activities

ACTIVITY 1

Who is a person you admire? Tell your partner about him or her. Then answer questions your partner may have.

EXAMPLE: I admire my mother. She loves our family. She enjoys her work. She cooks great food. She doesn't get angry.

Who is a person you are worried about? Tell your partner about him or her. Then answer the questions your partner may have.

EXAMPLE: I am worried about my friend. He doesn't eat healthy food. He doesn't exercise. He doesn't sleep. He sits in front of the TV all the time.

With your partner choose one person you admire or are worried about. Tell the class about the person.

ACTIVITY 2

What do you and your partner have in common? Write two affirmative statements and two negative statements with *like* for each of the categories below. Share your sentences with your partner and find out what you both have in common. Report your results to the class.

Music	Books	Food
I like to listen to classical music. I also like rock. I don't like rap. I don't like to listen to opera.		

Movies	Sports	Cars

ACTIVITY 3

Fill out your own daily schedule using only the base form of the verb. Then exchange schedules with a partner. Write ten affirmative and negative sentences about your partner's habits and routines. Report to the class.

EXAMPLE: My partner goes jogging on Mondays at 6:00 A.M.

	Mon.	Tues.	Wed.	Thurs.	Fri.	Sat.	Sun.
Morning		6:00 go jogging					
Afternoon				3:00 go to the library			
Evening							

Write ten statements about the habits of people in the country you come from. Share your information with your classmates. Compare the habits of people in different countries.

EXAMPLES:

1. In Korea,   women don't change their names when they get married.

                  people eat rice every day.

                  men go into the army.

2. In China,   people like to exercise in the morning.

                  people go to work by bicycle.

3. In Italy,   people eat pasta.

What is a typical day for you?
Look at the activities below and say how much time you spend on each activity.

sleep _____   eat _____   work _____

study in school _____   do exercise _____   clean my room _____

watch TV _____   do homework _____   talk on the phone _____

travel _____   cook _____   get dressed _____

other _____

Get into a group and talk about each activity. What is the average time the group spends on each activity? Each group should report to the class.

EXAMPLE: We sleep eight hours a night.

Listen to the two people talk about their jobs. Complete the chart.

S = Sunday
M = Monday
T = Tuesday
W = Wednesday
T = Thursday
F = Friday
S = Saturday

Job	Start	Circle workdays	Work on Sundays?
1.		S M T W T F S	
2.		S M T W T F S	

Which job do you like? 1 or 2? Why?

Simple Present Tense
Yes/No Questions, Adverbs of Frequency, Wh-Questions

What Do Good Language Learners Do?

You are all "language learners" in this class. But are you **good** language learners? What is a **good language learner**? What does a good language learner do?

STEP ❶ Read the text below. Then check Yes or No.

Good language learners think about how to learn. They try to use the new language every day. They read, write, and listen to the new language. They find people to speak to. When they don't understand, they don't get nervous. They try to guess the meanings of new words and expressions. They always ask questions about the language. They find ways to remember new words. They try to use new words and expressions in sentences. They listen to correct pronunciation. They repeat words out loud. They sometimes talk to themselves in the new language. They also think about grammar. They try to understand how the new language works.

Good language learners know that learning a new language is not easy. They don't feel bad when they make mistakes. They try to understand their problems in the new language. They review every day.

	Yes	No
1. _____ they think about how to learn?		
2. _____ they practice the new language?		
3. _____ they get nervous when they don't understand?		
4. _____ they ask questions about the new language?		
5. _____ they guess the meaning of new words?		
6. _____ they find ways to remember new words?		
7. _____ they listen to pronunciation?		
8. _____ they think about grammar?		
9. _____ they feel bad when they make mistakes?		
10. _____ they think language learning is easy?		

STEP ❷ Compare your answers with a partner's.

STEP ❸ With a partner, make up some comprehension questions about this text. For example: Do good language learners think about how to learn? Does a good language learner practice the new language?

Simple Present: *Yes/No* Questions

DO/DOES	SUBJECT	BASE FORM OF VERB	SHORT ANSWERS			
			AFFIRMATIVE		NEGATIVE	
Do	I you we they	work?	Yes,	you I we they do.	No,	you I we they do not. don't.
Does	he she it		Yes,	he she it does.	No,	he she it does not. doesn't.

EXERCISE 1

Are your classmates good language learners?

Ask one classmate *yes/no* questions with the words below. Then ask another classmate the questions.

EXAMPLE: You: Do you speak English outside of class?

Classmate: Yes, I do./No, I don't.

	Classmate 1		Classmate 2	
	Yes	**No**	**Yes**	**No**
1. speak English outside of class				
2. practice pronunciation				
3. ask people to correct your English				
4. ask people questions about English				
5. watch TV in English				
6. guess the meaning of new words				

1. speak English outside of class
2. practice pronunciation
3. ask people to correct your English
4. ask people questions about English
5. watch TV in English
6. guess the meaning of new words

	Classmate 1		Classmate 2	
	Yes	No	Yes	No
7. make lists of new words				
8. read something in English every day				
9. write something in English every day				
10. think about grammar				

7. make lists of new words

8. read something in English every day

9. write something in English every day

10. think about grammar

Discuss your answers with the class. Decide who is a good language learner.

EXERCISE 2

INFORMATION GAP

Nahal and Sang-Woo are two different types of language learners. Work with a partner to find out how they are different. Student A looks at the chart below. Student B looks at the chart on page E-4. Ask and answer questions to complete your chart.

EXAMPLE: **Student A:** Does Nahal want to meet English-speaking people?

Student B: Yes, she does.

Student B: Does Sang-Woo want to meet English-speaking people?

Student A: No, he doesn't.

Student A:

	Nahal		Sang-Woo	
	Yes	No	Yes	No
1. like to learn English	✔			
2. want to meet English-speaking people				✔
3. feel nervous when speaking English		✔		
4. like to work in groups			✔	
5. need grammar rules to learn English	✔			
6. learn by speaking and listening to English				✔
7. learn by reading and writing English		✔		
8. learn slowly, step by step			✔	
9. try new ways of learning	✔			

EXERCISE 3

What kind of language learner are you?
Look at Exercise 2 and write statements about yourself.

EXAMPLE: _I like to learn English. I want to meet English-speaking people. I don't feel_

nervous when speaking English.

EXERCISE 4

What are some of your habits? Ask a partner _yes/no_ questions with the words below. Check yes or no. Then your partner asks you.

EXAMPLE: You: Do you wake up early?

Your Partner: Yes, I do./No, I don't.

Your Partner's Answers

	Yes	No
1. wake up early	_____	_____
2. watch TV a lot	_____	_____
3. listen to loud music	_____	_____
4. cook	_____	_____
5. have parties on weekends	_____	_____
6. make friends easily	_____	_____
7. go to bed late	_____	_____
8. talk on the telephone a lot	_____	_____
9. study hard	_____	_____
10. clean your apartment every week	_____	_____

EXERCISE 5

Read about students in the United States.

(1) In the United States, a child usually starts kindergarten at age five. (2) In public schools, boys and girls study together. (3) Children go to school five days a week. (4) They don't go to school on Saturdays. (5) They go to school from 8:30 A.M. to 3:00 P.M. (6) They don't wear uniforms in school. (7) In public schools, children do not study religion.

(8) In high school, every student takes difficult exams to enter college. (9) A private college costs a lot of money. (10) The government doesn't pay for private colleges. (11) Parents pay for their children's education. (12) Many students work after school to help pay for college.

Write twelve *yes/no* questions from the sentences marked 1–12 in the reading. Interview a classmate about his or her country with the questions you wrote. Compare students in the United States to students in your countries.

QUESTIONS

1. Does a child usually start kindergarten at age five in your country ?
2. Do boys and girls usually study together ?
3. _____ ?
4. _____ ?
5. _____ ?
6. _____ ?
7. _____ ?
8. _____ ?
9. _____ ?
10. _____ ?
11. _____ ?
12. _____ ?

Now write five sentences about school in your partner's country.

1. In Korea, students study religion in school.
2. _____
2. _____
3. _____
4. _____
5. _____

FOCUS 2 ➢➢➢➢➢➢➢➢➢➢➢➢➢➢➢➢➢➢➢ MEANING

Adverbs of Frequency

Adverbs of frequency tell how often something happens.

QUESTION: HOW OFTEN DOES NAHAL WATCH TELEVISION?

	always		100%
	almost always		
	usually		
Nahal	**often/frequently**	watches television.	
	sometimes		
	seldom/rarely		
	never		0%

EXERCISE 6

Read the questions and answers. Circle the correct adverbs of frequency.

EXAMPLE: Q: Does Nahal read English/American newspapers?

　　　　　A: She ((often)/seldom) reads an English or American newspaper. She buys one every morning.

1. **Q:** Does Sang-Woo ever use his hands when he speaks English?

   A: He (never/always) uses his hands. His hands help him explain things.

2. **Q:** Does Nahal ever guess the meanings of words?

   A: She (never/always) guesses the meanings of new words. She uses her dictionary all the time.

3. **Q:** Does Sang-Woo ever think in English?

   A: He (never/usually) thinks in his own language first. Then he translates his words into English.

4. **Q:** Does Nahal ever sing in English?

   A: She (often/seldom) sings in English. She doesn't like to sing.

5. **Q:** Does Sang-Woo ever write letters in English?

A: He has an American friend in Boston. He misses him. He (rarely/sometimes) writes letters to him in English.

6. **Q:** Does Nahal ever make telephone calls in English?

   A: She lives with her aunt. Her aunt speaks English. Her aunt makes the phone calls. Nahal (never/always) makes phone calls in English.

7. **Q:** Does Nahal ever talk to herself in English?

   A: She likes English. She (usually/rarely) talks to herself in English.

8. **Q:** Does Sang-Woo ever think about how English works?

   A: He thinks grammar is very interesting. He (never/always) tries to understand how English works.

EXERCISE 7

The chart below shows learning habits and adverbs of frequency. Check the box that is true for you.

Learning Habits	Adverbs of Frequency						
	ALWAYS	ALMOST ALWAYS	USUALLY	OFTEN FREQUENTLY	SOMETIMES	SELDOM RARELY	NEVER
1. use a dictionary							
2. make telephone calls in English							
3. speak to native speakers							
4. discuss learning problems with classmates							
5. practice English pronunciation							
6. record your voice on tape							
7. read books or newspapers in English							
8. ask questions about English							
9. think in English							
10. dream in English							

Position of Adverbs of Frequency

EXAMPLES	EXPLANATIONS
(a) They **always** come to class. **(b)** He **sometimes** asks questions in class. **(c)** He **never** asks questions.	Adverbs of frequency usually come between the subject and the verb.
(d) **Sometimes** I ask questions in class. **(e)** That's not true. He asks questions **often.**	Adverbs of frequency can sometimes come at the beginning or at the end of a sentence for emphasis.
(f) They **are always** in class. **(g)** I **am never** late to class.	Adverbs of frequency come after the verb *be*.

EXERCISE 8

Go back to the chart in Exercise 7. Exchange books with a partner. Write statements about your partner's learning habits using adverbs of frequency.

EXAMPLE: He always uses a dictionary.

   She rarely speaks to native speakers.

EXERCISE 9

Add an adverb of frequency to make the statements below true about the country you come from.

Name of country: _____

In schools in the country I come from:

1. The students are of the same nationality.

   The students are usually of the same nationality.

2. The teachers are women.

   _____

3. Teachers hit students.

   _____

4. Teachers are young.

_____

5. Teachers give homework.

_____

6. Teachers are relaxed and friendly.

_____

7. Students work together to learn.

_____

8. The classrooms are noisy.

_____

9. Students take tests.

_____

10. Students cheat on tests.

_____

Now discuss what you think is true for the United States.

Simple Present: *Wh*-Questions

WH-QUESTION WORD	DO/DOES	SUBJECT	BASE FORM OF VERB	
(a) **What**		I	**do**	in class?
(b) **When**	**do**	you	**watch**	TV?
(c) **What time**		we	**begin**	class?
(d) **Where**		they	**study**	English?
(e) **Why**		he	**need**	English?
(f) **How**		she	**go**	to school?
(g) **How often**	**does**	Maria	**talk to**	native speakers of English?
(h) **Who(m)**		George	**meet**	after school?

EXERCISE 10

Match each question to its answer. Write the letter on the line.

_f___ 1. Why does he need English?

_____ 2. When does the semester begin?

_____ 3. What do they do in class?

_____ 4. What time does your class start?

_____ 5. Where does he study English?

_____ 6. How often does he speak English?

_____ 7. When does she go out with her girlfriends?

_____ 8. How does he go home?

a. on weekends

b. by car

c. at the City University of New York.

d. They speak, read, write, and listen to English.

e. at 8:30

f. because he wants to go to college in the United States

g. on September 10th

h. every day

Read the story of a student named Denise. Write Wh-questions with the words in parentheses. Then read the text again and answer the questions aloud.

Denise is a Haitian student in New York. She speaks three languages—Creole, French, and English. She wants to be a bilingual teacher. Her English is very good, but she speaks with an accent. Sometimes people don't understand her when she speaks. She often meets her Haitian friends to talk about her problem. Denise feels embarrassed and seldom speaks English. She feels angry at Americans. She says Americans only speak English. They don't understand the problems people have when they learn a new language.

EXAMPLE: (Denise/live) _Where does Denise live_ ?

1. (Denise/come from) _____ ?

2. (Denise/want to be) _____ ?

3. (Denise/speak English) _____ ?

4. (Denise/feel when she speaks English) _____ ?

5. (Denise/feel this way) _____ ?

6. (Denise/feel angry) _____ ?

Now ask two questions of your own about the story.

7. _____ ?

8. _____ ?

FOCUS 5 ➢➢➢➢➢➢➢➢➢➢ **FORM/MEANING/USE**

Wh-Questions with *Who/Whom*

EXAMPLES	EXPLANATIONS
(a) Q: Who usually meets her friends? **A:** Denise. **(b) Q: Who** speaks Creole? **A:** Denise and her Haitian friends.	*Who* asks a question about the subject (Denise) of the sentence. Do not use *do/does*.
(c) Q: Who(m) does Denise meet? **A:** Denise meets her friends.	*Who(m)* asks a question about the object (her friends) of the sentence.
(d) Whom does Denise call on Sundays? **(e) Who** does Denise call on Sundays?	Formal written English Informal or spoken English
(f) Q: What goes up but never comes down? **A:** Your age!	*What* can also be the subject of a question. Do not use *do/does* in this case.

EXERCISE 12

Fill in the blanks with *who* or *whom*.

EXAMPLE: __Who__ speaks English?

__Who(m)__ do you call every week?

1. _____ likes English?

2. _____ avoids English?

3. _____ bites his or her nails before a test?

4. _____ do you meet after class?

5. _____ do you usually visit on weekends?

6. _____ makes mistakes in English?

7. _____ do you call at night?

8. _____ understands the difference between *who* and *whom*?

9. _____ helps you with English?

Read about immigrant families in the United States.

Many families immigrate to the United States. At the beginning, the parents sometimes have problems. They don't speak English. They don't learn English fast. The children often learn English before the parents, so they translate for their parents. The children always help their parents. For example, the children sometimes pay the rent to the landlords. They often talk with doctors about their parents' health. The children take their parents to job interviews. They solve the family's problems. This is a big job for the children, and they feel important. But their parents sometimes feel sad and helpless. Life is often difficult for new immigrant families.

Fill in the blanks with *who* (subject) or *whom* (object).

EXAMPLE: Q: _Who_ learns English before the parents?

A: The children (learn English before the parents.)

Q: _Whom_ do the children help?

A: (The children help) their parents.

1. _____ translates for the parents?

2. _____ helps the parents?

3. _____ do the children pay the rent to?

4. _____ do the children often talk to about their parents' health?

5. _____ do the children take to job interviews?

6. _____ solves the family's problems?

7. _____ feels important?

8. _____ feels sad and helpless?

Getting Information about English

In a new language, you do not always know the words to say what you want. When you have a problem, ask for help.

EXAMPLES	EXPLANATIONS
You say:	**When you:**
(a) What does the word *decision* mean? **(b)** What does *strategy* mean?	• want to know the **meaning** of a word.
(c) How do you spell *remember*?	• want to know the **spelling** of a word.
(d) How do you pronounce *communicate*?	• want to know the **pronunciation** of a word.
(e) How do you say *a machine to clean floors*? **(f)** How do you say *the opposite of happy*?	• don't know the word for something, and you want to explain your meaning.

EXERCISE 14

Ask W*h*-questions for the answers below.

EXAMPLE: Q: How do you say special shoes you wear in the house?

A: You say slippers.

1. **Q:** _____ ?

   A: You pronounce it /ǽŋ-gwɪdʒ/.

2. **Q:** _____ ?

   A: The word *guess* means you don't know the answer, but you try to find the answer in your head.

3. **Q:** _____ ?

   A: You say *thin*.

4. **Q:** _____ ?

   A: You spell it: c-o-m-m-u-n-i-c-a-t-e.

5. **Q:** _____?

    A: *Strategy* means an action or actions you take to achieve a goal; for example. to learn English.

EXERCISE 15

Correct the mistakes in the following sentences.

1. Is he read books?
2. Do they good students?
3. What means *routines*?
4. I watch sometimes TV.
5. How often you listen to native speakers of English?
6. Does he studies in the library?
7. What does the class on Mondays?
8. How you say *not correct*?
9. I am never make mistakes.
10. Why you feel embarrassed to speak English?

Activities

ACTIVITY 1

Work with a partner. Ask each other *yes/no* and W*h*-questions in the simple present tense. Find five ways in which you are the same and five ways in which you are different. Write your questions and answers and then report to the class.

EXAMPLES: Do you eat breakfast?

                What do you eat for breakfast?

ACTIVITY 2

Find the perfect roommate. You want to share an apartment with another student. Write ten questions to ask your classmates. Find a good "roommate" in your class.

EXAMPLE: • Do you smoke?   • How often do you have parties?

            • What time do you get up?   • When do you go to bed?

ACTIVITY 3

What do you know about the countries your classmates come from? Write ten questions about customs, habits, etc. Find a classmate who comes from a different country and ask the questions. Use adverbs of frequency in your questions and answers. Then report to the class.

EXAMPLES: What do people usually do on weekends?

How often do people go to the movies?

How do people usually celebrate their birthdays?

ACTIVITY 4

GENERAL KNOWLEDGE QUIZ

STEP ❶ Get into two teams. Write ten general knowledge *Wh*-questions in the simple present.

STEP ❷ Team A asks Team B the first question. Team B can discuss the question before they answer. Then Team B asks Team A the second question and so on.

Score: Score 1 point for each grammatically correct question. Score 1 point for each correct answer. The team with the most points is the winner.

EXAMPLE: Where does the President of the United States live?

When do the Chinese celebrate the New Year?

ACTIVITY 5

Write about the educational system in your native country. Answer these questions:

- What do students usually do?
- What do teachers usually do?
- What are the differences between the school system in your native country and the United States?

ACTIVITY 6

STEP ❶ Listen to the conversation between Pedro and Yuko. Who is the hard-working student?

STEP ❷ Listen again. Make a list of the things Pedro and Yuko do on Sundays.

Pedro   Yuko

_____   _____

_____   _____

_____   _____

_____   _____

STEP ❸ Role-play the conversation with a partner.

UNIT

10

Imperatives and Prepositions of Direction

OPENING TASK

Who Says What?

1.

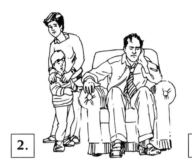

2.

3.

4.

5.

6.

(a) "Please give me change for a dollar, Sir." _____

(b) "Have a piece of cake with your coffee, Mary." _____

(c) "Don't ask your father now. He's very angry." _____

(d) "Don't throw your litter on the street. Pick it up!" _____

(e) "Go straight down Eighth Avenue and turn left at the bakery." _____

(f) "Watch out!" _____

STEP ❷ What is the mother saying? Write her words.

FOCUS 1

Imperatives: Affirmative and Negative

Affirmative

BASE FORM OF VERB	
(a) Have	a piece of cake.
(b) Give	me a dollar.

Negative

DON'T + BASE FORM OF VERB	
(c) Don't throw	your litter on the street.
(d) Don't ask	your father now.

Polite Imperatives

(e) Please give me change for a dollar.

(f) Please don't do that again.

(g) Don't do that again, **please.**

NOTE: Don't use a subject with imperatives:
Have a piece of cake. NOT: ~~You~~ have a piece of cake.

EXERCISE 1

Go back to the Opening Task on page 148. Underline all the affirmative imperatives and circle all the negative imperatives.

EXAMPLE: "Please <u>give</u> me change for a dollar, Sir."

FOCUS 2 ➤➤➤➤➤➤➤➤➤➤➤➤➤➤➤➤➤➤➤➤➤➤➤➤ USE

Uses of Imperatives

Imperatives have different uses or purposes. Look at the pictures and see what the imperative does in each situation.

a.

b.

c.

d.

e.

f.

150   Unit 10

IMPERATIVE	USE
(a) "Don't worry, Relax."	Give advice or make a suggestion
(b) "Be careful!"	Give a warning when there is danger.
(c) "Make a right at the corner."	Give directions or instructions.
(d) "Please give me some aspirin, Mom."	Make a polite request.
(e) "Have some coffee, dear."	Offer something politely.
(f) "Don't come home late again!"	Give an order.

EXERCISE 2

Look back at the Opening Task on page 147. Write the number of the picture that matches each use.

Use	Picture Number
A. Give advice	2
B. Give an order	
C. Give a warning when there is danger	
D. Make a polite request	
E. Offer something politely	
F. Give directions	

EXERCISE 3

Fill in each blank with an affirmative or negative imperative.

use	keep	drink	be	drive
wear	obey	leave	look	use

To be a good driver, remember these rules:

1. _____ prepared to stop.

2. _____ ahead.

3. _____ your rearview mirrors.

4. _____ the speed limit.

5. _____ space between your car and the car in front of you.

6. _____ your seat belt.

7. _____ if you are very tired or are on medication.

8. _____ and drive.

9. _____ your horn to warn others of danger.

10. _____ your car in good condition.

Work with a partner. You read each sentence on the left. Your partner gives an appropriate response from the right.

1. I don't like my landlord.
2. I have a headache.
3. I am overweight.
4. I have the hiccups.
5. I have a toothache.
6. I don't have any friends here.
7. I feel tired every morning.
8. I miss my family.
9. I worry too much.
10. I can't speak English very well.

a. Go on a diet.
b. Go to the dentist.
c. Make friends with your classmates.
d. Move to a different apartment.
e. Call home.
f. Go to bed early.
g. Practice speaking to native speakers.
h. Hold your breath for two minutes.
i. Take it easy.
j. Take some aspirin.

FOCUS 3 >>>>>>>>>>>>>>>>>>>>>>>>>>>>>> **USE**

Using Imperatives Appropriately

EXAMPLES	EXPLANATIONS
(a) Police Officer to woman: "Show me your license."	Use an imperative when: • the speaker has the right or authority to tell the listener to do something.
(b) A teacher to a teacher: "Pass me that book, please."	• the speaker and the listener are equals; for example, they work together.

Check Yes if the imperative is appropriate in each situation. Check (✔)No if the imperative is not appropriate.

Situation	Imperative	Yes	No
1. A student says to a teacher:	"Give me my paper."		
2. A student says to a classmate:	"Wait for me after class."		
3. A man stops you on the street. He says:	"Hey, mister. Tell me the time."		
4. A worker says to his boss:	"Don't bother me now. I'm busy."		
5. You get into a taxi and say:	"Take me to the airport, and please hurry!"		
6. Father says to a teenage son:	"Turn down that music! I can't take it anymore!"		

FOCUS 4 ➤➤➤➤➤➤➤➤➤➤➤➤➤➤➤➤➤ **MEANING**

Prepositions of Direction: To, Away From, On (to), Off (of), In (to), Out Of

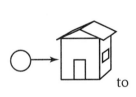
to

away from

on(to)

off (of)

in(to)

out of

EXAMPLES	EXPLANATIONS
(a) He gets **in (to)** the car.	Prepositions of direction show movement.
(b) He gets **on** the bus.	For cars, taxis, and vans, use *in* (*to*) and *out of*.
(c) He gets **out of** the taxi.	For buses, trains and planes, use *on* (*to*) and
(d) He gets **off** the train.	*off* (*of*).

EXERCISE 6

Here is a story about the hard life of a mouse. Fill in the blanks with a preposition of direction from Focus 4.

1. The mouse comes _____ his hole.

2. The cat jumps _____ the table.

3. The mouse runs _____ the cheese.

4. The cat jumps _____ the table and runs after the mouse.

5. The cat runs _____ the mouse.

6. The mouse runs _____ his hole.

Prepositions of Direction:
Up, Down, Across, Along, Around, Over, Through, Past

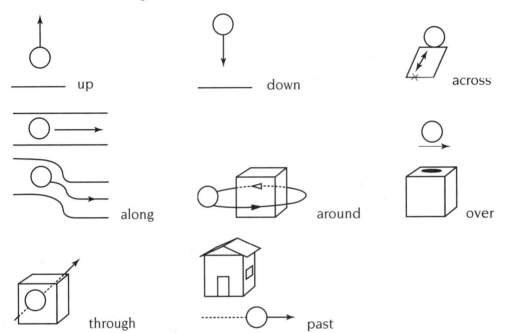

——— up   ——— down   across

along   around   over

through   past

EXERCISE 7

Here is a story about the hard life of a cat. Fill in the blanks with a preposition of direction from Focus 5.

1. The cat sees the dog. He runs _____ the field.

2. He runs _____ the grass.

3. He runs _____ the bridge.

4. He climbs _____ the tree.

5. The dog barks. He runs _____ the tree.

6. The dog's owner arrives and puts a leash on the dog. The cat climbs _____ from the tree.

7. The cat walks _____ the dog.

8. He walks _____ the road with a smile on his face.

FOCUS 6 ＞＞＞＞＞＞＞＞＞＞＞＞＞＞＞＞＞＞＞＞＞＞ USE

Giving Directions

Look at the map below and read the conversation on the following page.

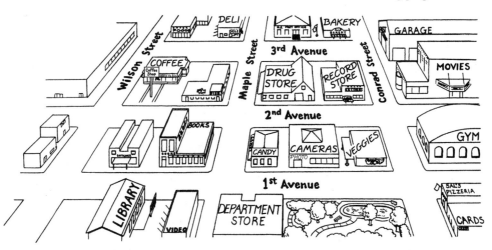

Imperatives and Prepositions of Direction　　**157**

(Person A is at the bakery.)

A: Excuse me, how do I get to the department store?

B: Walk **down** Conrad Street until you get to First Avenue. Then turn **right** at the corner. Go **straight**. Walk one block. The department store is on the corner on the left.

EXERCISE 8

Look at the map in Focus 6. Follow the directions. Then answer the questions.

EXAMPLE: You are at the record store on the corner of Second Avenue and Conrad Street. Walk down Conrad Street until you get to Third Avenue. Turn left at the corner. Walk one block. Cross Third Avenue. This place is on the right. Where are you? Answer: *At the Post Office.*

1. You are at the bakery. Walk down Conrad Street and make a right on Second Avenue. Go straight and make a left on Maple Street. Walk across the street. Where are you? _____

2. You are coming out of the coffee shop entrance on Second Avenue. Walk down Second Avenue and go two blocks. Turn right on Conrad Street. Go straight until you get to First Avenue. Make a left. Walk into the building on your right. Where are you? _____

3. You are at the library on First Avenue. Walk up Wilson Street. Make a right on Third Avenue. Go straight for two blocks. Then make a left on Conrad Street. Go across the street from the bakery. Where are you? _____

EXERCISE 9

Work with a partner. Take turns giving the commands. Your partner acts out the commands you give.

1. Step off the bus.   Step onto the bus.
2. Put your hand into your pocket.   Take your hand out of your pocket.
3. Walk to the blackboard.   Walk away from the blackboard.
4. Put a pencil into the desk drawer.   Put a pencil on the desk.
5. Climb up a mountain.   Climb down a mountain.
6. Walk on the grass.   Walk through tall grass.
7. Walk away from your classmate.   Walk around your classmate.
8. Walk past a group of people.   Walk through a group of people.
9. Walk across the room.   Walk over a book on the floor.

Activities

ACTIVITY 1

DO'S AND DON'TS

STEP ❶ Make a list of do's and don'ts for someone who plans to travel to your country.

EXAMPLE: Korea

	Do's	Don'ts
Hand and body movements	Bow to say goodbye.	Don't touch or pat a man on the back—only if you are very good friends.
Eating		
Manners for a guest at a person's house		
Other		

STEP ❷ Make an oral presentation of the do's and don'ts to your class.

ACTIVITY 2

PROBLEMS AND ADVICE

STEP ❶ Work with a partner. Write down three problems you have.

STEP ❷ Tell your partner your problems.

STEP ❸ Your partner gives you advice.

EXAMPLE: You: I can't sleep at night.

Your Partner: Drink a cup of hot milk.

Problems	Advice
1.	
2.	
3.	

ACTIVITY 3

Work in a group. Create an information booklet to give advice to new students in the United States. Choose from the ideas below.

- How to Learn English
- How to Find a Job
- How to Do Well in School
- How to Find an Apartment
- How to Meet People

ACTIVITY 4
DIRECTIONS GAME

STEP ❶ Work in groups of two or three. Write directions for someone to go to different parts of the building you are in (restrooms, snack bar, etc.).

> **EXAMPLE:** Go out of the room. Turn left and go to the end of the corridor. Turn right. It's on the right.

STEP ❷ Ask the rest of the class to find out where your group is directing someone.

ACTIVITY 5

Look around your neighborhood or your home. Find imperatives in public notices. Discuss the meaning of the notices.

ACTIVITY 6
REMEDIES

 STEP ❶ Listen to the three different remedies. Match the remedy to one of the titles below.

Remedies

(a) _____ How to cure a headache

(b) _____ How to cure a cold

(c) _____ How to treat a burn

STEP ❷ Describe a remedy you know.

Quantifiers

Who Eats a Healthy Breakfast?

The chart on page 162 shows the number of **calories** and the amount of **fat** and **cholesterol** in the foods Billy, Juanita, and Brad eat for breakfast every day.

Calories are the amount of energy a food produces in the body. To lose weight, we need to reduce our calories.

There is **fat** in foods like butter, cheese, and meat. Too much fat is bad for your health.

There is **cholesterol** in foods like eggs, butter, and cheese. Too much cholesterol can give you heart disease.

STEP ❶ Look at the chart and answer the questions.

	Calories	Fat (grams)	Cholesterol (milligrams)
Billy			
eggs (3)	140	9.8	399
sausages (2)	180	16.3	48
muffin	170	4.6	9
milk	165	8	30
Brad			
cereal	80	1.1	0
orange juice	80	0	0
nonfat milk	85	0	0
banana (1)	130	less than 1	0
Juanita			
pancakes (3)	410	9.2	21
vanilla milkshake	290	13	10
doughnuts (2)	240	20	18

1. Is there a lot of fat in Juanita's breakfast?

2. Who eats a breakfast with only a little fat?

3. Whose breakfast has a lot of calories?

4. Are there any calories in Brad's breakfast?

5. How much cholesterol is there in each breakfast?

6. Which foods don't have any cholesterol?

7. Which foods have little fat?

8. Which food has a lot of cholesterol?

STEP ❷ Whose breakfast is healthy? Write three sentences to explain why.

_____ has a healthy breakfast.

1. _____ calories

2. _____ fat.

3. _____ cholesterol.

Review of Count and Noncount Nouns

EXAMPLES	EXPLANATIONS
	Count nouns:
(a) Billy eats a **muffin** and an **egg.**	• can have *a/an* in front of them.
(b) Brad likes **pancakes.**	• can have plural forms.
(c) Billy eats three **eggs.**	• can have a number in front of them.
(d) There is a **fast-food restaurant** near here.	• can take singular or plural verbs.
(e) There are a lot of **calories** in a **milkshake.**	
(f) How many **eggs** does Billy eat?	• can be in questions with *how many.*
	Noncount nouns:
(g) **Cereal** is healthy.	• can't have *a/an* in front of them.
(h) He eats **bread** and **butter.**	• can't have plural forms.
(i) It has a little **cholesterol.**	• can't have a number in front of them.
(j) Nonfat **milk** is good for you.	• can't take plural verbs.
(k) How much **cholesterol** does an egg have?	• can be in questions with *how much.*

EXERCISE 1

Go back to the Opening Task on page 162. Make a list of the count and noncount nouns.

Count Nouns	Noncount Nouns
eggs	milk

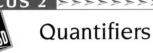

Quantifiers

Quantifiers are words or phrases that show how many things or how much of something we have.

Positive Meaning

COUNT NOUNS			
	Quantifiers		
(a) There are	**many**	eggs	
(b) There are	**a lot of**	apples	in the refrigerator.
(c) There are	**some**	bananas	
(d) There are	**a few**	potatoes	
NONCOUNT NOUNS			
	Quantifiers		
(e) There is	**a lot of**	milk*	
(f) There is	**some**	juice	in the refrigerator.
(g) There is	**a little**	cake	

Negative Meaning

COUNT NOUNS			
	Quantifiers		
(h) There aren't	**many**	potatoes	
(i) There aren't	**a lot of**	potatoes	
(j) There are	**few**	tomatoes	in the refrigerator.
(k) There aren't	**any**	onions	
(l) There are	**no**	onions	
NONCOUNT NOUNS			
	Quantifiers		
(m) There isn't	**much**	cake*	
(n) There isn't	**a lot of**	cake	
(o) There is	**little**	coffee	in the refrigerator.
(p) There isn't	**any**	jam	
(q) There is	**no**	jam	

*Use *much* in negative statements. Do not use *much* in affirmative statements.

NOT: There is much milk in the refrigerator

Match the picture to the statement. Write the letter next to each statement.

Community Bank	January 31
	Account #536
Debits: $325.00	
Credits: $325.00	
	Balance: $___.00

A.

Community Bank	January 31
	Account #741
Debits: $458.31	
Credits: $958.31	
	Balance: $500.00

C.

Community Bank	January 31
	Account #289
Debits: $312.80	
Credits: $412.80	
	Balance: $100.00

B.

Community Bank	January 31
	Account #125
Debits: $ 7,096.10	
Credits: $12,096.10	
	Balance: $5,000.00

D.

_____d_____ 1. Carlos has a lot of money in the bank.

_____ 2. François has a little money in the bank.

_____ 3. Kim has no money in the bank.

_____ 4. Lee has some money in the bank.

E.

F.

G.

_____ 5. The Greens have a lot of plants in their home.

_____ 6. The Smiths don't have any plants.

_____ 7. The Taylors have a few plants.

H.

I.

J.

_____ 8. Jody has no friends.

_____ 9. Irene has a few friends.

_____ 10. Helene has a lot of friends.

K.

L.

M.

_____ 11. Bill has a lot of hair.

_____ 12. Jim doesn't have any hair.

_____ 13. Albert has a little hair.

EXERCISE 3

Cross out the incorrect quantifier in each sentence.

EXAMPLE: My new apartment has furniture.

                                                  some

                                                  a lot of

1. Middletown has   a lot of   pollution.
                            a little
                            a few

2. The teacher gives us   some   homework.
                            many
                            a little.

3. Billy has   a little   girlfriends.
                            a few
                            many

4. Mario speaks   much   languages.
                            three
                            a few

5. Majid has   a lot of   money.
                            a little
                            many

EXERCISE 4

Test your knowledge about food. Check True or False. Then compare your answers to your partner's answers.

		True	False
1.	There are no calories in water.	✔	
2.	There's a lot of salt in fast food.		
3.	There are no calories in soda.		
4.	There's a lot of fat in cheese.		
5.	There are few calories in a small baked potato.		
6.	There's little cholesterol in fish.		
7.	There are few vitamins in orange juice.		
8.	There's some fat in low-fat yogurt.		
9.	There isn't any sugar in fruit.		
10.	There's a little caffeine in tea.		

EXERCISE 5

Use the chart in the Opening Task on page 162 to complete the statements by adding quantifiers.

1. Doughnuts have __a lot of__ calories.

2. A banana doesn't have _____ calories.

3. There is _____ cholesterol in eggs.

4. There is _____ cholesterol in a muffin.

5. There is _____ fat in bananas.

6. Orange juice has _____ calories.

7. Sausages have _____ fat.

8. Eggs and pancakes have _____ fat.

9. There are _____ calories in cereal.

10. There is _____ cholesterol in orange juice.

11. There is _____ fat in cereal.

12. There is _____ fat in whole milk.

FOCUS 3 ➤➤➤➤➤➤➤➤➤➤➤➤➤➤➤➤➤➤➤ MEANING

A Few/Few, A Little/Little

EXAMPLES	EXPLANATIONS
(a) She has **a few** books. = She has *some* books. **(b)** I have **a little** time. = I have *some* time.	A *few* and A *little* have a positive meaning. They mean *some*, or more than zero.
(c) They have **few** books. = They don't have many books. **(d)** They have **little** time. = They don't have much time.	*Few* and *Little* have a negative meaning. They mean *not much*, *not many*, almost zero.

EXERCISE 6

Linda and Kathy are both Americans living in Europe for a year. Their experiences are very different. Fill in the blanks with *few/a few* or *little/a little*.

Linda is very lonely. She doesn't have a full-time job. She has (1) __few__

friends and (2) _____ money. She works part-time as a baby sitter. She

doesn't like this kind of work. She has (3) _____ patience for children.

She speaks very (4) _____ Spanish.

Kathy loves to be in different countries. She speaks (5) _____ lan-

guages. She goes to a language school in Spain and she has (6) _____

very close friends. Kathy learns (7) _____ Spanish every day. She also

works as a baby sitter and makes (8) _____ extra money. Kathy works

hard, but she always has (9) _____ time to go out and have fun. She has

(10) _____ problems in Spain.

Questions with *How Many* and *How Much*

QUESTION			ANSWER	EXPLANATIONS
How many	**Count Noun**			
(a) How many	universities	are there?	A lot.	Use *How many* with count nouns.
(b) How many	brothers	do you have?	Two.	
(c) How many	oranges	do you eat every day?	A few.	
How much	**Noncount Noun**			
(d) How much	money	do you have in your account?	$200.	Use *How much* with noncount nouns.
(e) How much	time	do you have?	Five minutes.	
(f) How much	gas	do you need?	Not much.	

EXERCISE 7

Go back to the Opening Task on page 161. Make questions with *how much* or *how many*. Then answer the questions.

1. _How many_____ pancakes does Juanita usually eat for breakfast?

2. _How much_____ juice does Brad drink?

3. _____ eggs does Billy have?

4. _____ cholesterol is there in three eggs?

5. _____ calories are there in a vanilla milkshake?

6. _____ cholesterol is there in a bowl of cereal?

7. _____ fat is there in two doughnuts?

8. _____ calories are there in three pancakes?

9. _____ sausages can Billy eat?

10. _____ money does Brad spend on his breakfast?

Fill in the blanks with *how much* or *how many* or a quantifier (*a lot, a little, some, any, much, many*). Then answer the questions.

1. **Mom:** How was school today, dear?

   Child: O.K., Mom . . .

   Mom: (a) _____ homework do you have tonight?

   Child: I have (b)) _____ homework—three compositions plus a spelling test tomorrow!

   Mom: Don't worry, I have (c) _____ time to help you tonight.

2. **Doctor:** Please remember to take this medicine, Mr. Josephson.

   Patient: (a) _____ medicine do I need to take every day?

   Doctor: These are pills. You need three red pills a day, one after every meal. And you need two blue pills a day, one in the morning and one before bed.

   Patient: Say that again, please . . . (b) _____ red pills?
   (c) _____ blue pills? And (d) _____ pills do I need to take in all?

   Doctor: Three red pills and two blue pills. Five pills in all. Take these for a week. Then call me.

   Patient: O.K. Thanks, Doctor.

Ask your partner questions about a city he or she knows. First ask a *yes/no* question. Then ask a question with *how many* or *how much*.

1. skyscrapers   Are there any skyscrapers in your city?
   How many skyscrapers are there?

2. crime   Is there any crime in your city?
   How much crime is there?

3. noise
4. universities
5. pollution
6. trash on the streets
7. parks
8. poor people
9. traffic
10. museums
11. beaches
12. American fast-food restaurants
13. public transportation
14. shopping malls
15. hospitals

Measure Words

Measure words change the way we see a thing. A measure word before a noncount noun tells us about the specific quantity.

EXAMPLE: I have a lot of coffee.   (coffee = noncount noun)

I have four cans of coffee.   (specific quantity)

a **can** of tuna	a **box** of cereal	
a **jar** of jam	a **bottle** of beer	Containers
a **tube** of toothpaste	a **bag** of sugar	
a **slice** of pizza	a **glass** of milk	
a **piece** of pie	a **cup** of coffee	Portions
a **cup** of flour	a **quart** of milk	
a **pint** of ice cream	a **pound** of sugar	Specific quantities
a **teaspoon** of salt	a **gallon** of water	
a **head** of lettuce	a **loaf** of bread	
a **sheet** of paper	a **bar** of soap	Other
a **bag** of apples	a **can** of beans	Measure words can also
a **pound** of onions	a **box** of chocolates	be used with count nouns.
BUT: a **dozen** eggs	**five thousand** people	
NOT: a dozen of eggs	NOT: five thousand of people	

Here is Maggie at the checkout counter. Write down her shopping list. Use measure words in the list.

Shopping List

a pound of	coffee	_____	oil
_____	milk	_____	soda
_____	rice	_____	bread
_____	soup	_____	soap
_____	toothpaste	_____	lettuce
_____	candy	_____	toilet paper
_____	eggs	_____	beef
_____	butter	_____	peanut butter

How much food do you have at home? Use measure words to tell your classmate what you have.

EXAMPLE: I have a quart of milk.

Correct the mistakes in the following sentences.

1. **Jane:** Can I talk to you for a minute?

   Kevin: Sure, I have little time.

2. John has much friends.

3. How many money do you have?

4. My teacher gives us many homeworks.

5. Her hairs are black.

6. Elsie is in great shape. She runs few miles a day.

7. We don't sell no newspapers here.

8. There are much stores in this city.

9. I would like some informations please.

10. My best friend gives me many advices.

11. This school has little students.

12. We have few time to finish this book.

Activities

ACTIVITY 1

FOOD HABIT SURVEY

Ask three students questions with *how much* and *how many* to complete the chart.

EXAMPLES: How much coffee do you drink a day?

I drink three cups a day.

How much sugar do you put in your coffee?

Two teaspoons.

	Student 1	Student 2	Student 3
1. coffee or tea/drink/a day			
2. sugar/put in coffee or tea			
3. meat/eat/a week			
4. fish/eat/a week			
5. soda/drink/a day			
6. money/spend on food/a week			
7. bread/eat/a day			
8. fruit/eat/a day			
9. salt/put on food			
10. water/drink/a day			
11. eggs/eat/a week			
12. meals/have/a day			
13. other			
14. other			

Play a circle game with all the students in the class. Make a statement starting with "I want to buy . . ." One student says an item that begins with the letter A and uses a measure word. The second student repeats the statement and adds a second item that starts with the letter B. The third student does the same and adds on an item with the letter C and so on.

EXAMPLE: **Student 1:** I want to buy a bag of apples.

Student 2: I want to buy a bag of apples and a loaf of bread.

Student 3: I want to buy a bag of apples, a loaf of bread, and a head of cabbage.

ACTIVITY 3

Choose a recipe you like and write the ingredients without writing the quantity. The other students ask you questions with *how much* and *how many* to fill in the exact quantity. Make a book of the class's favorite recipes.

EXAMPLE: Recipe: *Italian Tomato Sauce*

Ingredients: tomatoes

onions

garlic

oil

salt and pepper

Questions: How many tomatoes do you use?

How many onions do you use?

How much garlic is there?

How much oil do you use?

How much salt do you need?

ACTIVITY 4

Go to a supermarket. Look at three food labels. Write down the nutrition facts on the next page.

Nutrition Facts
Serving Size 1 Container

Amount Per Serving	
Calories 170	Calories from Fat 15

	% Daily Value*
Total Fat 2g	3%
Saturated Fat 1g	5%
Cholesterol 10mg	3%
Sodium 110mg	4%
Total Carbohydrate 31g	10%
Dietary Fiber 0g	0%
Sugars 28g	
Protein 7g	

Vitamin A 2%	•	Vitamin C	6%
Calcium 25%	•	Iron	2%

*Percent Daily Values are based on a 2,000 calorie diet.

	Example	Label 1	Label 2	Label 3
Calories per serving	120			
Fat	2g			
Cholesterol	10 mg			
Sodium	110 mg			
Sugars	28g			
Protein	7g			

Tell the class about the foods. Are they healthy or not?

ACTIVITY 5

Make your own health survey like the one in Exercise 4. Write five true statements and five false statements about calories, cholesterol, fat, and salt (sodium) in different foods. Read your statements aloud. Your partner says if the statement is True or False.

EXAMPLES: There are a lot of calories in a steak.   False

There's a little cholesterol in cheese.   False

There isn't any fat in a carrot.   True

ACTIVITY 6

Sara is calling a supermarket. She has a shopping order.

STEP ❶ Listen to her order and check the things she wants.

STEP ❷ Listen again. Write the amount she wants.

_____ onions	_____ potatoes	_____ carrots
_____ milk	_____ water	_____ yogurt
_____ lettuce	_____ cabbage	_____ tomatoes
_____ tuna	_____ eggs	_____ oil

UNIT

Adverbs of Manner

Does Bill Rogers Get Life Insurance?

STEP ❶ You work for a life insurance company. Look at Bill Rogers' record and read the sentences below. Check True, False, or I Don't Know.

Long Life Insurance Company
Health and Accident Record

Name:	Bill Rogers	*Sex:*	Male
Date of Birth:	9/20/58	*Marital Status:*	Single
Height:	5'7"	*Weight:*	225 pounds
Health Information:	Heart problems		
	Smokes 2 packs a day		

Offenses: Ticket for speeding: 5/19/92, 8/15/96
Not stopping at a red light: 7/14/89, 9/21/93, 12/31/94, 7/4/95
Drunk driving: 12/31/95
Crashing into a wall: 3/17/96

	True	False	I Don't Know
1. Bill is a careful driver.			
2. He eats moderately.			
3. He drives slowly.			
4. He's a heavy drinker.			
5. He works hard.			
6. He drives carefully.			
7. He is a big eater.			
8. He drives fast.			
9. He dresses neatly.			
10. He is a heavy smoker.			

STEP ❷ Work with a group. Are you going to give Bill Rogers life insurance? Tell why or why not.

Adverbs of Manner

EXAMPLES	EXPLANATIONS
(a) He is a **careful** driver.	*Careful* is an adjective. It describes the noun *driver*. The adjective goes before the noun.
(b) He drives **carefully.**	*Carefully* is an adverb of manner. It describes the verb *drive*. The adverb answers the question "how?" The adverb goes after the verb.
(c) He drives his car **carefully.** NOT: He drives carefully his car.	When there is an object after the verb, the adverb goes after the object (*his car*).

EXERCISE 1

Go back to the Opening Task on page 178. Underline all the adjectives and circle all the adverbs of manner.

EXAMPLE: Bill is a <u>careful</u> driver.

He eats (moderately.)

Spelling of Adverbs of Manner

ADJECTIVE	ADVERB	RULE
slow beautiful	slowly beautifully	Add -*ly*.
heavy	heavily	Adjectives that end in -*y*: change *y* to *i* and add -*ly*.
fantastic	fantastically	Adjectives that end with -*ic*: add -*ally*.
terrible	terribly	Adjectives that end with -*le*: drop the -*e*, and add -*y*.

EXAMPLES		EXPLANATIONS
(a) She's a **fast** driver.	**(b)** She drives **fast**.	Some adverbs have the same form as adjectives.
(c) We have an **early** dinner.	**(d)** We have dinner **early**.	
(e) We eat a **late** lunch.	**(f)** We eat lunch **late**.	
(g) We are **hard** workers.	**(h)** We work **hard**.	
(i) Joel's a **good** cook.	**(j)** He cooks **well**.	Some adverbs are irregular.
(k) He works **hard**.		Do not confuse *hard* with *hardly*.
(l) He **hardly** works.		In example (l), *hardly* means "he doesn't work very much."
(m) She is lovely. **(n)** Marco is lonely. **(o)** That dress is ugly. **(p)** Maria is friendly. **(q)** The party is lively.		Some words that end in -*ly* are not adverbs. They are adjectives.

Find three sentences that describe each occupation. Write the letters next to the occupation.

Occupations

1. I am a teacher.   _c_   a. I respond to medical emergencies very quickly.

    _____   b. I defend my clients well.

    _____   c. I prepare lessons carefully.

2. I am a lawyer.   _____   d. I draw beautifully.

    _____   e. I take care of international problems urgently.

    _____   f. I give medical treatment to people carefully.

3. I am an artist.   _____   g. I paint well.

    _____   h. I speak three languages fluently.

4. I am a Secretary for the United Nations.   _____   i. I stay at the office very late.

    _____   j. I drive very fast.

    _____   k. I talk to my students politely.

5. I am an emergency medical technician in an ambulance.   _____   l. I use colors creatively.

    _____   m. I study the law constantly.

    _____   n. I write on the blackboard neatly.

    o. I act diplomatically.

How are the speakers saying the sentences below? Match each sentence with the best adverb. Write the adverb in the blank.

EXAMPLE: "Shhh, don't say a word." she said _quietly_.

politely	sadly	nervously	quickly	shyly
incorrectly	impolitely	happily	angrily	kindly

1. "I just got engaged!" she said _____.

2. "My dog just died," he said _____.

3. "I'm in a hurry," she said _____.

4. "I ain't got no mistakes," he said _____.

5. "May I make a telephone call?" she asked _____.

6. "Bring me a menu, fast!" he said _____.

7. "This is the last time I'm telling you! Clean up your room!" she said

   _____.

8. "WWWWWWWWWWill yyyyou mmmmmmmmmmarry mmmmmmmmmmmme?" he
   asked _____.

9. "Please, don't ask me to speak in front of the class," she said _____.

10. "Can I help you?" he asked _____.

EXERCISE 4

Read each statement. Use the adjective in parentheses to make another statement
with an adverb.

EXAMPLE: My son is a safe driver. (careful)

My son drives carefully. _____

1. Baryshnikov is an excellent dancer. (graceful)

   _____

2. Uta Pippig is a great runner. (fast)

   _____

3. My father is a smoker. (heavy)

   _____

4. The President is a good speaker. (effective)

   _____

5. Pavarotti is a wonderful singer. (beautiful)

   _____

6. Teachers are hard workers. (diligent)

   _____

7. He is a careless writer. (incorrect)

   _____

8. Some children are fast learners. (quick)

   _____

9. These painters are messy workers. (sloppy)

_____

10. She is a good thinker. (quick/clear)

_____

Take turns with a partner asking and answering the questions below.

1. Why is Carrie an excellent teacher?

   (a) speak/slow

   She speaks slowly.

   (b) pronounce words/clear

   (c) prepare/careful

2. Why is Mark a good secretary?

   (a) type/fast

   (b) answer the phone/ polite

   (c) take message/accurate

3. Why is Mike a good truck driver?

   (a) drive/slow

   (b) respond/quick

   (c) work/hard

4. Why is Paula Abdul a popular performer?

   (a) sing/good
   (b) dance/fantastic

5. Why is Miyuki a good language learner?

   (a) study/hard

   (b) guess/accurate

   (c) ask questions/constant

Talking about a Person or an Action

EXAMPLES	EXPLANATIONS
(a) Isabelle Allende is a **good** writer.	When you want to say something about a person, place, or thing, use an adjective.
(b) Isabelle Allende **writes** well.	When you want to say something about a verb or action, use an adverb.
(c) She is a **very good** writer. **(d)** She writes **very well.**	You can use *very* in front of an adjective or adverb.

EXERCISE 6

Do these sentences tell us about the person or the action? Check the correct column.

	Person	Action
1. Meryl Streep is a fantastic actress.		
2. My students learn easily.		
3. Steven dances slowly.		
4. Karl's a fast runner.		
5. My children are good cooks.		
6. Bill Rogers drives carelessly.		
7. My accountant is an honest person.		
8. Marco speaks to his parents impolitely.		
9. Gloria works very hard.		
10. Our teacher is a clear speaker.		

EXERCISE 7

Read the statements on the following page. Write one sentence that tells about the person and another that tells about the action.

EXAMPLE: Can you believe it! Jeryl is the winner of the race! (runner)

She is a great runner. She runs very fast.

1. Just look at Joe! He finishes one cigarette and then starts on another. (smoker)

2. My mom cooks a great meal every night. She loves to make new dishes. (cook)

3. Gloria goes to work at 8:00 in the morning and leaves at 6:00 in the evening. She never takes a break. (worker)

4. He got another speeding ticket. This is his third ticket this year! (driver)

5. Bob can sing, dance, and play the piano too. (performer)

EXERCISE 8

Read each sentence and give three reasons why the sentence is true. Use adverbs in the reasons.

EXAMPLE: I don't want Henry to drive me downtown.

Reasons: He doesn't drive very carefully.

He drives very fast.

He's a careless driver.

1. Harold drives forty miles an hour in a sixty-five-mile-an-hour zone!
2. I can't understand Bruce when he speaks.
3. Patricia is now the chef at that expensive restaurant downtown.
4. Rose is a great secretary.
5. Lucia is a good language learner.
6. Ms. Wu is a great boss.

EXERCISE 9

Correct the mistakes in the following sentences.
1. Sarah comes to work in a suit every day. She dresses elegant.
2. Melanie speaks fluently French.

3. Sam studies three hours every night. He studies hardly.

4. Dinner starts at 8:00. They always arrive at 9:30. They always come very lately.

5. Johan plays the piano very good.

6. She speaks slow.

7. She sings lovely.

Activities

ACTIVITY 1

Work in a group. One person in the group chooses an adverb of manner, but does not tell the other students the adverb. The students in the group tell the person to do something "in that manner." The person mimes the action and the other students guess the adverb.

EXAMPLE: (First student chooses the adverb *slowly*.)

Students in the group say: "Walk to the door in that manner."

Students in the group guess: *slowly*

(Example adverbs: *slowly, fast, nervously, happily, angrily, loudly, sadly, romantically.*)

ACTIVITY 2

Work in a group. Are you a good student? A good mother? A good friend? A good worker? Choose one and tell your group five reasons to explain why or why not. Use adverbs of manner.

ACTIVITY 3

Think about the Opening Task on page 177–178. Interview your partner. Role-play a conversation between an insurance agent and a person like Bill Rogers. The person tries to convince the agent to give him/her insurance. Then explain to the class why your partner can or cannot get insurance easily.

ACTIVITY 4

 STEP ❶ Listen to the three people. What are their occupations? Choose from the occupations below.

waiter   salesperson   flight attendant   doctor   receptionist

STEP ❷ Describe an occupation to the class. Use adverbs. The class guesses the occupation.

Direct and Indirect Objects, Direct and Indirect Object Pronouns

Giving Gifts

You need to give a gift to the people on your list below. Look at the gifts you have and decide which gift you want to give to each person.

Gifts

A.
Camera

B.
Flowers

C.
Toaster

D.
Doll

E.
Earrings

F.
Running Shoes

G
Compact Disc Player

People

1. a single thirty-five-year-old athletic male friend
2. your sixty-three-year-old grandmother
3. your friend's four-year-old daughter
4. an artistic twenty-seven-year-old friend
5. your mother
6. your music-loving boyfriend/girlfriend
7. a newlywed couple

Direct Objects

EXAMPLES			EXPLANATIONS
Subject	**Verb**	**Direct Object**	
(a) My friend	sings.		Some sentences have only a subject and a verb.
(b) He	loves	music.	Some sentences have a subject, a verb, and an object.
(c) He	buys	compact discs.	A direct object answers the question "What?" *Compact discs* is the direct object.
(d) He	loves	the Beatles.	A direct object also can answer the question "Who(m)?" *The Beatles* is the direct object.

EXERCISE 1

Underline the direct object in each sentence below.

EXAMPLE: My friend loves <u>sports</u>.

1. My grandmother loves flowers. She always has fresh flowers on the dining room table.

2. Andrea and Bob have a new home.

3. My mother adores jewelry.

4. My friend's daughter has a doll collection. She owns ten different dolls.

5. Akiko takes beautiful pictures.

6. My friend enjoys classical music. She prefers Mozart.

7. In my family, we always celebrate our birthdays together.

Direct Object Pronouns

EXAMPLES	EXPLANATIONS
Subject **Verb** **Direct Object** **(a)** My mother loves my father. **(b)** My mother loves him.	The direct object can also be a pronoun.
(c) My mother loves **my father.** She thinks about **him** all the time. **(d)** My father loves **my mother.** He thinks about **her** all the time.	Object pronouns refer to a noun that comes before. In (c), *him* refers to "my father." In (d), *her* refers to "my mother."

SUBJECT	VERB	OBJECT PRONOUN	SUBJECT	VERB	OBJECT PRONOUN
I	am				me.
You	are				you.
He	is				him.
She	is	a good person.	She	loves	her.
It	is				it.
We	are				us.
You	are				you.
They	are				them.

EXERCISE 2

Fill in the correct subject or object pronouns.

1. My grandmother is a very special person. (a) _____ has a vegetable garden in her backyard. (b) _____ plants tomatoes, cucumbers, eggplant, leeks and carrots. She picks (c) _____ fresh every day. We love her fresh vegetables. (d) _____ taste delicious. We eat (e) _____ in salads and soup. Her vegetable garden gives (f) _____ great pleasure.

2. Mariela and Juan are newlyweds. (a) _____ have a new home, and

   (b) _____ really love (c) _____. Their appliances are

   on order, but they don't have (d) _____ yet, so Mariela and Juan

   have a lot of work to do. He helps (e) _____ with the cooking. She

   helps (f) _____ with the laundry.

3. Sally: Billy, do you like heavy metal music?

   Billy: (a) _____ (b) love _____!

   Sally: Really? I hate heavy metal. (c) _____ bothers

   (d) _____. I hate all that noise.

EXERCISE 3

This is a story about three people in a love triangle. Maggie has a steady boyfriend, Ted. She also has a male friend, Jim. Read the text below. Cross out the incorrect pronouns and write the correct pronouns above them.

Jim   Ted   Maggie

Maggie loves her boyfriend, Ted. She also likes Jim. (1) Jim works with ~~she~~ *her*.

(2) She sees he every day. (3) She sometimes invites he to dinner. (4) She likes to

talk with he. (5) Maggie doesn't love Jim, but Jim loves she. (6) Jim thinks about

she all the time. Jim knows about Ted, but Ted doesn't know about Jim. Ted is very

jealous. (7) So, Maggie can't tell he about Jim. (8) Maggie doesn't want to leave he.

But she cares for both Ted and Jim. She doesn't know what to do. (9) She doesn't

want to hurt they. She says to herself, "What's wrong with me? (10) Ted loves I and

I love he. (11) Jim is my friend and I like he. So what can I do?"

Direct and Indirect Objects, Direct and Indirect Object Pronouns   **191**

Ted finds out about Jim. He talks to Maggie on the phone late one night. Fill in the correct object pronouns.

1. **Ted:** Hello, Maggie. Do you remember (a) __me_____ ?

    Maggie: Of course, I remember (b) _____ , Ted. You're my boyfriend!

2. **Ted:** I know about Jim, Maggie.

    Maggie: What? You know about (a) _____ ?

3. **Ted:** That's right, Maggie. I know everything about (a) _____ .

    Maggie: How do you know?

    Ted: John—your secretary—told me. I meet (b) _____ for lunch sometimes. He knows about (c) _____ and Jim.

4. **Ted:** Jim can't come between (a) _____ , Maggie.

    Maggie: I know, Ted. Don't worry. I don't love (b) _____ .

    We're just friends.

    Ted: Do you love (c) _____ ?

    Maggie: Of course, I love (d) _____ , Ted. I want to marry (e) _____ .

5. **Ted:** You can't see (a) _____ so much, Maggie.

    Maggie: Ted, please trust (b) _____ .

Ask your partner questions with *how often*. Your partner answers with object pronouns.

EXAMPLE: You: How often do you call your parents?

      Your Partner: I call them every week.

1. clean your room?
2. do your laundry?
3. see your dentist?
4. buy the newspaper?
5. cut your nails?

6. wash your hair?
7. visit your friends?
8. drink coffee?
9. do the grocery shopping?
10. watch the news?

Indirect Objects

EXAMPLES				EXPLANATIONS
Subject	**Verb**	**Direct Object**	**Indirect Object**	
(a) I	want to give	the toaster	to **the newlyweds.**	Some sentences have two objects: a direct object and an indirect object. *The toaster* is the direct object. It tells **what** I want to give. *The newlyweds* is the indirect object. It tells to **whom** I give the toaster.
(b) I	buy	flowers	for **my grand-mother.**	*My grandmother* is the indirect object. It tells for **whom** I buy flowers.
(c) I	want to give	the toaster	to **the newlyweds.**	The indirect object can be a noun or a pronoun.
(d) I	want to give	the toaster	to **them.**	

(e) I fix the car **for** my grandmother.	**For and To** *For* tells us one person does the action to help or please another person.
(f) I give earrings **to** my mother.	*To* tells us about direction of the action: The earrings go from you to your mother.

Write sentences telling what you want to give to each of the people in the Opening Task. Underline the direct object and circle the indirect object. Then tell why you want to give that item to that person.

EXAMPLE: I want to give <u>the toaster</u> to the (newlyweds.) They have a new home and don't have any appliances.

New Year's Resolutions. Every January 1st, North Americans decide to change their lives and do things differently. Read the resolutions below. Change each underlined noun to a pronoun. Then add the information in parentheses.

EXAMPLE: Every year, I give <u>my father</u> a tie. (golf clubs)

This year, I want to give him golf clubs.

1. Used car salesman:

   I always sell <u>my customers</u> bad cars. (good cars)

   This year, I want to . . .

2. Child away at college:

   I always write to <u>my parents</u> once a month. (once a week)

   This year, I want to . . .

3. People with money problems:

   Every year, the bank sends <u>my husband and me</u> a big credit card bill. (a very small bill)

   This year, I want the bank to . . .

4. Boyfriend:

   I usually buy <u>my girlfriend</u> flowers for her birthday. (a diamond ring)

   This year, I want to . . .

5. Teenager:

   Sometimes I lie to <u>my mother</u>. (tell the truth)

   This year, I want to . . .

6. Mother:

   I never have time to read to <u>my children</u> at night. (every night)

   This year, I want to . . .

7. Student:

I always give my homework to <u>the teacher</u> late. (on time)

This semester, I want to . . .

8. Friend:

Every year, I lend money to <u>you and your brother</u>. (lend money)

This year, I don't want to . . .

Now say three things you want to do differently this year.

 FOCUS 4 ➤➤➤➤➤➤➤➤➤➤➤➤➤➤➤➤➤➤➤➤➤➤➤ **FORM**

Position of the Indirect Object

All verbs that take indirect objects can follow Pattern A.

Pattern A

SUBJECT	VERB	DIRECT OBJECT	INDIRECT OBJECT
(a) I	give	presents	to my mother on her birthday.
(b) I	give	presents	to her.
(c) I	give	them	to her.
(d) We	have	a party	for our twin daughters on their birthday.
(e) We	have	a party	for them.
(f) We	have	it	for them.

Some of these verbs also follow Pattern B. In Pattern B, put the indirect object before the direct object. Do not use *to* or *for.*

Pattern B

SUBJECT	VERB	INDIRECT OBJECT	DIRECT OBJECT
(g) People	send	their friends	birthday cards.
(h) People	send	them	birthday cards.
(i) I	make	my friends	birthday cakes.
(j) I	make	them	birthday cakes.

NOTE: Do not put an indirect object pronoun before a direct object pronoun.

            I make my friend a cake.

            I make her a cake.

NOT: I make her it.

Verbs that follow both Pattern A and B

give	send	pass	mail	make	do (a favor)
write	bring	read	offer	buy	find
show	hand	lend	pay	bake	get
tell	sell	teach	throw	cook	

EXERCISE 8

Work with a partner and make sentences about North American customs with the words below.

BIRTH: When a baby is born:

1. mother /flowers /the /to /give /friends

   Friends give flowers to the mother.

2. cigars /gives /friends /father /his /the

3. send /and /parents /friends /family /to /birth /announcements /their /the

4. baby /family /friends /gifts /the /buy /and

5. make /for /grandmothers /sweaters /new /the /baby

6. grandfathers /for /toys /make /baby /the

7. child /the /the /parents /everything /give

ENGAGEMENT/MARRIAGE: When a couple gets engaged or married:

8. diamond / man / a / woman / the / gives / ring / the / to / sometimes

9. friends / couple / an / party / the / for / have / engagement

10. gifts / woman / give / friends / at a party / the

11. at the wedding / to / couple / gifts / give / guests / the

DEATH: When someone dies:

12. send / family / some / flowers / people / the

13. people / special cards / the / send / family / to

14. some / to / give / people / money / charities

15. some / food / for / family / bring / people / the

FOCUS 5 ➤➤➤➤➤➤➤➤➤➤➤➤➤➤➤➤➤➤➤➤➤ **USE**

Position of New Information

New information in a sentence comes at the end. You can write a sentence in two different ways. Both are correct, but the emphasis is different.

EXAMPLES	EXPLANATIONS
(a) Whom do you give earrings to? I usually give earrings to **my mother.**	The emphasis is on **who(m)**. *My mother* is the new information.
(b) What do you usually give your mother? I usually give my mother **earrings.**	The emphasis is on **what**. *Earrings* is the new information.

EXERCISE 9

Answer the following question. The new information is in parentheses ( ).

EXAMPLES: Who(m) do you usually give presents to at Christmas? (my family)

I usually give presents to my family.

What do you usually give your father? (a good book)

I usually give him a good book.

1. Who(m) do you want to give a present to at work? (three of my co-workers)

2. What do you usually give your parents for their anniversary? (tickets to a play)

3. Who(m) do you tell jokes to? (my friend)

4. What do you sometimes send your sister? (some new recipes)

5. Does she teach English to your brother or sister? (my brother)

6. Which story do you usually read to your little sister—"Cinderella" or "Snow White"? ("Cinderella")

7. Who(m) do you need to mail the application to? (the admissions office)

8. What do you usually buy for your son on his birthday? (compact discs)

EXERCISE 10

Choose the best sentence.

EXAMPLE: You are waiting for a friend in front of a restaurant.

You do not have your watch. You want to know the time.

You see someone coming. You ask him:

((a)) Could you please tell me the time?

(b) Could you please tell the time to me?

1. You are alone at a restaurant. You finish your meal. You see the waiter. You ask him:

   (a) Could you please give the check to me?

   (b) Could you please give me the check?

2. You are celebrating someone's birthday with a group of friends. You finish your meal. You want to be sure you pay the check. You tell the waiter:

   (a) Please give the check to me.

   (b) Please give me the check.

3. What do your children usually do for you on Mother's Day?

   (a) They usually serve breakfast in bed to me.

   (b) They usually serve me breakfast in bed.

4. You are at a friend's house for dinner. The food needs salt. You say:

   (a) Please pass me the salt.

   (b) Please pass the salt to me.

5. You realize you don't have any money on you for the bus. You ask a friend:

   (a) Could you lend a dollar to me?

   (b) Could you lend me a dollar?

6. You are in class. It is very noisy. You say to a classmate:

   (a) Do me a favor. Please close the door.

   (b) Do a favor for me. Please close the door.

7. Why does your class look so sad on Mondays?

   (a) because our teacher gives us a lot of homework.

   (b) because our teacher gives a lot of homework to us.

8. You are speaking to the Director of the English Language Institute. You want to apply to the City University. You have the application form in your hand.

   Director: (a) Please send the application form to the City University.

             (b) Please send the City University the application form.

9. You come home from the supermarket. Your car is full of groceries. You need help. You say to your roommate:

   (a) Can you please give a hand to me?

   (b) Can you please give me a hand?

10. There are three children at a table. They are finishing a box of cookies. A fourth child sees them and runs toward them. The child says:

    (a) Wait! Save me one!

    (b) Wait! Save one for me!

Verbs that Do Not Omit *To* with Indirect Objects

EXAMPLES	EXPLANATIONS
S + V + DO + IO **(a)** My mother reads stories to us. **S + V + IO + DO** **(b)** My mother reads us stories.	Many verbs follow both Pattern A and B. (See Focus 4.)
DO + IO **(c)** The teacher explains the grammar to us. **(d)** NOT: The teacher explains us the grammar.	Some verbs only follow Pattern A.
explain *describe* *repeat* *introduce* *report* *say* *solve* *open* *carry* *clean* *do* *prepare* *fix* *repair* *spell*	Verbs that follow Pattern A ONLY. Do not omit *to/for.*

Read the following pairs of sentences or questions aloud. Check any sentence that is not possible. In some pairs, both patterns are possible.

EXAMPLE 1:

Pattern A: My husband sends flowers to me every Valentine's Day.

Pattern B: My husband sends me flowers every Valentine's Day.

   (Both patterns are possible.)

EXAMPLE 2:

Pattern A: The teacher always repeats the question to the class.

NOT: **Pattern B:** The teacher always repeats the class the question.

Pattern A

1. Tell the truth to me.
2. Please explain the problem to me.
3. Spell that word for me, please.
4. I need to report the accident to the insurance company.
5. My father usually reads a story to my little brother every night.
6. He always opens the door for me.
7. Let me introduce my friend to you.
8. Cynthia gives her old clothes to a charity.
9. The students write letters to their parents every week.
10. Please repeat the instructions to the class.
11. Can you describe your hometown to me?
12. Can you carry that bag for me?

Pattern B

Tell me the truth.

Please explain me the problem.

Spell me that word, please.

I need to report the insurance company the accident.

My father usually reads my little brother a story every night.

He always opens me the door.

Let me introduce you my friend.

Cynthia gives a charity her old clothes.

The students write their parents letters every week.

Please repeat the class the instructions.

Can you describe me your hometown?

Can you carry me that bag?

Activities

ACTIVITY 1

Think of the different things people have. Then give clues so that your classmates can guess the object.

EXAMPLE: Clues: The Japanese make a lot of them. We drive them. What are they?

Answer: Cars!

ACTIVITY 2

STEP ❶ Write down the names of ten occupations on ten pieces of paper.

STEP ❷ Choose one of the pieces of paper and make sentences for the class so they can guess the profession. You get one point for each sentence you make.

STEP ❸ When the class guesses the profession, another student picks a piece of paper. The person with the most points at the end wins.

> **EXAMPLE:** (You choose "firefighter.")
>
> > **You say:** *This person wears a hat.*
> >
> > *He or she drives a big vehicle.*
> >
> > *He or she saves people's lives.*

ACTIVITY 3

STEP ❶ Each person in the class writes down a personal habit—good or bad.

STEP ❷ Each person reads his or her statement to the class.

STEP ❸ The class asks questions to find out more information.
(Possible habits: playing with your hair, tapping your feet.)

> **EXAMPLE: You:** I *bite my fingernails.*
>
> > **Class:** *Why do you bite them?*
> >
> > **You:** *Because I'm nervous!*

ACTIVITY 4

What customs do you have in your country for events such as birth, engagement, marriage, death? Tell the class what people do in your country.

> **EXAMPLE:** In Chile, when a baby is born . . .
>
> > when a couple gets married . . .
> >
> > when someone dies . . .
> >
> > when a person turns thirteen . . .
> >
> > OTHER . . .

ACTIVITY 5

Work in a small group. On small slips of paper, write the numbers 1 to 16 and put them in an envelope. One person in the class is the "caller" and only he or she looks at the grid below. The first student picks a number from the envelope. The caller calls out the command in that square for the student to follow. Then a second student picks out a number and the caller calls out the command. Continue until all the commands are given.

EXAMPLE: You pick the number 7.

Caller: Lend some money to Maria.

1. Whisper a secret to the person across from you.	2. Give a penny to the person on your left.	3. Write a funny message to someone in your group.	4. Hand your wallet to the person on your right.
5. Make a paper airplane for the person across from you.	6. Tell a funny joke to someone.	7. Lend some money to a person in your group.	8. Describe a friend to someone.
9. Explain indirect objects to the person across from you.	10. Tell your age to the person on your right.	11. Introduce the person on your left to the person on your right.	12. Offer candy to someone.
13. Call up the police and report a crime to them.	14. Open the door for someone in the class.	15. Throw your pen to the person across from you.	16. Pass a secret message to one person in your group.

STEP ❶ Listen to the conversation between Linda and Amy. Then read the statements below. Check True or False.

	True	False
1. Linda is giving her mother perfume on Mother's Day.		
2. Linda's mother tells her what gift she wants.		
3. Amy's mother always tells her daughter what gift she wants.		
4. Linda's father only takes Linda's mother to a restaurant on Mother's Day.		
5. Linda's father does not buy his wife a gift.		

STEP ❷ Work with a partner. If a statement is false, make a true statement.

STEP ❸ Tell your classmates what you do and give to a person on a special day like Mother's Day or a birthday.

UNIT 14

Can, Know How To, Be Able To, And/But/So/Or

OPENING TASK

Find Someone Who Can . . .

STEP ❶ Find someone in your class who can do these things:

1. dance

2. swim

3. draw

4. sing

5. cook

6. use a computer

7. drive a car

8. play a musical instrument

9. speak three languages

STEP ❷ Report to the class what you know about your classmates.

Can

Can expresses ability.

AFFIRMATIVE	NEGATIVE	NEGATIVE CONTRACTION
I You He She **can** speak We English. You They	I You He She **cannot** We speak Chinese. You They	I You He She **can't** speak We French. You They
(a) She can DANCE. **(b)** He can SING.	In the affirmative, we pronounce *can* as /kən/ and stress the base form of the verb.	
(c) He CAN'T DANCE. **(d)** She CAN'T SING.	In the negative, we stress both *can't* and the base form of the verb.	

EXERCISE 1

Go back to the Opening Task on page 205. With a partner, take turns saying what you can or can't do.

EXAMPLE: I can cook.

I can't play a musical instrument.

Make affirmative or negative statements about the pictures.

1. He/hear his mother
   He can't hear his mother.

2. She/swim

3. They/play basketball

4. She/open the jar

5. He/walk

6. He/go to work

7. They/see the screen

8. They/speak Korean

What can you do in English? Check *Yes* or *No*.

	Yes	No
1. I can introduce someone.		
2. I can ask about prices.		
3. I can describe people and places.		
4. I can make a polite request.		
5. I can give directions.		
6. I can give advice.		
7. I can ask for information about English.		

Now, exchange books with a partner. Tell the class what your partner can or can't do in English.

EXAMPLE: My partner can introduce someone.

FOCUS 2 >>>>>>>>>>>>>>>>>>>>>>>>> **FORM**

Questions with *Can*

| (a) **Can** you use a computer? |
| Yes, I can. No, I can't. |
| (b) **Can** he cook? |
| Yes, he can. No, he can't. |

| (c) **What** *can* he cook? |
| He can boil water! |
| (d) **Who** *can* cook in your family? |
| My mother can. |
| My father can't. |

EXERCISE 4

STEP ❶ Write *yes/no* questions with *can*. Then, under Your Response, check *Yes* or *No* to give your opinion about each question. Leave the columns under *Total* blank for now.

	Your Response		Total	
	Yes	No	Yes	No
1. a woman/work as a fire fighter _Can a woman work as a firefighter?_ ?				
2. women/be good soldiers _____ ?				
3. a man/be a good nurse _____ ?				
4. men/raise children _____ ?				

	Your Response		Total	
	Yes	**No**	**Yes**	**No**

5. women/be police officers

_____?

6. a woman/be a construction worker

_____?

7. a man/work as a housekeeper

_____?

8. a woman/be President of a country

_____?

9. a man/work as a baby sitter

_____?

STEP ❷ Go back to Exercise 4. Read the questions aloud. Do a survey in your class. Count how many students say "yes" and how many say "no." Write the *total* number of Yes and No answers in the Total column. Do you agree or disagree with your classmates? Give reasons for your answers.

    EXAMPLE: Women can be police officers.

            They can help people in trouble. They can use guns when necessary.

EXERCISE 5

Work in a group of four to six people. Take turns asking the following questions.

    EXAMPLE: a. Who/type?   Who can type?

                b. How fast/type?   How fast can you type?

1. a. Who/cook?   b. What/cook?
2. a. Who/speak three languages?   b. What/say in your third language?
3. a. Who/play a musical instrument?   b. What/play?
4. a. Who/sew?   b. What/sew?
5. a. Who/fix a car?   b. What/fix?
6. a. Who/draw?   b. What/draw?
7. a. Who/run a marathon?   b. How fast/run a marathon?

Asking for Help with English

EXAMPLES	EXPLANATIONS
(a) Can I say, "She can to swim" **in English?**	When you are not sure your English is correct, use the expression: *Can I say . . . in English?*
(b) How can I say, "…" **in English?**	When you don't know how to say something in English, ask the question: *How can I say,* "…" *in English?*
	To explain your meaning: Use your hands to show "tremendous." Use your face to show "sour." Use your whole body to show action like "sweeping."

Look at the pictures. First mime each action and then ask your classmates questions to find out how to say each word.

EXAMPLE: How can I say (mime the action) in English?

1.

2.

3.

4.

5.

6.

FOCUS 4 >>>>>>>>>>> **FORM/MEANING/USE**

Expressing Ability: *Can, Know How to*, and *Be Able to*

EXAMPLES	EXPLANATIONS
(a) She **can** cook. **(b)** She **knows how to** cook. **(c)** She **is able to** cook.	To express learned ability, use *can, know how to,* or *be able to*.
(d) A blind person **can't** see. **(e)** A blind person **isn't able to** see. **(f)** NOT: A blind person **doesn't know how to** see.	To express natural ability, use *can* or *be able to* only. *Be able to* is more formal than *can*. Use *be able to* in all tenses; not *can*.

Make affirmative or negative statements with the words below. To express learned ability, make one statement with *can* and one statement with *know how to*. To express natural ability, make only one statement with *can*.

EXAMPLES: fix/a flat tire

I can fix a flat tire.

I know how to fix a flat tire.

see/without glasses

I can see without glasses.

1. A blind person/see
2. A dog/live for twenty-five years
3. Infants/walk
4. A deaf person/hear
5. Fish/breathe on land

6. Mechanics/fix cars
7. Men/take care of babies
8. A man/have a baby
9. Doctors/cure some diseases

Fill in the blanks with the affirmative or negative forms of *can* or *be able to*.

Fran: Hello, Vanna. How are you today?

Vanna: I'm sorry to say I'm still not well, Fran. My back still hurts. I (1) _can_ sit up now, but I (2) _am not able to_ walk very well.

Fran: What? You mean you (3) _____ come in to work today? Vanna, I (4) _____ do my work without you. I (5) _____ use my

computer. I (6) _____ find any of my papers. I (7) _____
remember any of my appointments. This office is a mess. I (8) _____ do
all this work myself.

Vanna: What about your temporary secretary? What (9) _____ he do?

Fran: This temporary secretary is terrible. He (10) _____ do anything.
He (11) _____ even make a good cup of coffee! I need you here, Vanna.
Only you (12) _____ do everything in this office.

Vanna: Well, Fran, do you remember our conversation about my pay raise?

Fran: O.K., O.K., Vanna. You can have your raise. But please come in today!

Vanna: O.K., calm down, Fran, and listen to me. I (13) _____ come in
to the office this morning, but I (14) _____ come in this afternoon.

Vanna: Oh . . . thank you, Vanna . . . See you later.

EXERCISE 9

Test your knowledge. Make Yes/No Questions and discuss your answers.

1. people/live without food for six months

   Can people live without food for six months?

   > Yes, they can.

   > No, they can't.

   Are people able to live without food for six months?

   > Yes, they are.

   > No, they aren't.

2. a computer/think
3. smoking/cause cancer
4. an airplane/fly from New York to Paris in four hours
5. a person/run twenty-five miles an hour
6. a river/flow uphill
7. we/communicate with people from other planets
8. a person/learn a language in one week
9. modern medicine/cure AIDS

10. a two-year old child/read

11. the United Nations/stop wars

12. you/think of any more questions

FOCUS 5 ➤➤➤➤➤➤➤➤➤➤➤➤ **FORM/MEANING**

Sentence Connectors:
And/But/So/Or

And, but, so, and **or** are sentence connectors. We use them to connect two complete sentences.

EXAMPLES	EXPLANATIONS
(a) I can rollerskate **and** I can ski.	**And** adds information.
(b) I can dance, **but** I can't sing. He can swim, **but** his brother can't.	**But** shows contrast.
(c) I can't cook, **so** I often go out to eat.	**So** gives a result.
(d) You can go **or** you can stay.	**Or** gives a choice.
(e) I can speak English, but I can't speak Spanish. **(f)** I can speak Spanish, and my sister can speak Japanese.	When you connect two complete sentences, use a comma (,) before the connector.
(g) I can say it in English, or I can say it in French. **(h)** I can say it in English or French.	When the subject is the same for the two verbs, it is not necessary to repeat the subject or *can*. Do not use a comma.

EXERCISE 10

What can you do? Write sentences about yourself with *can* or *know how to* with *and* or *but.*

EXAMPLE: 1. use a typewriter/use a computer

I can use a typewriter, but I can't use a computer.

I can use a typewriter and a computer.

2. rollerskate/rollerblade

3. ride a bicycle/drive a car

4. use a camera/use a video camera

5. use a telephone/use a fax machine

6. cook rice/cook Chinese food

7. sew a button/sew a dress

8. walk fast/run fast

Now make three statements of your own:

9. _____

10. _____

11. _____

EXERCISE 11

Look back at the pictures in Exercise 2. Fill in the blanks with *and*, *but*, or *so*.

1. (Look at Picture 7 in Exercise 2)

    Bob and Andrea love the movies, (a) __but__ they are often too busy to go to the movies on Saturdays. They usually go to the first show on Sundays. On Sunday afternoon, the tickets are half-price, (b) _____ the theater is very crowded. There is one woman in the audience who is always a problem. Today, Bob and Andrea are behind her. The woman has very bushy hair, (c) _____ Bob and Andrea can't see the movie screen. She loves pop-corn (d) _____ eats it non-stop during the movie. Popcorn is delicious, (e) _____ it is also very noisy, (f) _____ Bob and Andrea can't hear the movie. Sometimes they think it's better to stay home and rent a movie!

2. (Look at Picture 6 in Exercise 2)

    Larry is in the hospital. He has a high fever (a) _____ he is very sick. The doctor wants him to stay in the hospital, (b) _____ Larry wants to go home. The doctor says he needs to rest, (c) _____ Larry wants to go back to work. He is bored in the hospital (d) _____ he misses his family. He is unhappy, (e) _____ he decides to leave.

3. (Look at Picture 1 in Exercise 2)

    Tommy loves to listen to loud music, (a) _____ his mom hates his music. Tommy's mom has a headache, (b) _____ she asks Tommy to use his walkman. Tommy has a walkman, (c) _____ it's broken.

Give your partner a choice.

EXAMPLE: listen to rock music / listen to classical music

You: We can listen to rock music or classical music.

Your Partner: Let's listen to rock music.

1. eat at home / go out to a restaurant

2. watch the baseball game on TV / go to the game at the stadium

3. go to an opera / go to a ballet

4. study physics / study biology

5. play cards / watch a movie

6. drive to the mountains / drive to the beach

7. eat Italian food / eat Indian food

8. go to the movies / rent a film and stay home

Activities

ACTIVITY 1

Read the job advertisement in the newspaper for a baby sitter. Interview your partner for the job. Ask questions with *can, know how to,* and *be able to.*

EXAMPLE: Do you know how to cook?

Can you work full-time?

> **WANTED: Baby sitter** Responsible person. Full-time work five days a week 8:00-5:00, some evenings and weekends. Must speak English and be able to drive. Laundry, light housekeeping, and cooking required. Experience with children necessary. References requested.

ACTIVITY 2

What can you/do you know how to do that your parents or other people you know cannot/do not know how to do? Write six sentences.

EXAMPLE: My mother can't ride a bicycle, but I can.

My sister knows how to sew, but I don't.

ACTIVITY 3

Do you think it's better to be a man or a woman?
Give as many reasons as you can for your opinion.

EXAMPLE: It's better to be a woman. A woman can have children.

ACTIVITY 4

Make a list of ten jobs.
Say what you can or are able to do. The class decides what job is good for you. Use *and* and *but*.

EXAMPLE: You say: I can help sick people, and get along with them. I am able to follow directions.

Your group: Then you can be a nurse!

ACTIVITY 5

STEP ❶ Ask a classmate if he or she can do one of the activities in the box on the next page.

EXAMPLE: Can you touch your toes?

STEP ❷ If the person says *yes*, write his/her name in the box. Then go to another student and ask another question.
If the person says *no*, ask the other questions until he or she says *yes*. Then write his or her name in the box.

STEP ❸ Each student who answered *yes* must perform the action in the box!

touch your toes	dance	whistle
_____	_____	_____
sing a song in English	say "Hello" in four languages	tell a joke in English
_____	_____	_____
draw a horse	pronounce the word "Psychology"	juggle
_____	_____	_____

 STEP ❶ Listen to Ken's interview for a job. Then answer the questions. Check Yes or No.

	Yes	No
1. Ken can speak French, Spanish, and German.		
2. Ken can stay in another country for a year.		
3. Ken can drive.		
4. Ken can use computers.		
5. Ken can sell computers.		
6. Ken can repair computers.		

STEP ❷ Discuss with your classmates.

1. What kind of job is the interview for?
2. Can Ken get the job? Why or why not?

Present Progressive Tense

A Bad Day at the Harrisons'

Robin's babysitter cannot come today, so her husband Regis is staying at home and taking care of the children and the house.

Talk about what is happening in the picture. Use the subjects on the left and the verbs in the box.

the food

Suzy

the telephone

the baby and the dog

the baby

Jimmy

the dog

Regis

bark
play cowboy
burn on the stove
go crazy
watch TV
cry
ring
fight

Present Progressive:
Affirmative Statements

EXAMPLES	EXPLANATIONS
(a) The food **is burning.** **(b)** The baby **is crying.** **(c)** The dog and the baby **are fighting.**	Use the present progressive to talk about an action that is happening right now; an action in progress.
now *right now* *at the moment*	Use these time expressions with the present progressive.

SUBJECT	BE	BASE FORM OF THE VERB + -ING
I	am	
You	are	
He She It	is	working.
We You They	are	

Affirmative Contractions

SUBJECT + BE CONTRACTION	BASE FORM OF THE VERB + -ING
I'm	
You're	
He's She's It's	working.
We're You're They're	

EXERCISE 1

Underline all the present progressive verbs in the text.

EXAMPLE: Regis <u>isn't having</u> a good day.

Today is not a normal day at the Harrisons'. Usually, Robin's babysitter comes at 3:00 when Robin leaves for work. But today, Robin is attending an all-day meeting at the college, and her babysitter can't come. So Regis is spending the day at home. He's taking care of the children and the house. He's trying very hard, but everything is going wrong. Regis isn't having a good day. Actually, poor Regis is going crazy. He's thinking about Robin. He's learning something today. It's not easy to stay home with the children. He's beginning to understand this.

Spelling of Verbs Ending in *-ing*

VERB END	RULE	EXAMPLES	
1. consonant + *e*	Drop the *-e*, add *-ing*.	write	writing
2. vowel + consonant (one syllable) Exception: verbs that end in *-w*, *-x*, and *-y*.	Double the consonant, add *-ing*. Do not double *w*, *x*, and *y*.	sit show fix play	sitting showing fixing playing
3. consonant + vowel + consonant. There is more than one sylla-ble, and the stress is on the last syllable If the stress is not on the last syllable	Double the consonant, add *-ing*. Do not double the conso-nant.	beGIN forGET LISten HAPpen	beginning forgetting listening happening
4. *-ie*	Change *-ie* to *y*, add *-ing*.	lie die	lying dying
5. All other verbs	Add *-ing* to the base form of verb.	talk study do agree	talking studying doing agreeing

EXERCISE 2

Fill in the blanks with the present progressive.

Today's a normal day at the Harrisons'. It is 4:00. Robin (1) _____ (prepare) dinner in the kitchen. She (2) _____ (slice) onions and (3) _____ (wipe) the tears from her eyes. The house is quiet, so she (4) _____ (listen) to some music. She (5) _____ (think) about her class tonight. She (6) _____ (wait) for her babysitter to arrive.

The baby (7) _____ (sleep). The dog (8) _____ (chew) on a bone. Jimmy (9) _____ (play) with his toys. Suzy (10) _____ (clean) her room. Everything is under control.

EXERCISE 3

Who's talking? Fill in the blanks with the present progressive of the verb. Then match each statement to a picture.

EXAMPLE: "You're ___*driving*___ (drive) me crazy. Turn off the TV!"

1. "That crazy dog _____ (bite) me!"

a.

2. "I _____ (walk) into a zoo!"

b.

3. "Quiet! You _____ (make) a lot of noise. I can't hear the TV."

c.

4 "Stop that, Jimmy. You _____ (hurt) me."

d.

5. "Oh no! The food _____ (burn)!"

e.

6. "I _____ (die) to take off my shoes. My feet _____ (kill) me."

f.

Present Progressive: Negative Statements

SUBJECT + BE + NOT			NEGATIVE CONTRACTION			BE CONTRACTION + NOT		
I	am		*			I'm		
You	are		You	aren't		You're		
He She It	is	not working.	He She It	isn't	working.	He's She's It's		not working.
We You They	are		We You They	aren't		We're You're They're		

*There is no standard English contraction with I am not.

Make sentences with negative contractions.

EXAMPLE: Robin/take care of the children today

              Robin isn't taking care of the children today.

1. Robin/wear comfortable shoes today
2. Robin's babysitter/come today
3. The baby and the dog/get along
4. Regis/relax
5. The children/listen to Regis
6. Suzy/do her homework
7. Suzy/help Regis
8. Regis/pay attention to the dinner in the oven
9. Regis/laugh
10. Regis/enjoy his children today

Look at the picture. Make affirmative or negative statements.

EXAMPLE: Mrs. Bainbridge _is having_ (have) a party at her home this evening.

Mrs Bainbridge _isn't talking_ (talk) to her guests at the moment.

Mrs. Bainbridge is having a party at her home this evening. The guests

(1) _____ (talk) in the living room. But Mr. and Mrs. Parker

(2) _____ (talk) to the other guests. They (3) _____

(enjoy) the party. They (4) _____ (feel) very bored right now. They

(5) _____ (think of) a way to escape. Mrs. Bainbridge

(6) _____ (stand) in the doorway. She (7) _____

(turn) her back to the Parkers. The Parkers (8) _____ (leave),

but they (9) _____ by the front door. Mr. and Mrs. Parker

(10) _____ (climb) out of the bedroom window at the moment.

Mr. Parker (11) _____ (hold) his hat between his teeth.

He (12) _____ (help) Mrs. Parker climb out. Mr. and

Mrs. Parker (13) _____ (say) good-bye to the other guests.

FOCUS 4 ▷▷▷▷▷▷▷▷▷▷▷▷▷▷▷▷▷▷▷▷▷▷▷▷▷ USE

Choosing Simple Present or Present Progressive

The simple present and the present progressive have different uses.

USE THE SIMPLE PRESENT FOR:	USE THE PRESENT PROGRESSIVE FOR:

• **habits and repeated actions**
(a) Suzy usually does her homework in the afternoon.
• **things that are true in general**
(c) Women usually take care of children.
	• **actions in progress now**
	  (b) Suzy's watching TV right now.
	• **actions that are temporary, not habitual**
	  (d) Regis is taking care of the children today.
	• **situations that are changing**
	  (e) These days, men are spending more time with their children.

Time Expressions *always* *rarely* *often* *never* *usually* *every day* *sometimes* *once a week* *seldom* *on the weekends*	**Time Expressions** *right now* *now* *today* *at the moment* *this week* *this evening* *this year* *this month* *these days*

EXERCISE 6

Read each statement. If the statement is in the simple present, make a second statement in the present progressive. If the statement is in the present progressive, make a second statement in the simple present.

Simple Present	Present Progressive
1. Suzy usually does her homework in the evening.	a. <u>Tonight she is watching cartoons on TV.</u>
2. _____	b. Tonight, Robin isn't cooking dinner.
3. Robin usually takes care of the children.	c. _____
4. _____	d. Today, Regis is spending the day at home.
5. The baby sitter usually takes care of the children when Robin goes to work.	e. _____
6. _____	f. Right now, the baby and the dog are fighting.
7. The babysitter usually doesn't go crazy.	g. _____

EXERCISE 7

Make sentences with *these days* or *today* to show changing situations.

EXAMPLE: women/get more education

These days, women are getting more education.

1. Women/get good jobs
2. Fifty percent of American women/ work outside the home
3. Women/earn money
4. Women/become more independent

5. Men/share the work in the home
6. Husbands/help their wives
7. Fathers/spend more time with their children
8. The roles of men and women/change

Add two sentences of your own.

9. _____

10. _____

Verbs Not Usually Used in the Progressive

There are some verbs we usually do not use in the present progressive. These verbs are *not* action verbs. They are called nonprogressive (or stative) verbs.

EXAMPLES	NONPROGRESSIVE (STATIVE) VERBS
(a) Robin **loves** her job. **(b)** NOT: Robin is loving her job. **(c)** The children **need** help. **(d)** NOT: The children are needing help.	**FEELINGS AND EMOTIONS** (*like, love, hate, prefer, want, need*)
(e) Regis **understands** his wife.	**MENTAL STATES** (*think, believe, understand, seem, forget, remember, know, mean*)
(f) Regis **hears** the telephone ringing.	**SENSES** (*hear, see, smell, taste, feel, sound*)
(g) Robin and Regis **own** a house.	**POSSESSION** (*belong, own, have*)

There are some stative verbs you can use in the present progressive, but they have a different meaning.

SIMPLE PRESENT	PRESENT PROGRESSIVE
(h) I **think** you're a good student. (*Think* means "believe.")	**(i)** I **am thinking** about you now.
(j) I **have** two cars. (*Have* means "possess.")	**(k)** I'm **having** a good time. (*Have* describes the experience.)
(l) This soup **tastes** delicious. (*Taste* means "how the food is.")	**(m)** I'm **tasting** the soup. (*Taste* here means the person is putting soup in his or her mouth.)

Fill in the blanks with the present progressive or simple present form of the verb. Read the dialogues aloud. Use contractions.

EXAMPLE: Regis: _I'm going_ (go) crazy in this house.

Robin: _I think_ (think) you need a vacation!

1. **Regis:** Suzy, I need your help here.

   Suzy: But, Dad, you (a) _____ (need) my help every five minutes! I (b) _____ (watch) TV right now!

2. It is 3:00. The telephone rings.

   Regis: Hello.

   Laura: Hello, Regis. What are you (a) _____ (do) home in the middle of the afternoon?

   Regis: Oh, hi, Laura. I know I (b) _____ (be) never home in the afternoon, but today I (c) _____ (try) to be a househusband!

   Laura: Oh really? Where's Robin?

   Regis: Robin (d) _____ (attend) a meeting at the college, so I (e) _____ (take care of) the kids.

3. Jimmy interrupts Regis's telephone conversation:

   Regis: Hold on a minute, Laura . . . Jimmy (a) _____ (pull) on my leg! Jimmy, I (b) _____ (talk) to Mommy's friend Laura right now. You (c) _____ (know) Laura. She (d) _____ (come) to see Mommy every week. Now, just wait a minute, please . . .

   Laura: Is everything O.K., Regis?

   Regis: Oh, yes, Laura, don't worry. We (e) _____ (do) just fine. Talk to you later; bye!

4. It is 5:30. The telephone rings.

   Regis: Hello.

   Robin: Hi, honey! The meeting (a) _____ (be) over. I (b) _____ (be) on my way home. What (c) _____ (happen)? I hope the children (d) _____ (behave).

Regis: They (e) _____ (act) like wild animals, Robin. I
(f) _____ (yell) at them all the time, but they don't listen to me. I
(g) _____ (not/have) a very good day today. Please come home
soon.

Robin: You (h) _____ (sound) terrible! Can I bring anything home,
dear?

Regis: Yes, a bottle of aspirin!

EXERCISE 9

Work with a partner. You describe a picture by making one statement with *seem, look,* or *feel* and an adjective from the box and another statement with the present progressive to say what the person is doing. Your partner tells you the number of the picture you are talking about. Take turns.

EXAMPLE: You say: The boy looks sad. He is crying.

Your partner says: Picture Number 1.

sad ✔	sick	scared	tired
angry	happy	cold	hot
bored	surprised	nervous	confused

1.   4.   7.   10.

2.   5.   8.   11.

3.   6.   9.   12.

Present Progressive: *Yes/No* Questions and Short Answers

YES/NO QUESTIONS			SHORT ANSWERS						
Am	I		Yes,	you	are.	No,	you	aren't.
Are	you		Yes,	I	am.	No,	I'm	not.
Is	he he it	working?	Yes,	he she it	is.	No,	he she it	isn't.
Are	you we they		Yes,	we you they	are.	No,	we you they	aren't.

EXERCISE 10

With a partner, take turns asking and answering questions about the Harrisons. Give short answers. Use the verbs from the box below.

EXAMPLE: Suzy/ . . . /her father

Is Suzy helping her father? No, she isn't.

watch	ring	play	bite	come
	burn	help	fight	smile

1. children / their father
2. Frankie and the dog/ . . .
3. Suzy / TV
4. their dinner/ . . .
5. the phone/ . . .

6. Jimmy / cowboy
7. the dog / the toy
8. Robin / home
9. Robin

Work with a partner and ask each other Yes/No questions about your life these days. Check Yes or No.

EXAMPLE: enjoy English class

Are you enjoying your English class?

your English/improve

Is your English improving?

You		Your Partner	
Yes	**No**	**Yes**	**No**

1. enjoy English class?

2. your English/improve?

3. take other classes?

4. learn a lot?

5. get good grades?

6. make progress?

7. do a lot of homework?

8. cook for yourself?

9. go out with friends?

10. meet lots of people?

11. eat well?

12. sleep well?

13. get exercise?

14. work after school?

Present Progressive: *Wh*-Questions

WH-WORD	BE	SUBJECT	VERB + -ING	ANSWERS
What	am	I	doing?	(You're) getting ready for the beach.
When Where Why How	are	you	going?	(I'm going) at 2:00. (We're going) to the beach. (We're going) because we don't have school today. (We're going) by car.
Who(m)	is	she	meeting?	(She's meeting) her friends.
Who*	is		having a nice day?	Clara (is having a nice day).

Who is asking about the subject.

EXERCISE 12

Write the question that asks for the underlined information.

1. **Q:** <u>Who is watching television?</u>

   A: <u>Suzy</u> is watching television.

2. **Q:** <u>Who(m) is Regis taking care of tonight?</u>

   A: Regis is taking care of <u>the children</u>.

3. **Q:** _____

   A: Frankie and the dog are fighting <u>because they both want the toy.</u>

4. **Q:** _____

   A: Robin is meeting <u>her colleagues</u> at the college.

5. **Q:** _____

   A: Robin's thinking that <u>she's lucky to be at work!</u>

6. **Q:** _____

   A: They're eating sandwiches for dinner <u>because Regis's dinner tastes terrible.</u>

7. **Q:** _____

   A: <u>Regis</u> is watching the children today.

8. **Q:** _____

   A: Regis is taking two aspirin <u>because he has a terrible headache.</u>

9. **Q:** _____

   A: Robin's meeting is taking place <u>at the college.</u>

10. **Q:** _____

    A: <u>Robin</u> is coming home right now.

11. **Q:** _____

    A: Regis is feeling <u>very tired</u> right now.

12. **Q:** _____

    A: <u>The children</u> are making a lot of noise.

EXERCISE 13

Correct the mistakes in the following sentences.

EXAMPLE: Is the pizza tasting good?

Does the pizza taste good?

1. Frankie and the dog are fight.
2. He's having a new TV.
3. Why you are working today?
4. Are you needing my help?
5. What Robin is thinking?
6. Is she believing him?
7. Right now, he plays cowboy on his father's back.
8. The soup is smelling bad.
9. Where you are going?
10. People no are saving money nowadays.
11. You working hard these days.
12. How you doing today?

Activities

Your teacher will divide the class into two groups.

STEP ❶ Group A should look at the statements in Column A. One student at a time will mime an action. Students in Group B must guess the action. Group B students can ask questions of Group A. Then Group B mimes statements from Column B and Group A guesses the action.

Column A	Column B
1. You are opening the lid of a jar. The lid is on very tight.	2. You are reading a very sad story.
3. You are watching a very funny TV show.	4. You are an expectant father waiting in the delivery room.
5. You are trying to sleep and a mosquito is bothering you.	6. You are sitting at the bar in a noisy disco. At the other side of the bar, there is someone you like. You are trying to get that person's attention.
7. You are crossing a busy street. You are holding a young child by the hand and carrying a bag of groceries in the other hand.	8. You are a dinner guest at a friend's house. Your friend is not a good cook. You don't like the food!
9. You are trying to thread a needle, but you're having trouble finding the eye of the needle.	10. You are cutting up onions to cook dinner.

STEP ❷ Make up three situations like those above. Write each situation on a separate piece of paper and put all the situations in a hat. Every student will then pick a situation and mime it for the others to guess.

ACTIVITY 2

In this unit, we see that family life is changing in the United States. Is family life changing in the country you come from or in a country that you know? Write sentences using the simple present and present progressive tense about the following.

Mothers . . .   Grandparents . . .
Fathers . . .   Couples . . .
Children . . .   Men . . .
Teenagers . . .   Women . . .

LISTEN AND DECIDE

 STEP ❶ Look at the three pictures. Listen to the conversation. Decide which picture fits the description. Check A, B, or C.

A.   B.   C.

The woman is describing Picture   A _____   B _____   C _____

STEP ❷ Describe the other two girls in the picture.

STEP ❶ Look at the picture. Give this person a name, nationality, occupation, age, and so on. Write a story about this person. What is the woman doing? Where is she? How does she look? What is she thinking about? Why is she there?

STEP ❷ Tell the class your story.

Adjective Phrases

Another, The Other, Other(s),
The Other(s), Intensifiers

Meeting the Staff at P.S. 31

Identify the people below by describing them. Do not point to the pictures. Say what each person does at P.S. 31.

1. _____ is the school principal.

2. _____ teaches science.

3. _____ is the school nurse.

4. _____ is the girls' basketball coach.

5. _____ works in the school cafeteria.

6. _____ teaches art.

Adjective Phrases

EXAMPLES			EXPLANATIONS
NOUN	ADJECTIVE PHRASE	VERB	
(a) The man	**in the suit**	is the school principal.	Adjective phrases are groups of words that describe nouns.
(b) The food	**on the table**	is delicious.	
The woman is in a white coat. The woman is the school nurse.			Adjective phrases can combine two sentences.
(c) The woman	**in a white coat**	is the school nurse.	
(d) The **man** with the books **is** the science teacher.			The verb agrees with the subject, not with the noun in the adjective phrase.

EXERCISE 1

Put parentheses around the adjective phrases. Underline the subject and the verb in each sentence.

EXAMPLE: <u>The man</u> (in the suit) <u>works</u> in an office.

1. The man in the suit and tie is the school principal.
2. The man with the books and microscope is the science teacher.
3. The woman in the white coat is the school nurse.
4. The woman with the whistle is the girls' basketball coach.
5. The man with the white hat works in the school cafeteria.
6. The woman with the easel and paints is the art teacher.

Each chair belongs to one of the people on the next page. Match each person to a chair. Then write a sentence with an adjective phrase.

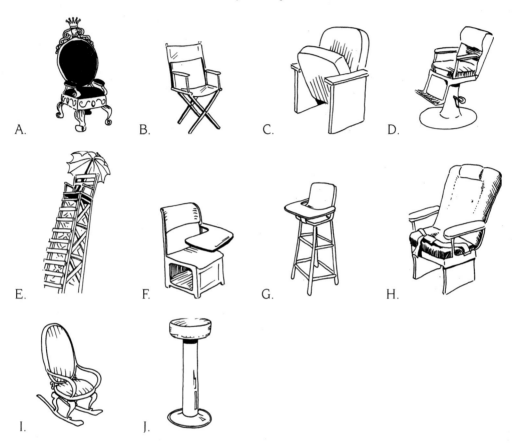

A.   B.   C.   D.

E.   F.   G.   H.

I.   J.

Chair	Person	
1. A	7	The man with the crown sits in chair A.
2.		
3.		
4.		
5.		
6.		
7.		
8.		
9.		
10.		

Combine each of the sentence pairs into one sentence with an adjective phrase. Then identify the person in the picture and write the number of your sentence next to the person.

1. The girl has pigtails. She is kicking her partner.

   The girl with pigtails is kicking her partner.

2. The boy has a striped shirt and black pants. He is throwing a paper airplane across the room.

   _____

3. The girls are near the window. They are waving to their friends outside.

   _____

4. The boy is in a baseball uniform. He is standing on the teacher's desk.

   _____

5. The boys are in the back of the room. They are fighting.

   _____

6. The boy is in the corner. He is reading.

   _____

7. The girl is in the closet. She is crying.

   _____

8. The girl has a Walkman. She is singing.

   _____

9. The man has a rope around him. He is the new teacher.

   _____

10. The man is in a suit and tie. He is the school principal.

    _____

FOCUS 2 ➤➤➤➤➤➤➤➤➤➤➤➤➤➤➤ **FORM/MEANING**

Questions with *Which*

EXAMPLES	EXPLANATIONS
(a) Which woman is wearing a white coat? the school nurse **(b) Which** teachers are women? the coach and the art teacher	Use *which* when there is a choice between two or more people or things.
(c) Which coat do you like, Mom? I like the black **one.** **(d) Which** shoes do you like, Dad? the brown **ones**	Substitute the words *one* or *ones* for nouns so you do not repeat the noun.
(e) Which shoes do you want? the ones **in the window**	You can also use adjective phrases after *one* and *ones*.

Julie's house was robbed. She is talking to her husband on the phone, describing the damage. Work with a partner. Find the differences between the pictures. You say Julie's statements. Your partner is the husband, and asks questions with *which* to get more specific information.

EXAMPLE: Julie: The window is broken.

Husband: Which window?

Julie: The one over the kitchen sink.

BEFORE

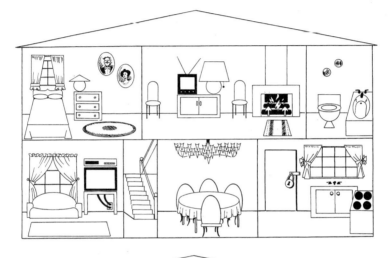

AFTER

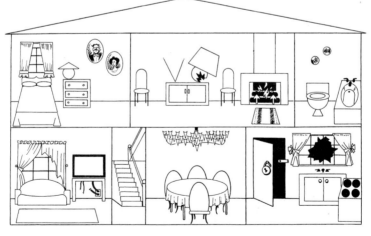

1. The window is broken.
2. The curtains are torn.
3. The TV is missing.

4. The door is open.
5. The lamp is broken.
6. The VCR over the TV is missing.

7. The lock is broken.
8. The rug is missing.

Another, The Other, Other(s), The Other(s)

	ADJECTIVE	PRONOUN	MEANING
A: I'm hungry. B: Here. Have a cookie. A: I am still hungry. Can I have **another** cookie? (Can I have **another**?)	**another** cookie	**another**	one more cookie; one more from a group
B: There are no more cookies in the box. A: There are two **other boxes** in the closet. (There are two **others** in the closet.)	**other** boxes	**other**s	more than one more
B: I found one box. Where is **the other box**? (Where is **the other**?) B: **The other box** is behind it. A: How many more cookies can I have?	**the other** box	**the other**	the one you spoke about; the last one in a group
B: You can have one more. **The other cookies** are for me! (**The others** are for me!)	**the other** cookies	**the others**	the ones you spoke about; the last ones in a group

EXERCISE 5

Thor is visiting Earth from another planet. Ed Toppil interviews Thor on television.

Fill in the blanks with *another, the other, other(s),* or *the other(s)*.

Ed: We on Earth are really excited to know there is (1) _____ planet

out there, Thor. Many of us know there are (2) _____, but we are not able

to find them. Do you know of any (3) _____ planets?

Thor: Yes, we do. We know two (4) _____: Limbix and Cardiax. I have photos of the people from both of (5) _____ planets.

The Limbix are the ones on the left. The Cardiax are (6) _____ ones. We also now know the planet Earth. We are sure there are (7) _____ out there, but (8) _____ are very far away.

Ed: I am surprised that you speak English so well, Thor. Do the Thoraxes have (9) _____ language too?

Thor: Yes, of course. We speak Thoracic, but English is a universal language, you know, so we all learn it in school. People on (10) _____ two planets speak English too!

Ed: So what brings you to Earth?

Thor: Well, Ed, we are looking for (11) _____ intelligent beings in the universe.

Ed: On Earth?!! I don't know if you can find many intelligent beings on Earth, Thor! But we can discuss this at (12) _____ time. Right now, let's stop for a station break.

EXERCISE 6

Thor tours America. Fill in *another*, *other(s)*, or *the other(s)*.

1. **George:** You only have one tie, Thor. You need to buy (a) _____ one.

Thor: Why?

George: Because Americans are consumers. They like to buy things.

Thor: But I don't like any (b) _____ ties here.

George: O.K. Look at (c) _____ over there. Maybe you can find (d) _____ one.

2. Thor is in a candy store with a child:

   Thor: Which candy is good here?

   Child: This one is good, but first taste (a) _____ one in the brown and green paper. It's out of this world!

   Thor: Hmmmm, excellent. Is it O.K. to take (b) _____ one?

3. **Soaprah:** So, Thor, tell us about your family. Are you married?

   Thor: Yes. I am, and I have two children. One is a specialist in interplanetary communication and (a) _____ owns a spaceship factory.

   Soaprah: And what does your wife do?

   Thor: My wife is a spaceship pilot.

   Soaprah: What about (b) _____ people on Thorax? What do they do?

   Thor: (c) _____ do different jobs. We have doctors, teachers, artists, and so on. We don't have any tax collectors.

   Soaprah: Are there any (d) _____ professions you don't have?

   Thor: We don't have any lawyers, I'm happy to say.

   Soaprah: That sounds great to me!

   Thor: Do you have any (e) _____ questions?

   Soaprah: I have a million (f) _____ questions! But our time is up. It was nice meeting you, Thor. Thanks so much for coming.

Intensifiers

Intensifiers are words that make adjectives more or less strong.

SUBJECT	BE	INTENSIFIER	ADJECTIVE
(a) Earth	is	very	beautiful.
(b) The people on Thorax	are	quite	similar.
(c) The people on Earth	are	rather/pretty* fairly	different.
(d) Thorax	isn't	very**	beautiful.

SUBJECT	BE	ARTICLE	INTENSIFIER	ADJECTIVE	NOUN
(e) Earth	is	a	very	special	place.
(f) Thorax	is	a	rather/pretty fairly	small	planet.
(g) Thorax	isn't	a	very	attractive	place.

*Pretty has the same meaning as rather, but is very informal.
**Very is the only intensifier we use in negative sentences.

SUBJECT	BE	INTENSIFIER	ARTICLE	ADJECTIVE	NOUN
(h) Thorax	is	quite	a	small	planet.

Test Thor's knowledge. How many of the objects can Thor (and you) guess?

1. This is fairly long and thin.

   People eat it.

   It is very popular in Italy.

   What is it? _____

2. This is a liquid.

   People usually drink it hot.

   They like its rather strong smell.

   It is brown.

   What is it? _____

3. This is an electrical appliance.

   It is quite common in people's homes.

   Sometimes it is very hot.

   You put bread into it.

   What is it? _____

4. This is very cold.

   It's also pretty hard.

   People put it in drinks on hot days.

   It's quite slippery.

   What is it? _____

5. This is quite a big metal box.

   It's electrical and pretty practical.

   It's very useful in tall buildings.

   People go inside the box.

   The box goes up and down.

   What is it? _____

6. This is a very popular piece of plastic.

   It isn't very big.

   With it, we can buy rather expensive things without money.

   What is it? _____

7. There are different kinds of candy.

   All of them are good.

   But this one is very special.

   It comes in brown or white.

   It's pretty fattening.

   It's quite delicious.

   What is it? _____

8. This thing is quite colorful.

   It isn't very common.

   It sometimes follows rainstorms.

   It is quite a beautiful sight.

   What is it? _____

EXERCISE 8

Ed Toppil continues his interview with Thor. Write an intensifier in each blank. There is more than one possible answer.

Ed: So tell me, Thor, what do you think of our planet?

Thor: Well, Earth is a beautiful planet, but it's (1) __quite_____ a strange place. Many of your leaders are not doing a (2) _____ good job. Some people on Earth are (3) _____ rich. Others are (4) _____ poor. There can be a (5) _____ big difference among people. On Thorax, we are all equal. Money isn't (6) _____ important. Learning is

(7) _____ important. That's why we're visiting Earth. Your knowledge can be (8) _____ useful to us. Also, your art and music are (9) _____ beautiful.

   Ed: That's (10) _____ interesting. I'm sure we can learn many (11) _____ useful and exciting things from you, too, Thor.

EXERCISE 9

How necessary or important is each thing? Make statements about Thor's opinion, and give your opinion. Use intensifiers. Explain your answers.

1. a spaceship

   For me, a spaceship is not necessary. I travel by car.

   For Thor, a spaceship is very important. Thor travels by spaceship.

2. a car
3. a spaceship
4. a credit card
5. music
6. knowledge
7. money

8. a good leader for the country
9. a computer
10. teachers
11. a beautiful planet
12. friends

EXERCISE 10

Fill in a verb (affirmative or negative) and an intensifier in each blank. There are many possible answers. Talk about your answers with a partner.

1. A walkman _is fairly_____ useful.
2. A cordless telephone _____ practical.
3. Big cars _____ economical.
4. A microwave oven _____ necessary.
5. A driver's license _____ important.
6. A credit card _____ dangerous.
7. Fast food _____ popular in my country.
8. American movies _____ violent.
9. Airplanes _____ safe.
10. A university degree _____ important.

Activities

STEP ❶ Write ten sentences that give information about your country or city. Use adjective phrases.

> **EXAMPLE:** The beaches in the south are beautiful.
>
> The market in the center of the city is always crowded.
>
> The coffee in Brazil is delicious.

STEP ❷ Now tell the class about your country or city.

ACTIVITY 2

STEP ❶ In a group, write sentences about ten students in the class. Use adjective phrases. Do not use names.

STEP ❷ Read your sentences to the class. The class guesses the person you are talking about.

> **EXAMPLE:** The student from Bogota has pretty eyes.
>
> The student next to Miyuki wears glasses.
>
> The student with the big smile is from Ecuador.

ACTIVITY 3

STEP ❶ Check (✔)the adjectives that describe you, and write *very/quite/rather/pretty/fairly/not very* under You in the chart on the next page.

STEP ❷ Ask your partner questions to find out which adjectives describe him or her. Then ask questions with *how* and write *very/quite/rather/pretty/fairly/not very* under Your Partner in the same chart.

> **EXAMPLE: You ask:** Are you shy?
>
> **Your partner answers:** Yes, I am.
>
> **You ask:** How shy are you?
>
> **Your partner answers:** I'm very shy.

Adjective	You		Your Partner	
		very quite rather pretty fairly not very		very quite rather pretty fairly not very
shy				very
lazy				
quiet				
romantic				
friendly				
old-fashioned				
organized				
jealous				
talkative				
athletic				
healthy				

ACTIVITY 4

Use the information in Activity 3 to write five sentences about you or about your partner using *very/quite/rather/pretty/fairly/not very*.

EXAMPLE: My partner is a very romantic person. He is pretty old-fashioned, and he is very jealous.

Imagine you are starting life on a new planet. Look at the list of people. Then choose only ten people to move to the new planet. Say how necessary each one is and why.

EXAMPLE: A doctor is very necessary because we need to stay healthy.

an actor	an artist	a police officer	a political leader
a scientist	a religious leader	a young man	a young woman
a historian	a writer	a musician	a lawyer
a farmer	a teacher	a journalist	a pilot
a doctor	a mechanic	a computer specialist	a dancer
a military person		an elderly person	an engineer

ACTIVITY 6

Make up descriptions of objects using intensifiers like those in Exercise 7. Test your classmates' knowledge of these objects.

ACTIVITY 7

STEP ❶ Listen to the descriptions of Bob, Don, and Tom. Write the number of the correct description next to each man.

Bob: Number_____   Don: Number_____   Tom: Number_____

STEP ❷ Work in a group. Each student draws a face. Then, the student describes the face to the rest of the group. The rest of the group draws what the student describes.

Past Tense of B*e*

Test Your Memory

Look at the photos and the information about famous people from the past. Make statements about each person. Correct any facts that are not true. See answers on page AK-1.

		Nationality	Occupation
	1. Martin Luther King, Jr.	African	civil rights leader
	2. The Beatles	British	hairdressers
	3. Marilyn Monroe	American	actress

4. Indira Gandhi   Indian   rock singer

5. Pierre and Marie Curie   French   fashion designers

6. Mao   Chinese   political leader

7. Jacqueline Kennedy Onassis   Greek   millionaire

8. George Washington,   Canadian   presidents
   Thomas Jefferson,
   Abraham Lincoln,
   Theodore Roosevelt

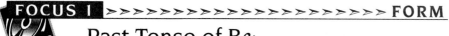
Past Tense of Be:
Affirmative Statements

SUBJECT	VERB	
I	was	
You	were	
He She It	was	famous.
We You They	were	
There	was	a famous actress in that film.
There	were	many political leaders at the meeting.

EXERCISE 1

Use the past tense of *be* to make correct statements about the famous people in the Opening Task.

1. The Beatles _____ a famous British rock group in the 1960s.

2. Indira Gandhi _____ the Prime Minister of India.

3. Marie and Pierre Curie _____ French scientists.

4. Mao Tse Toung _____ a revolutionary and political leader in the People's Republic of China.

5. George Washington, Thomas Jefferson, Abraham Lincoln, and Theodore Roosevelt _____ presidents of the United States.

6. Martin Luther King, Jr., _____ an American civil rights leader.

7. Marilyn Monroe _____ an American movie star.

8. Jacqueline Kennedy Onassis _____ the wife of president John F. Kennedy and of Aristotle Onassis, a Greek millionaire.

EXERCISE 2

Fill in the blanks in the postcard. Use *be* in the simple past.

Dear Grandma and Grandpa,

Here we are in Florida. What a place! Yesterday
we (1) _____ at Disneyworld all day. The sun
(2) _____ really strong and it (3) _____ very hot.
The lines (4) _____ long, but the rides and the shows
(5) _____ fun. Disneyworld (6) _____ crowded,
but all the people (7) _____ friendly and polite. Our
favorite place (8) _____ Cinderella's palace! The
fireworks at night (9) _____ beautiful! It
(10) _____ great for us, but Dad (11) _____
really hot and tired at the end of the day!

    We miss you! See you soon.

      Love, Melanie and Michele

Orlando FL
FL
34624

USA
20

The Grandparents
Homestead Lane
Harvard, MA
01451

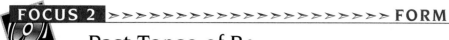

FOCUS 2

Past Tense of Be: Negative Statements

SUBJECT	BE + NOT		NEGATIVE CONTRACTIONS		
I	was not		I	wasn't	
You	were not		You	weren't	
He She It	was not	famous.	He She It	wasn't	famous.
We You They	were not		We You They	weren't	
There	was	no time to eat.	There	wasn't	any time to eat.
There	were	no dates in the Task.	There	weren't	any dates in the Task.

EXERCISE 3

How do Michael and Carol remember their trip to Disneyworld? Fill in the blanks with the affirmative or negative of *be* in the simple past. Then role-play the dialogue aloud.

Alice: Oh, hi, Michael. Hi, Carol. How (1) __was__ your trip to Disneyworld last week?

Carol: Hi, Alice. Oh, it (2) _____ fun.

Michael: Fun! That vacation (3) _____ (not) fun, it (4) _____ terrible!

Carol: But Michael, how can you say that? I think the children and I (5) _____ very satisfied with our vacation.

Michael: Carol, the weather (6) _____ boiling hot.

Carol: It (7) _____ (not) boiling hot, it (8) _____ very comfortable.

Michael: The food (9) _____ (not) very good . . .

Carol: The food (10) _____ fine, Michael.

Michael: The people (11) _____ (not) friendly.

Carol: Of course, they (12) _____ friendly.

Michael: The kids (13) _____ very difficult.

Carol: The kids (14) _____ (not) difficult, Michael. Come on, they (15) _____ great.

EXERCISE 4

Make sentences about last weekend with the adjectives in the box.

cheap	cold	rainy	polite	sunny	rude	good
interesting	friendly	windy	comfortable	terrible	slow	charming
warm	small	wet	nice	delicious	crowded	wonderful

Last weekend, you were in the country with your friends . . .

1. The weather? How was the weather?

   It was cold. _____

2. In the evening, you were at an expensive restaurant.

   How was the restaurant? The food and service?

   _____

3. After the restaurant, you were at a party.

   How were the people?

   _____

EXERCISE 5

Do you remember the story *Cinderella*. Fill in the blanks with the affirmative or negative form of *be*.

Once upon a time, there (1) _____ a young woman named Cinderella. She (2) _____ rich, but she (3) _____ very beautiful and kind. Her two stepsisters (4) _____ beautiful. They (5) _____ jealous of Cinderella. Cinderella's stepmother (6) _____ good to her.

Yes/No Questions and Short Answers with *Be* in the Simple Past

YES/NO QUESTIONS			SHORT ANSWERS				
VERB	SUBJECT		AFFIRMATIVE			NEGATIVE	
Was	I			you	were.	you	were not.
						you	weren't.
Were	you			I	was.	I	was not.
						I	wasn't.
Was	he she it	right?	Yes,	he she it	was.	No,	he/she/it was not. he/she/it wasn't.
Were	we you they			you we they	were.		you/we/ were not. they
							you/we/ weren't. they
Was there any good food at Disneyworld?			Yes,	there was.		No, there	was not.
						No, there	wasn't.
Were there long lines at Disneyworld?			Yes,	there were		No, there	were not.
						No, there	weren't.

Detective Furlock Humes is questioning a police officer about a crime. Fill in the blanks with *there + be* in the simple past.

EXAMPLE: ___Was there___ a crime last night?

___There were___ several police officers at the house.

Police Officer: The body was here, Detective Humes.

Furlock: (1) _____ a weapon?

Police Officer: Yes, (2) _____ a gun next to the body.

Furlock: (3) _____ any fingerprints on the gun?

Police Officer: No, sir, (4) _____.

Furlock: (5) _____ any motive for this crime?

Police Officer: We don't know, sir.

Furlock: How about witnesses? (6) _____ any witnesses to the crime?

Police Officer: Yes, sir. (7) _____ one witness—a neighbor. She said (8) _____ loud noises in the apartment at midnight.

Furlock: Where is she? Bring her to me . . .

EXERCISE 7

Ask your classmates Yes/No questions about the events below. Give short answers. Correct the facts if necessary.

EXAMPLE: Margaret Thatcher/the first female Prime Minister of Great Britain.

Was Margaret Thatcher the first female Prime Minister of Great Britain?

Yes, she was.

1. Tom Hanks/the first man to walk on the moon
2. AIDS/a known disease in 1949
3. Yugoslavia/a country in 1980
4. Europeans/the first people on the American continent
5. Nelson Mandela/in prison for many years in South Africa
6. The Wright Brothers/the first men to cross the Atlantic Ocean by plane
7. a big earthquake/in Kobe, Japan in 1995
8. any women/in the Olympic Games in 1920

Wh-Questions with Be

WH-QUESTION	BE	SUBJECT	ANSWERS
What		November 22, 1963?	It was the day of President Kennedy's assassination.
Where		the assassination?	It was in Dallas, Texas.
How	was	the day?	Very sad.
Who		the assassin?	Lee Harvey Oswald, we think.
When		the assassination?	November 22, 1963.
Why	were	people sad?	because Kennedy was a popular president.
Whose gun	was	it?	Lee Harvey Oswald's.

EXERCISE 8

Fill in the *wh*-question word and the correct form of *be* to complete each question.

Andrea: (1) _____ you on the day of Kennedy's assassination?

Helene: I was in school. There was an announcement over the loud speaker.

Andrea: (2) _____ you with at the time?

Helene: I was with my friend Patty.

Andrea: (3) _____ it in school that day?

Helene: It was terrible. We were all very upset and silent.

Andrea: (4) _____ you all silent?

Helene: because it was hard to believe he was dead.

Andrea: And at home? (5) _____ things at home?

Helene: At home, things were very bad. My parents were in shock too.

Andrea: (6) _____ their feelings after the assassination?

Helene: They were angry, sad, confused, and afraid.

Look at the photo and write a *wh*-question for each answer.

1. _____?

   These people were mountain climbers.

2. _____?

   They were in the Himalayas.

3. _____?

   They were there for the adventure and the challenge.

4. _____?

   They were there in 1996.

5. _____?

   The name of the mountain was Mount Everest.

6. _____?

   It was their idea to take this trip.

7. _____?

   The trip was a disaster; eight people died on this trip.

Work in a group. Take turns. One student makes a statement about last weekend. The other students ask questions. Use *wh*-questions and the past tense of *be*.

EXAMPLE: Statement: I was at the movies on Saturday.

Questions: What was the movie? Who were you with?

Who was in the movie? How was the movie?

Correct the mistakes in the following sentences.

1. Do was Indira Gandhi and Golda Meir Prime Ministers?
2. The Beatles wasn't fashion designers.
3. Was hot the weather at Disneyworld last week?
4. Where the earthquake was in Japan in 1996?
5. Why the people were on Mount Everest?
6. Was good the service at the restaurant?
7. No was any dates in the Opening Task.
8. How it was the trip to Disneyworld?

Activities

ACTIVITY 1

Work with a partner, finish writing the story of Cinderella in Exercise 5 (page 262).

ACTIVITY 2

Work with a partner. Ask your partner the questions below and other questions to find out about a special place he or she knows.

QUESTIONS: Where were you last summer? When were you there?

Why were you there? What was special about this place?

How was the weather? Were the people friendly? How was the food?

ACTIVITY 3

With the information from Activity 1, tell the class about your partner's special place.

EXAMPLE: Last summer, my partner was in Greece. She was there with her boyfriend. Greece was very beautiful and interesting.

ACTIVITY 4

Work in a group.

STEP ❶ Write the dates below on pieces of paper. Mix all the papers together.

STEP ❷ Pick a piece of paper and say something about your life at that time and your life now. Take turns with the classmates in your group.

EXAMPLE: In 1995, I was a doctor in the Philippines, but now I am an ESL student in the United States.

July	1995	September	1996	December	1995
	1994		1991		1993
	1990		in the 1980s		1992
	1970		1960		

ACTIVITY 5

STEP ❶ Listen to the beginning of the stories on tape. Decide what kind of story type each one is. Write the number of the story you hear next to the story type.

A horror story   _____   A murder mystery   _____

A love story   _____   A children's story/fairy tale   _____

STEP ❷ Finish one of the stories. Tell the story to the class.

UNIT

Past Tense

OPENING TASK

Solve the Mystery: Who took the VCR?

STEP ❶ Read the mystery.

For most students, Ms. Ditto was the best ESL teacher in the English Language Center. Three years ago, she began to use a VCR in her classes. She brought in interesting videotapes for her students to watch every week. The students enjoyed her classes and really liked her.

Only one student, Harry, didn't like Ms. Ditto. Harry's writing wasn't very good, so he failed Ms. Ditto's class twice. Last summer, he got a job in the language lab to pay the tuition for her class again this semester. Yes, Harry felt angry at Ms. Ditto.

Just before the new semester started, the Director of the English Language Center heard the university didn't have money to pay the teachers. They were not able to give Ms. Ditto a job this semester. Everyone was sad. Harry just laughed!

On the first day of class, Professor Brown wanted to use the VCR. He asked Harry to open the language lab. But when Harry opened the door to the lab, the VCR was not there. In its place, there was a typed note with a signature on it. The note said:

```
    Today, I very sad. I no can work in English Language
Center because there no have money to pay me. What I
can do now? How I can live? I take this VCR because I
have angry. Please understand my. I sorry . . .
                                          C. Ditto
```

STEP ❷ Read the sentences and check True or False.

	True	False
1. Ms. Ditto's students didn't like her.		
2. Harry needed money.		
3. Harry worked in the language lab.		
4. Ms. Ditto didn't have a job this semester.		
5. Harry disliked Ms. Ditto.		
6. Harry did well in Ms. Ditto's class.		

STEP ❸ Solve the mystery. Discuss your answers with the class.

Who took the VCR? How do you know?

Spelling of Regular Past-Tense Verbs

SUBJECT	BASE FORM + -ED
I You He She It We You They	started three years ago.

Regular verbs can change spelling in the simple past tense.

IF THE VERB ENDS IN:	SPELLING RULE
(a) a consonant **want** **need**	Add *-ed* **wanted** **needed**
(b) a vowel + *y* **enjoy** **play**	Add *-ed* **enjoyed** **played**
(c) a consonant + *e* **like** **smile**	Add *-d* **liked** **smiled**
(d) a consonant + *y* **study** **worry**	Change *-y* to *-i*, add *-ed* **studied** **worried**
(e) consonant + vowel + consonant (one syllable verbs) **stop** **drop**	Double the consonant, add *-ed* **stopped** **dropped**
(f) *-x, -w* (one syllable verbs) **show** **fix**	Do not double the consonant, add *-ed* **showed** **fixed**
(g) two-syllable verbs stress on the last syllable **oCCUR** **preFER**	Double the consonant, add *-ed* **occurred** **preferred**
(h) two-syllable verbs stress on the first syllable **LISten** **VISit**	Do not double the consonant, add *-ed* **listened** **visited**

Go back to the Opening Task on page 270 and underline all the regular past-tense verbs in the mystery.

EXAMPLE: They <u>enjoyed</u> her classes and really <u>liked</u> her.

Fill in the blanks with the past tense of the verbs.

1. Ms. Ditto _enjoyed_____ (enjoy) her classes.

2. Ms. Ditto _____ (use) interesting videotapes in her classes.

3. She _____ (help) her students to understand the tapes.

4. The students _____ (study) new vocabulary.

5. They _____ (learn) about American life.

6. They _____ (discuss) the tapes in class.

7. The students _____ (play) language learning games in class.

8. Many students _____ (register) for her class every semester.

9. All the students really _____ (love) her.

10. Ms. Ditto _____ (stop) teaching because the university didn't have money to pay her.

11. Ms. Ditto's students _____ (cry).

12. One day, a robbery _____ (occur) at the English Language Center.

13. A VCR _____ (disappear) from the language lab.

Pronunciation of the *-ed* Ending

VERB END	EXAMPLES
Group I After voiceless sounds*, the final *-ed* is pronounced /t/.	/t/ *asked* *kissed* *stopped*
Group II After voiced sounds**, the final *-ed* is pronounced /d/.	/d/ *robbed* *killed* *played*
Group III After /t/ and /d/, the final *-ed* is pronounced /ɪd/.	/ɪd/ *pointed* *wanted* *waited*

*Voiceless sounds: s, k, p, f, sh, ch, x.
**Voiced sound: b, g, l, m, n, r, v, z, or a vowel

EXERCISE 3

STEP ❶ Put each verb in the simple past and read each sentence aloud. Check the column that shows the pronunciation of each verb.

Bookworm Benny was an excellent student.

	/t/	/d/	/ɪd/
1. Teachers always __liked__ (like) Bookworm Benny.	✔		
2. He _____ (work) hard in school.			
3. He always _____ (finish) his work first.			
4. The teacher always _____ (call) on him.			
5. He always _____ (answer) questions correctly.			

	/t/	/d/	/ɪd/
6. He _____ (remember) all his lessons.			
7. He never _____ (talk) out of turn.			
8. The other students _____ (hate) Benny.			
9. One day, they _____ (decide) to get him into trouble.			
10. They _____ (roll) a piece of paper into a ball.			
11. They _____ (wait) for the teacher to turn his back.			
12. They threw the paper ball at the teacher. It _____ (land) on the teacher's head.			
13. The teacher was really angry. He _____ (yell) at the class.			
14. "Who did that?" he _____ (ask).			
15. All the students _____ (point) to Benny.			
16. But the teacher _____ (trust) Benny.			
17. The teacher _____ (punish) the other students.			

STEP ❷ The pictures about Bookworm Benny are not in the correct order. Number the pictures in the correct order. Then use the pictures to retell Bookworm Benny's story.

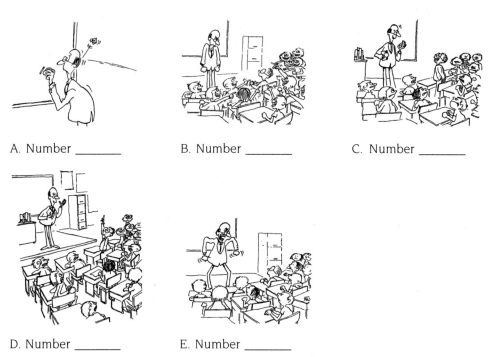

A. Number _____

B. Number _____

C. Number _____

D. Number _____

E. Number _____

EXERCISE 4

The solution to the Ms. Ditto story is in this exercise. Fill in the blanks with the past tense of the verbs in the box.

discuss	look	remember	fire	notice	learn
type	confess	believe	lock	ask	sign

When the Director of the English Language Center (1) __learned__ about the robbery, she was sad. She (2) _____ Ms. Ditto was an honest person.

To solve the mystery, the Director (3) _____ herself in her office alone. She (4) _____ the problems between Harry and Ms. Ditto. Then, the Director (5) _____ at the note again. She (6) _____ all the grammar mistakes! And the signature on the note was not Ms. Ditto's signature.

The Director (7) _____ Harry to come to her office. She (8) _____ the problem with him. Finally, Harry (9) _____ to the crime. Harry said, "I (10) _____ the note and

(11) _____ Ms. Ditto's name." In the end, the Director

(12) _____ Harry.

FOCUS 3 ＞＞＞＞＞＞＞＞＞＞＞＞＞＞＞＞＞＞＞＞＞＞＞ **FORM**

Irregular Past-Tense Verbs: Affirmative Statements

Many verbs in the past tense are irregular. They do not have the *-ed* form.

SUBJECT	VERB	
I You He She It We You They	went	to New York last year.

You can learn irregular past-tense forms in groups.

BASE FORM	SIMPLE PAST
/I/ sound	**/ae/ sound**
begin	began
drink	drank
ring	rang
sing	sang
sink	sank
swim	swam

BASE FORM	SIMPLE PAST
	ought/aught
buy	bought
bring	brought
catch	caught
fight	fought
teach	taught
think	thought

BASE FORM	SIMPLE PAST	BASE FORM	SIMPLE PAST
	Base form and past-tense forms are the same	become	**Change of vowel**
			became
cost	cost	come	came
cut	cut	dig	dug
hit	hit	draw	drew
hurt	hurt	fall	fell
put	put	forget	forgot
quit	quit	get	got
shut	shut	give	gave
let	let	hold	held
		hang	hung
-ow	**-ew**	run	ran
blow	blew	sit	sat
grow	grew	win	won
know	knew		
throw	threw	break	**/o/ sound**
			broke
/iy/ sound	**/ɛ/ sound**	choose	chose
feed	fed	sell	sold
feel	felt	tell	told
keep	kept	speak	spoke
lead	led	steal	stole
leave	left	drive	drove
meet	met	ride	rode
read	read	wake	woke
sleep	slept	write	wrote
-d	**-t**		
lend	lent		
send	sent		
spend	spent		
bend	bent		
build	built		

BASE FORM	SIMPLE PAST
	Other
be	was
bite	bit
do	did
eat	ate
find	found
fly	flew
go	went
have	had
hear	heard
hide	hid
lose	lost
make	made
pay	paid
say	said
see	saw
shake	shook
shoot	shot
stand	stood
take	took
tear	tore
understand	understood
wear	wore

(See Appendix 8 for an alphabetical list of common irregular past-tense verbs.)

EXERCISE 5

Go back to the Opening Task on page 270. Circle the irregular past-tense verbs.

EXAMPLE: For most students, Ms. Ditto (was) the best ESL teacher in the English Language Center.

EXERCISE 6

Liisa and Kate are from Finland. They had a dream vacation in New York last fall. Fill in the blanks with the past tense of the verbs in parentheses.

1. Liisa and Kate __flew__ (fly) to New York on Sunday, November 4.

2. They _____ (find) many interesting things to do in the city.

3. They _____ (eat) great food every day.

4. They _____ (go) to the Statue of Liberty.

5. They _____ (take) a ferry to the Immigration Museum at Ellis Island.

6. They _____ (stand) at the top of the World Trade Center.

7. They _____ (spend) an evening at a jazz club.

8. Liisa _____ (buy) gifts for her friends in Finland.

9. They _____ (see) an exhibit at the Museum of Modern Art.

10. They _____ (meet) a nice woman at the museum.

11. They _____ (speak) English with her all afternoon.

12. They _____ (think) New York was a beautiful, friendly city.

EXERCISE 7

Monique and Daniel are from France. Their vacation in New York was a nightmare. Fill in the blanks with the past tense of the verbs in parentheses.

1. On Sunday, November 4, Monique and Daniel's flight to New York was late, so they __sat__ (sit) in the airport for four hours.

2. The airline company _____ (lose) all their luggage, so on Monday they _____ (go) shopping for new clothes.

3. On Tuesday, they _____ (get) stuck in the subway when their train _____ (break) down.

4. On Wednesday, they _____ (pay) ninety dollars to rent a car, and _____ (drive) to the Aquarium.

5. They _____ (leave) the car on the street and _____ (get) a fifty-dollar parking ticket!

6. A thief _____ (throw) a rock through the car window and _____ (steal) Monique's camera.

7. On Thursday, they _____ (buy) a new camera downtown.

8. On Friday, they _____ (go) ice skating at Rockefeller Center. Monique had the new camera around her neck.

9. Monique _____ (fall) on the ice _____ (hurt) her knee.

10. She _____ (break) her new camera.

11. Monique was wet and frozen, so she _____ (catch) a cold.

12. On Saturday night, they _____ (eat) some unusual food in a restaurant.

13. On Sunday morning, they each _____ (wake) up with stomach problems.

14. Later that Sunday, they _____ (take) a taxi to the airport and finally _____ (leave) for home.

FOCUS 4 >>>>>>>>>>>>>>> **FORM/MEANING**

Time Expressions

Time expressions tell us when the action occurred in the past.

yesterday morning afternoon evening	last night week month year summer	an hour ago two days six months a year	in 1988 on Sunday at 6:00 the day before yesterday

EXAMPLES	EXPLANATIONS
(a) **On Sunday,** they flew to New York. **(b)** Liisa and Kate went to Spain **two years ago.**	Time expressions can come at the beginning or at the end of a sentence.
(c) **Yesterday morning,** a VCR disappeared from the English Language Center.	Use a comma after the time expression if it is at the beginning of the sentence.

Think back to Monique and Daniel's nightmare vacation in New York. Use time expressions to complete the sentences.

EXAMPLE: <u>Last</u> Sunday, Monique and Daniel left Paris for New York City.

1. Monique and Daniel left New York _____ Sunday.

2. Their plane took off _____ 8 o'clock _____ the evening.

3. It is now Tuesday, November 13. Monique and Daniel are back in Paris. Monique and Daniel returned to Paris _____.

4. They left New York _____.

5. _____ week, they had bad luck every day.

6. It was exactly a week _____ that they got stuck on the subway in New York.

Make true statements about yourself. Use each of the time expressions below.

EXAMPLE: Six months ago

Six months ago, <u>I took a trip to Mexico.</u>

1. Two months ago, _____

2. In 1988, _____

3. Last year, _____

4. Last summer, _____

5. Two days ago, _____

6. On Sunday, _____

7. The day before yesterday, _____

8. Yesterday morning, _____

9. At six o'clock this morning, _____

10. An hour ago, _____

FOCUS 5 ➤➤➤➤➤➤➤➤➤➤➤➤➤➤➤➤➤➤➤➤➤➤ FORM

Past Tense: Negative Statements

SUBJECT	DID + NOT DIDN'T	BASE FORM OF VERB
I You He She It We You They	**did not** **didn't**	work.

EXERCISE 10

Make affirmative or negative statements aloud about the people in this unit.

EXAMPLE: the teacher/like Benny

<u>The teacher liked Benny.</u>

the teacher/get angry at Benny.

<u>The teacher didn't get angry at Benny.</u>

1. The other students/like Bookworm Benny
2. The teacher/trust Benny
3. The students/try to get Benny into trouble
4. The students' plan for Benny/succeed
5. Liisa and Kate/lose their luggage
6. Liisa's camera/break
7. Liisa and Kate/get stuck on the subway
8. Liisa and Kate/enjoy their vacation in New York
9. Harry/notice the grammar mistakes in his note
10. Ms. Ditto/sign the note

11. Harry/steal the VCR

12. The Director/believe Harry

13. Monique and Daniel/spend an evening at a jazz club

14. Monique and Daniel/visit the United Nations

15. Monique and Daniel/enjoy their vacation in New York

 FOCUS 6 ➤➤➤➤➤➤➤➤➤➤➤➤➤➤➤➤➤➤➤➤➤ **FORM**

Past Tense: *Yes/No* Questions and Short Answers

Yes/No Questions

DID	SUBJECT	BASE FORM OF THE VERB	
Did	I you he she we you they	visit	New York last year?

Short Answers

AFFIRMATIVE			NEGATIVE		
Yes,	I you he she we you they	did.	No,	I you he she we you they	did not. didn't.

EXERCISE 11

Ask a partner *yes/no* questions about the mystery story.

EXAMPLES: Q: understand the mystery

Did you understand the mystery?

A: Yes, I did.

1. like the Ms. Ditto story
2. enjoy being a detective
3. think Ms. Ditto took the VCR
4. guess that Harry was the thief
5. find the grammar mistakes in Harry's note
6. correct the mistakes in the note
7. feel sorry for Harry
8. want to give Harry any advice

EXERCISE 12

Look at the cartoon about Jerry, a man with very bad luck. He went on a two-week cruise last winter and there was a big storm at sea.

STEP ❶ Ask a partner *yes/no* questions with the words below. The pictures can help you answer the questions.

EXAMPLE: Jerry/go on a cruise last winter

Did Jerry go on a cruise last winter?

Yes, he did.

1. Jerry's ship/reach its destination
2. Jerry/know how to swim
3. Jerry/die
4. he/find an island
5. he/meet anyone on the island
6. the island/have stores
7. he/have enough food
8. he/write postcards home
9. he/make tools
10. he/build a good boat

STEP ② Remember, Jerry has very bad luck. Ask each other Yes/No questions and guess the end of the story. See the Appendix for the conclusion to Exercise 12 (page E-4).

11. Jerry's luck/change
12. a helicopter/find Jerry
13. Jerry/find his way back home
14. the story/have a happy ending
15. Jerry/ever take another cruise again

FOCUS 7 ➤➤➤➤➤➤➤➤➤➤➤➤➤➤➤➤➤➤➤➤➤ **FORM**

Past Tense: *Wh*-Questions

WH-WORD	DID	SUBJECT	BASE FORM OF VERB	ANSWERS
What		I	do last summer?	You went to Paris.
When		you	make plans?	(I made plans) last month.
Where		he	go last summer?	(He went) to Scotland.
Why		the ship	sink?	(It sank) because there was a storm.
How	**did**	she	get to Paris?	(She got there) by plane.
How long		they	stay in New York?	(They stayed there for) two weeks.
How long ago		you	visit Alaska?	(I visited Alaska) ten years ago.
Who(m)		Liisa and Kate	meet in New York?	(They met) a nice woman.

WH-WORD AS SUBJECT	PAST TENSE VERB	ANSWERS
What	happened to Jerry's ship?	It sank.
Who	had a terrible vacation?	Monique and Daniel.

EXERCISE 13

Write Wh-questions about Jerry. Then ask your partner the questions. Your partner gives an answer or says "I don't know."

EXAMPLE: Jerry/eat on the island?

      Q: What _did Jerry eat on the island_ ?

      A: _(He ate) fruit from the trees and fish from the sea._

1. Jerry/go on vacation

   Q: Where _____ ?

   A: _____

2. Jerry/go on vacation

   Q: When _____ ?

   A: _____

3. Jerry/leave home

   Q: How long ago _____ ?

   A: _____

4. Jerry's ship/sink

   Q: Why _____ ?

   A: _____

5. Jerry/do after the ship sank

   Q: What _____ ?

   A: _____

6. Jerry/meet on the island

   Q: Who(m) _____ ?

   A: _____

7. Jerry/build the boat

    Q: How _____?

    A: _____

8. Jerry/put on the boat

    Q: What _____?

    A: _____

9. Jerry/feel when he finished the boat

    Q: How _____?

    A: _____

10. the story end

    Q: How _____?

    A: _____

EXERCISE 14

Make questions that ask for the underlined information. Use *who*, *whom*, or *what*.

EXAMPLE: Q: _What did the students enjoy_ _____?

    A: The students enjoyed <u>Ms. Ditto's classes.</u>

1: **Q:** _____?

    A: The students loved <u>Ms. Ditto.</u>

2: **Q:** _____?

    A: Ms. Ditto used <u>a VCR</u> in her classes.

3: **Q:** _____?

    A: Harry wanted to hurt <u>Ms. Ditto.</u>

4: **Q:** _____?

    A: <u>Harry</u> got hurt in the end.

5: **Q:** _____?

    A: <u>Professor Brown</u> found the note.

6: **Q:** _____?

    A: <u>The Director</u> fired Harry.

7: **Q:** _____ ?

    A: Harry stole <u>the VCR</u>.

8: **Q:** _____ ?

    A: The Director fired <u>Harry</u>.

9: **Q:** _____ ?

    A: The moral of the story was "<u>crime doesn't pay</u>."

EXERCISE 15

Information Gap B. This is a story about a very special woman named Doina. Work with a partner. You look at Text A, and ask questions to get the information for the sentences with the blanks. Your partner looks at Text B on page E-5, and asks questions to get the information for the blanks in Text B.

EXAMPLE: **Your Partner:** (Look at Text B)   1. Where did Doina grow up?

         You: (Look at Text A)   1. She grew up in Romania.

TEXT A:

1. Doina grew up in Romania.

2. She married _____ (who/m)

3. She had a daughter in 1976.

4. Doina was unhappy because she was against the government in Romania.

5. She thought of _____ (what) every day.

6. She taught her daughter how to swim.

7. On October 9, 1988, she and her daughter swam across the Danube River. They swam to _____ (where)

8. The police caught them.

9. Doina and her daughter went _____ (where)

10. They tried to escape several months later.

11. Finally, they left Romania _____ (how)

12. They flew to New York in 1989.

13. Doina went to school _____ (why)

14. She wrote the story of her escape from Romania in her ESL class.

Correct the mistakes in the following sentences.

1. This morning, I waked up early.

2. I saw him yesterday night.

3. Harry didn't felt sad.

4. They don't met the Mayor of New York last week.

5. What Harry wanted?

6. Harry didn't noticed his mistakes.

7. Who did signed the note?

8. What did the Director?

9. What did happen to Harry?

10. Where Liisa and Kate went on vacation?

11. Who did go with Lisa to New York?

12. How Jerry built a boat?

13. They no had dinner in a Greek restaurant.

14. Whom did trust the teacher in the Bookworm Benny story?

15. The ship sank before a long time.

Activities

ACTIVITY 1

STEP ❶ Get into groups. One person in the group thinks of a famous person from the past.

STEP ❷ The others in the group can ask up to twenty *yes/no* questions to guess who the person is. After twenty questions the group loses if they haven't guessed.

EXAMPLE: Did this person sing?

Did this person live in North America?

Was this person a woman?

ACTIVITY 2

Write your own ending for the story about Jerry. Compare your ending with your class-mates'. Who has the best ending? When you are finished, look at the cartoons that tell the end of Jerry's story on page E-4. How does your ending compare with the ending in the cartoon?

ACTIVITY 3

Work in groups of three.

STEP ❶ Each person tells a true personal story. The group chooses one story. Then each of you learns as much as you can about that story.

STEP ❷ Each of you tells the same beginning to the class. Your classmates ask each of you questions to find out who is telling the truth. Your job is to make the class believe this is your story.

> **EXAMPLE:** **Student 1 says:** When I was ten years old, I went on a long trip.
>
> **Student 2 says:** When I was ten years old, I went on a long trip.
>
> **Student 3 says:** When I was ten years old, I went on a long trip.
>
> **The Class asks:** Where did you go?
>
> Who(m) did you go with? etc.

ACTIVITY 4

Interview a partner about a past vacation. Ask as many *wh*-questions as you can. Report back to the class about your partner's trip.

> **EXAMPLE:** Where did you go?   How long did you stay?
>
> When did you go?   With whom did you go?
>
> How did you get there?   Why did you go there?
>
> What did you do there?

ACTIVITY 5

 STEP ❶ Listen to the three students talking about their vacations. Match the students to the titles of the essays they wrote about their vacations.

Names	**Essay Titles**
Pedro	A Great Vacation
Hakim	My Terrible Trip
Angela	A Boring Vacation

STEP ❷ In a group discuss why each vacation was good or bad. What is your opinion of each vacation?

ACTIVITY 6

Jeopardy Game. Your teacher will choose one student to be the host. Only the host can look at the complete game board (page E-5). The rest of the class will be divided into two teams. Team 1 chooses a category and an amount of money from the game board. The host reads the answer. Team 1 has one minute to ask a correct question. If Team 1 can't, Team 2 gets a chance to ask a question. There can be more than one correct question for each answer. The team with the most money wins.

> **EXAMPLE: Team 1 chooses:** People for $10.
>
> **Host reads:**   Ms. Ditto
>
> **Team 1 asks:**   Who lost her job?
>
>   Who(m) did Harry hate?

GAME BOARD

$$$	Category 1 PEOPLE	Category 2 WH-QUESTIONS	Category 3 YES/NO QUESTIONS
$10 $20 $30 $40 $50			

ACTIVITY 7

The stories in this unit are about unfair or unlucky things that happen to people. Think about a time when something unfair or unlucky happened to you. Write your story and tell the class what happened. Your classmates can ask you questions.

UNIT 19

Reflexive Pronouns, Reciprocal Pronoun: *Each Other*

Advice Columns

STEP ❶ Read the letters to "Dear Darcy" in Part A. Match each one to a "Letter of Advice" in Part B. Fill in the name of the person who wrote each letter in the blanks in Part B.

PART A

Dear Darcy,

I'm married and have two children. I'm trying to be a super-woman. I do all of the housework, shopping, and the cleaning. I help my children with their school work. I never have time for myself. I am tired and unhappy. Please help!

—*Supermom in Seattle*

Dear Darcy,

My wife and I never go out anymore. We have a new baby, and my wife doesn't want to get a baby sitter. I'm starting to talk to myself! Can you help me?

—*Bored in Boston*

Dear Darcy,

My mom and dad got divorced last month. They fought with each other a lot, and finally, my dad moved out. Maybe I wasn't a good daughter to them. Maybe the break-up was my fault. What do you think?

—*Guilty in Gainesville*

PART B

A. Dear _____,

   Don't blame yourself. You did not cause the problems. This is your parents' problem.

B. Dear _____,

   You need to explain how you feel to her. Tell her you want to go out once a week. Life is short. Go out and enjoy yourselves!

C. Dear _____,

   You need to make time for yourself. Go out with your friends. Do yourself a favor and join a gym. Take care of yourself too. Buy yourself something special.

STEP ❷ Read the last letter from *Lonely in Los Angeles*. Circle the correct pronouns in Darcy's answer.

Dear Darcy:

   I'm a rather shy and lonely high school student. I'm doing well in school, but I don't have many friends. The girls in my class always call each other, but they never call me. I don't go out. I don't enjoy myself. I don't even like myself very much anymore.

                                                        Lonely in Los Angeles

Dear Lonely in Los Angeles:

   Remember, the teenage years are difficult. At 16, many girls don't like (they/them/themselves). You're doing well in school. Be proud of (you/yourself). Try to like (you/yourself) first. Then others will like (you/yourself). Teenage girls need (each other/themselves). Force (you/yourself) to open up to other girls. Relax and try to enjoy (you/yourself).

                                                        Darcy

Reflexive Pronouns

Use a reflexive pronoun when the subject and object are the same.

EXAMPLE: Sara bought **herself** a new car.

NOT: Sara bought Sara a new car.

EXAMPLES	REFLEXIVE PRONOUNS
(a) I bought **myself** a new car.	*myself*
(b) Look at **yourself** in the mirror.	*yourself*
(c) He doesn't take care of **himself.**	*himself*
(d) She blames **herself** for the accident.	*herself*
(e) A cat licks **itself** to keep clean.	*itself*
(f) We enjoyed **ourselves** at the theater.	*ourselves*
(g) Help **yourselves** to some food.	*yourselves*
(h) Babies can't feed **themselves.**	*themselves*

EXERCISE I

Go back to the Opening Task on page 293. Underline all the reflexive pronouns and the subjects.

EXAMPLE: <u>I</u> never have time for <u>myself.</u>

EXERCISE 2

Fill in each blank with a reflexive pronoun.

EXAMPLE: I lost my wallet yesterday, and I wanted to kick __myself__ .

1. **Mary:** Do you sometimes talk to _____ ?

   Bill: Well, sometimes, when I'm alone.

2. **Monica:** Thanks for such a lovely evening. We really enjoyed (a) _____ .

   Gloria: Well, thanks for coming. And the children were just wonderful. They really behaved (b) _____ all evening. I hope you can come back soon.

3. **Jane:** I can't believe my bird flew out the window! It's my fault. I forgot to close the birdcage.

   Margaret: Don't blame _____. He's probably happier now. He's free.

4. **Cynthia:** What's the matter with Bobby's leg?

   Enrique: He hurt _____ at the soccer game last night.

5. **Jason:** My girlfriend Judy really knows how to take care of _____. She eats well, exercises regularly, and gets plenty of sleep.

6. **Sylvia:** Hello Carol, hello Eugene. Come on in. Make (a) _____ at home. Help (b) _____ to some drinks.

7. **Mother:** Be careful! that pot on the stove is very hot. Don't burn _____.

FOCUS 2 ➤➤➤➤➤➤➤➤➤➤➤➤➤➤ **MEANING/USE**

Verbs Commonly Used with Reflexive Pronouns/By + Reflexive Pronoun

EXAMPLES	EXPLANATIONS
(a) I fell and **hurt myself.** (b) He **taught himself** to play the guitar. (c) Be careful! Don't **cut yourself** with that knife. (d) Did you **enjoy yourself** at the party?	These verbs are commonly used with reflexive pronouns: *hurt* *cut* *tell* *burn* *blame* *enjoy* *teach* *introduce* *behave* *take care of*
(e) He got up, washed, and shaved.	The verbs *wash*, *dress*, and *shave* do not usually take reflexive pronouns. In sentence (e) it is clear he washed and shaved himself and not another person.
(f) He's only two, but he wants to get dressed **by himself.** (g) I sometimes go to the movies **by myself.**	Use *by* + a reflexive pronoun to show that someone is doing something alone (without company or help).

Write a sentence with a reflexive pronoun for each picture.

EXAMPLE: <u>The woman is introducing herself to the man.</u>

1. 2. 3. 4

5. 6. 7. 8.

cut	dry	enjoy	look at/admire
clean/lick	hurt	talk to	weigh

1. _____
2. _____
3. _____
4. _____
5. _____
6. _____
7. _____
8. _____

Reciprocal Pronoun: *Each Other*

The reciprocal pronoun *each other* is different in meaning from a reflexive pronoun.

(a) John and Ann blamed **themselves** for the accident.

(b) John and Ann blamed **each other** for the accident.

Work with a partner. Draw pictures to show the differences in meaning between the following sentences.

1. **(a)** The weather was very hot. The runners poured water on themselves after the race.

   (b) The weather was very hot. The runners poured water on each other after the race.

2. **(a)** They love themselves.

   (b) They love each other.

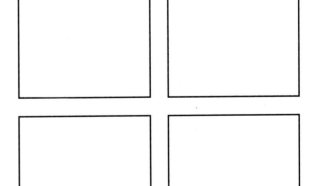

Act out the following sentences to show the difference between *each other* and reflexive pronouns.

1. You and your classmate are looking at yourselves in the mirror.
2. You and your classmate are looking at each other.
3. You and your classmate are talking to yourselves.
4. You and your classmate are talking to each other.
5. You're playing ball with a friend, and you break a neighbor's window. Blame yourself for the accident.
6. You're playing ball with a friend, and you break a neighbor's window. Blame each other for the accident.
7. You introduce yourself to your partner.
8. You and your partner introduce each other to a third person.

Choose a reflexive pronoun or *each other* to complete the statements.

1. An egotistical person loves _himself/herself_____.
2. Divorced people can be friends if they forgive _____.
3. Good friends protect _____.
4. Close friends tell _____ their secrets.
5. A self-confident person believes in _____.
6. In a good relationship, the two people trust _____.
7. A realistic person doesn't lie to _____.
8. Independent people take care of _____.
9. Caring people help _____.
10. Angry people say things to hurt _____.
11. Young children can't always control _____.
12. An insecure person doesn't have confidence in _____.

Circle the correct word in the "Dear Darcy" letters below.

EXAMPLE: ((He) Him, Himself) cares about (I, (me,) myself).

Dear Darcy,

(1) (I, My, Mine) boyfriend loves himself. (2) (He, His, Him) is very pleased with (3) (he, him, himself). He always looks at (4) (he, him, himself) in store windows when he passes by. (5) (Himself, He, Him) only thinks about (6) (his, himself, him). He never brings (7) (my, me, myself) flowers. The last time he told (8) (my, me, myself) that he loved me was two years ago. He's also very selfish with (9) (he, his, him) things. For example, he never lends me (10) (him, himself, his) car. He says that the car is (11) (himself, him, his), and he doesn't want me to use it. Do (12) (yourself, your, you) have any advice for me?

"Unhappy"

Dear Unhappy:

(13) (You, Your, Yourself) boyfriend is very selfish. (14) (You, Your, Yourself) can't really change (15) (he, himself, him). Get rid of (16) (he, himself, him)! Find (17) (you, yourself, yours) a new guy!

Darcy

Correct the mistakes in the following sentences.

1. I hurt me.
2. They're looking at theirselves in the mirror.
3. I shave myself every morning.
4. I have a friend in Poland. We write to ourselves every month.
5. We enjoyed at the circus.
6. Larry blamed Harry for the accident. Harry blamed Larry for the accident. They blamed themselves for the accident.
7. He did it hisself.

Activities

ACTIVITY 1

Read the following riddle and try to find the answer. Discuss it with a partner. The answer is on page AK-1.

A prison guard found a prisoner hanging from a rope in his prison cell. Did he hang himself or did someone murder him? There was nothing else in the prison cell but a puddle of water on the floor.

ACTIVITY 2

Who is the most independent person in your class?
Make up a survey with ten questions. Then go around to all the students in your class and ask your questions. Tell the class who the independent people are.

EXAMPLE: Do you like to do things by yourself?

Do you usually travel by yourself?

Do you ever go to the movies by yourself?

ACTIVITY 3

Interview another classmate, using the questions below.

1. Do you believe in yourself?

2. When you go shopping for clothes, do you like to look at yourself in the mirror?

3. Do you ever compare yourself to other people?

4. Do you ever buy yourself a present?

5. In a new relationship, do you talk about yourself or try to learn about the other person?

6. Do you ever talk to yourself?

7. Do you cook for yourself?

8. Do you blame yourself for your problems or do you blame others?

9. Do you take care of yourself? (Do you eat well? Do you get enough sleep?)

10. Do you ever get angry at yourself?

Add questions of your own.

ACTIVITY 4

Listen to the people talk about their problems.

STEP ❶ Match the problems to the people.

Person #1   _____   (a) Serious

Person #2   _____   (b) Lonely

Person #3   _____   (c) Unhealthy

STEP ❷ What advice can you give to each of these people? Tell your classmates.

Future Time
Will and *Be Going To*, *May* and *Might*

Looking into Wanda's Crystal Ball

What is Wanda the Fortune-teller saying about each person? Match the phrases to the correct person (or people). Then, make a statement about each person's future.

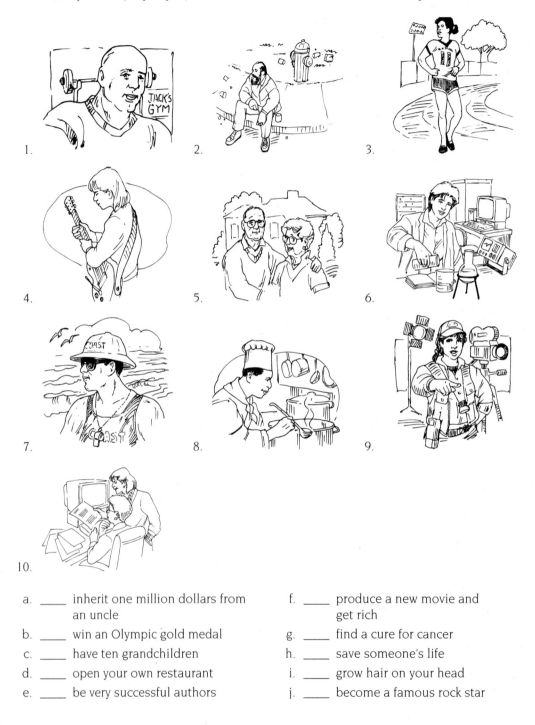

1.
2.
3.
4.
5.
6.
7.
8.
9.
10.

a. ____ inherit one million dollars from an uncle

b. ____ win an Olympic gold medal

c. ____ have ten grandchildren

d. ____ open your own restaurant

e. ____ be very successful authors

f. ____ produce a new movie and get rich

g. ____ find a cure for cancer

h. ____ save someone's life

i. ____ grow hair on your head

j. ____ become a famous rock star

FOCUS 1 >>>>>>>>>>>>>>>> MEANING/USE

Talking about Future Time

Use *will* and *be going to* to make predictions about the future or to say what you think will happen in the future.

EXAMPLES	EXPLANATIONS
(a) One day, he **will** be rich.	Use *will* for a prediction (what we think will happen).
(b) Look at those big black clouds. It **is going to** rain. NOT: It will rain.	Use *be going to* for a prediction based on the present situation (what we can see is going to happen).
(c) Teacher to student: Your parents **will** be very upset about this.	*Will* is more formal.
(d) Father to daughter: Your mother**'s going to** be very angry about this.	*Be going to* is less formal.

EXERCISE 1

Match the sentences to the pictures.

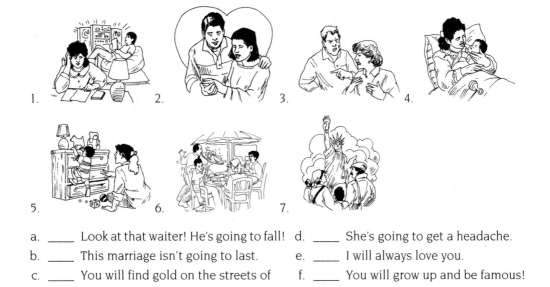

1.   2.   3.   4.

5.   6.   7.

a. ____ Look at that waiter! He's going to fall!

b. ____ This marriage isn't going to last.

c. ____ You will find gold on the streets of America!

d. ____ She's going to get a headache.

e. ____ I will always love you.

f. ____ You will grow up and be famous!

g. ____ Be careful, Julian. You're going to fall.

FOCUS 2 >>>>>>>>>>>>>>>>>>>>>>> FORM

Will

AFFIRMATIVE STATEMENTS		NEGATIVE STATEMENTS	
I You He She It We You They	**will arrive** next week. **'ll arrive** next week.	I You He She It We You They	**will not arrive** next week. **won't arrive** next week.
There	**will be** peace in the world. **'ll be**	There **will not be** any wars. **won't be**	
Men **will be able** to have babies.		Men **will not be able to** have babies. **won't**	

YES/NO QUESTIONS			SHORT ANSWERS						
Will	I you he she it we you they	arrive next week?	Yes,	you I he she it we you they	**will.**	No,	you I he she it we you they	**won't.**

WH-QUESTIONS	ANSWERS
(a) **When will** the scientists discover a cure?	(They **will discover** a cure) in ten years.
(b) **Where will** the couple go on their honeymoon?	(They **will go**) to Hawaii.
(c) **What will** the homeless man do with the money?	He**'ll buy** a new house.
(d) **How will** the couple travel?	(They**'ll travel**) by plane.
(e) **How** long **will** they be on the plane?	(They**'ll be** on the plane) for five hours.
(f) **Who will** get an Olympic medal?	The athlete.
(g) **Who(m)** **will** the lifeguard save?	(He**'ll save**) a lucky person.

EXERCISE 2

Think about the people in the Opening Task on page 304. Try to remember the predictions for each person. Say the prediction aloud.

EXAMPLE: The scientist *will find a cure for cancer.*

1. The bald man . . .
2. The athlete . . .
3. The teenager . . .
4. The movie director . . .
5. The lifeguard . . .
6. The chef . . .
7. The homeless man . . .
8. The authors . . .
9. The elderly couple . . .

How will our lives be different in fifty years? Make predictions with *will* or *won't*. Discuss your predictions with a partner.

1. The climate _____ change.

2. Pollution _____ be under control.

3. People _____ take vacations on the moon.

4. There _____ be few fish left in the oceans.

5. All countries _____ share the world's money equally.

6. Most people _____ move back to the countryside.

7. The traditional family with a husband, wife, and two children
    _____ disappear.

8. Men and women _____ continue to marry.

9. People of different races _____ learn to live together peacefully.

10. People _____ speak the same language.

11. Crime _____ stop.

12. People _____ drive electric cars.

13. We _____ discover life on other planets.

14. Science _____ continue to be very important.

15. People _____ live to be 130 years old.

16. A woman _____ be President of the United States.

Think about the year 2025. Where will you be? What will you be able to do? Write *yes/no* questions with *will*. Interview your classmates and report their answers to the class.

	Classmate 1	**Classmate 2**
1. be in the United States	_____	_____
Will you be in the United States?		
2. speak English fluently	_____	_____
3. be back in the country you come from	_____	_____

4. have a good job   _____   _____

5. earn a living   _____   _____

6. take care of a family   _____   _____

7. have a nice house   _____   _____

8. be content   _____   _____

9. want something different   _____   _____

Add two questions of your own.

10. _____   _____   _____

11. _____   _____   _____

EXERCISE 5

Work with a partner. You are Janice Williams and your partner is Wanda the Fortune-teller. Ask your partner *yes/no* and *wh*-questions with *will* and *will be able to*. Your partner looks into the crystal ball to answer your questions.

EXAMPLE: You: Will my husband lose his job?

         Your Partner: Yes, he will.

Wanda's Crystal Ball

Husband will find another job in 3 months

Daughter will get married to a computer specialist

Husband will lose job

Will have 5 grandchildren

You and your husband will retire to Tahiti!

Son will drop out of high school

Janice's Questions

1. my husband/lose his job?
2. my husband/be able to find another job?
3. when/my husband/find another job?
4. my daughter/get married?
5. who(m)/she/marry?
6. I/have grandchildren?
7. how many grandchildren/I/have?
8. my son/go to college?
9. what/he/do?
10. my husband and I/be able to retire?
11. where/we/retire?

FOCUS 3 ▷▷▷▷▷▷▷▷▷▷▷▷▷▷▷▷▷▷▷▷▷ FORM

Be Going To

AFFIRMATIVE STATEMENTS		NEGATIVE STATEMENTS	
I — am / 'm		I — am not / 'm not	
You — are / 're		You — are not / aren't	
He She It — is / 's	**going to** leave.	He She It — is not / isn't	**going to** leave.
We You They — are / 're		We You They — are not / aren't	

YES/NO QUESTIONS		SHORT ANSWERS			
Am I			you **are.**		you **aren't.**
Are you	**going to** leave?	Yes,	I **am.**	No,	I'm **not.**
Is he she it			he she **is.** it		he she **isn't.** it
Are we you they			we you **are.** they		we you **aren't.** they

310 Unit 20

WH-QUESTIONS			ANSWERS	
When		leave?		leave in two weeks.
Where		go?		go to Colorado.
What	**are you going to**	do there?	**I'm going to**	go skiing.
How		get there?		go by car.
How long		stay?		stay for one week.
Who(m)		visit?		visit my cousin.
Who**'s**	**going to**	drive?	My friend (is going to drive).	

Remember: *Going to* is often pronounced "gonna" when we speak. We do not usually write "gonna."

EXERCISE 6

Look at the pictures. Then fill in the blanks with the affirmative or negative form of *be going to*.

1.   "Watch out! That bag _____ fall!"

2.   "Hurry up! We _____ miss the bus."

3.   "This _____ hurt you."

4. "I am so tired! I _____ take a nap."

5. "Hello, dear. I _____ be home on time tonight."

6. **George:** What are you _____ to have, Fred?
Fred: I _____ to have a pizza, as usual.

7. "Watch her, Jack! She _____ fall into the pool!"

8. "They _____ have a baby."

9. "Hello, boss. I'm sorry, I _____ be able to come
in today. I have a terrible backache and I can't get out of bed."

10. **Ben:** I have a test tomorrow. I _____ to study.

Roommate: I have a test tomorrow too, but I _____ study. I
_____ to watch the game on TV!

Read the answers. Write a *yes/no* or *wh*-question with *be going to*.

Richard: My doctor says I need to leave my job and get away somewhere.

Robert: (1) _Where are you going to go?_ ?

Richard: To California.

Robert: (2) _____ ?

Richard: I don't know (what I'm going to do there).

Robert: (3) _____ ?

Richard: (I'm going to stay) with some old friends.

Robert: (4) _____ ?

Richard: For about a month.

Robert: (5) _____ ?

Richard: By plane.

Robert: (6) _____ ?

Richard: I don't know (if I'm going to come back to my job).

Use your imagination to answer these questions about the people in the Opening Task on page 304. Use *be going to* in writing your answers. Compare your answers with your classmates'.

1. What is going to happen to the elderly people?

   They're going to live to a ripe old age.

2. What is the poor person going to do with the million dollars?

3. Who is the lifeguard going to save?

4. What kind of movie is the director going to make?

5. What kind of food is the chef going to have in his restaurant?

6. How are the authors going to celebrate their success?

7. What is the athlete going to do after the Olympics?

8. What kind of life is the rock star going to have?

FOCUS 4 >>>>>>>>>>>>>> FORM/MEANING

Time Expressions

EXAMPLES	EXPLANATIONS
(a) I'm going to visit you **tomorrow evening.** **(b) A month from now,** Wanda will be on a tropical island.	Future time expressions can come at the beginning or at the end of the sentence. Put a comma (,) after the time expression when it is at the beginning of the sentence.

Future Time Expressions

(Later) this	morning
	afternoon
	evening
		next	week
			month
			year
			Sunday
			weekend
				tomorrow	morning
					afternoon
					evening
					night
						soon
						later
						the day after
						  tomorrow
						a week from
						  today
						tonight

EXAMPLES				EXPLANATIONS
I'll see you	**(c)**	**in**	fifteen minutes two weeks. March. 2015.	We also use prepositions of time to talk about future time.
	(d)	**on**	Tuesday May 21st.	
	(e)	**at**	4:00 midnight.	
(f) We are going to go to the Bahamas **for** three weeks.				*For* shows how long the action will last.
(g) I'll be there **until** 3:00. (At 3:00, I will leave. I will not be there after 3:00.) **(h)** I won't be there **until** Monday. (Before Monday, I won't be there. After Monday, I'll be there.)				*Until* shows the specific time in the future when the action will change.

EXERCISE 9

Make statements about yourself. Use *be going to*.

EXAMPLE: In a few days, I'm going to call my parents .

1. In a few days, _____.

2. Next summer, _____.

3. The day after tomorrow, _____.

4. This evening, _____.

5. Tomorrow night, _____.

6. This weekend, _____.

7. At 9:00, _____.

8. In December, _____.

9. On Wednesday night, _____.

Anthony and Sally are planning a vacation in Europe. They are going to visit four countries in seven days. Sally is telling Anthony about their travel plans. Fill in the blanks with *in, on, at, for,* or *until.*

1. We are going to arrive in London (a) __at__ 6:00 P.M.
   (b) __on__ Sunday.

2. We'll stay in London _____ two days.

3. Then, we'll fly to Paris _____ Tuesday morning.

4. We'll stay in Paris _____ Wednesday afternoon.

5. Then, we'll fly to Rome _____ the evening.

6. We won't leave Rome _____ Friday morning.

7. _____ 10:00 A.M. on Friday morning, we'll fly to our final destination, Athens, Greece.

8. We'll stay in Greece _____ two days.

9. We'll return home _____ Sunday. Then, we'll need a vacation!

Look at Wanda's calendar. Imagine it is now 2 p.m. on Wednesday, April 10, 1996. Read the sentences about Wanda's plans and fill in the blanks with a time expression or a preposition of time. There may be more than one correct answer.

SUNDAY	MONDAY	TUESDAY	WEDNESDAY	THURSDAY	FRIDAY	SATURDAY
APRIL	1	2	3	4	5	6
7	8	9	10 Last client 6:00 pm	11 polish crystal ball	12 deposit money in bank	13
14	15	16 buy new fortune cards	17	18 secretary goes on vacation	19 Fortune Tellers' conference	20
21	22	23	24	25	26	27
28	29	30	31			

Still To Do:
First Edition of "How to Make Predictions" magazine arrives on June 10th
—Retire 2015!
—Write autobiography 2020

SUNDAY	MONDAY	TUESDAY	WEDNESDAY	THURSDAY	FRIDAY	SAT...
MAY			1	2	3	4
5	6 place ad in newspaper	7	8	9	10	11
12	13	14				

1. Wanda is going to see her last client _at 6:00 this evening; in four hours_ .

2. She's going to attend the Fortune-tellers' Conference _____ .

3. She's going to polish her crystal ball _____ .

4. She's going to deposit all her money in the bank _____ .

5. Her secretary is going to go on vacation _____ .

6. She is going to buy new fortune cards _____ .

7. She's going to put an advertisement about herself in the newspaper

   _____ .

8. She will receive her first *How To Make Predictions* magazine

   _____ .

9. She will retire to a tropical island _____ .

10. She will write a book called *How to Be a Successful Fortune-teller in 10 Easy Lessons*

   _____ .

FOCUS 5 ⪢⪢⪢⪢⪢⪢⪢⪢⪢⪢⪢⪢⪢⪢⪢⪢⪢⪢⪢⪢⪢⪢ **USE**

Talking about Future Intentions or Plans

EXAMPLES	EXPLANATIONS
(a) A: The phone is ringing. B: O.K. I**'ll get** it.	Use *will* when you decide to do something **at** the time of speaking.
(b) Mother: Where are you going? Daughter: I**'m going to** take a drive with Richard tonight. Remember, Mom? You said it was okay . . . Mother: I did?	Use *going to* when you made a plan to do something **before** the time of speaking.

Work with a partner. You read the first five statements in Column A aloud. Your partner chooses an answer from Column B. After the first five, your partner reads from Column A and you choose the answer from Column B.

EXAMPLE: Do you have any plans for tonight?

(B.) Yes, we're going to the theater.

Column A

1. Christine called. She's coming over for dinner.

2. What are you doing with that camera?

3. Do you need a ride home today?

4. We don't have a thing to eat in the house.

5. Help! The car died again.

6. Why are you meeting Jenny in the library tonight?

7. Look, those thieves are robbing the bank!

8. Mom, can you brush my hair?

9. Are you off the phone yet?

10. Why did Maria cancel her date for Saturday night?

Column B

A. Great! I'll cook.
B. Great! I'm going to cook.

A. I'll take your picture.
B. I'm going to take your picture.

A. No, thanks. Jason will take me home.
B. No, thanks. Jason's going to take me home.

A. I'll call up and order a pizza.
B. I'm going to call up and order a pizza.

A. Calm down. I'll be right there.
B. Calm down. I'm going to be right there.

A. She'll help me with my homework.
B. She's going to help me with my home work.

A. I'll call the police.
B. I'm going to call the police.

A. I'll do it in a minute, sweetie.
B. I'm going to do it in a minute, sweetie.

A. I'll be off in a minute!
B. I'm going to be off in a minute!

A. Her parents will take her away for the weekend.
B. Her parents are going to take her away for the weekend.

May and Might

Use *may* or *might* to say something is possible in the future.

EXAMPLES	EXPLANATIONS
(a) I **will go** to Mexico next year.	(a) shows certainty. The speaker is 100% sure.
(b) I **may/might go** to Mexico next year.	(b) shows possibility.

AFFIRMATIVE STATEMENTS			NEGATIVE STATEMENTS		
I You He She We You They	**may** **might**	study abroad next year. be able to stay abroad for two years.	I You He She We You They	**may not** **might not**	take a vacation. be able to stay for two years.
It		rain later.	It		rain later.
There		be cheap flights to Mexico.	There		be any discounts on flights.

NOTE:
- You cannot use *may* or *might* in *yes/no* questions.
- There are no contractions for *may* or *might*.

Fill in the blanks with *may* or *might* in the affirmative or negative.

EXAMPLE: Peter: How are you going to go to Boston next weekend?

Al: I _may_ drive or I _may_ take the train. I won't fly because it's expensive.

1. **Joanne:** Is Ilene going to come to your New Year's Eve party?

   Paula: She (a) _____ be able to come. She went out of town on business and she (b) _____ be back in time for the party.

2. **Tamara:** Where are you and Chip going to go on vacation this summer?

   Susan: Chip (a) _____ start a new job in July, so we (b) _____ be able to go on vacation. We (c) _____ stay home and go to the beach.

3. **Eugene:** What's Jason going to major in at the university?

   Carol: Well, he really loves the ocean, so he (a) _____ major in marine biology, or he (b) _____ major in environmental science.

4. **Priscilla:** Will you go back to your country after you finish college here?

   Arnaldo: I don't know. I (a) _____ want to go back to visit my family, but I (b) _____ want to go back to live. There (c) _____ be more job opportunities for me here in the United States.

What are your plans for the future? Complete your chart with a base verb. Exchange charts with your partner. Report your partner's plans to the class.

EXAMPLE: He**'s going to, might, may, will go to** see a movie this evening.

	Base Verb	Will/Going to	May/Might
1. This evening,	to see a movie	X	
2. This weekend,			
3. Tomorrow night,			
4. A week from today,			
5. In 3 months,			
6. Next summer,			
7. In 5 years,			

EXERCISE 15

What is our future in the computer age? Make statements with affirmative or negative forms of *will*, *be going to*, *may*, or *might*.

EXAMPLE: Computers/always be part of our lives

Computers will always be part of our lives.

1. People/want to go back to a time before computers
2. The number of computers in the world/increase
3. We/all have pocket computers
4. The Internet/connect people in every home all over the world
5. Students in classrooms all around the world/be able to "talk" to each other
6. People/learn languages easily with computers
7. People/prefer to communicate by computer
8. Books/disappear
9. People who cannot use computers/be able to find jobs
10. Computers/take away our privacy.

Activities

What do you think the world will be like in 2050? Think about changes in travel, the home, food, technology, and people, etc. With your group, write down ten changes. Discuss your group's ideas with the rest of the class.

ACTIVITY 2

Imagine that you and your partner win $1,000. You have one day to spend it. What are you going to do together? Give details of your activities. For example, if you rent a car, say what kind of car you are going to rent (a sports car, a limousine, a jeep?). Share your plans with the class. Decide which pair has the most interesting plans.

ACTIVITY 3

Make a weekly calendar and fill in your schedule for next week. Write different activities for each day. Try to make a date to do something with your partner in the future.

EXAMPLE: What are you going to do on Sunday?

I'm going to go jogging in Central Park.

ACTIVITY 4

You are a group of tourists going to Europe. You are at the airport and the tour guide is giving you some information.

 STEP ❶ Listen to the tour guide, and complete the travel plan below.

Day	Place	Number of Days/Nights
Sunday	Paris	
		3 nights
	Milan	
Saturday		
	Vienna	
Thursday		
Saturday		

STEP ❷ Compare your plan with a partner's.

STEP ❸ Tell the class your travel plans, real or imaginary. Say when you are going to go, how you are going to go there, where you are going to stay, etc.

> **EXAMPLE:** In June, I'm going to go to Vancouver alone. I'm going to fly there. I'm going to visit my uncle, who lives there.

ACTIVITY 5

STEP ❶ Sit in a circle with your whole class or a group of six to eight people. On the top of a blank piece of paper write:

On _____ in the year 2015, _____
     (today's date)   (your name)

STEP ❷ Pass the sheet of paper to the person on your left. This person writes a prediction about you for the year 2015. Then he or she passes the paper to the left for the next person to write a second prediction.

STEP ❸ Continue until everyone has written their predictions. At the end of the activity, you will have a list of predictions. Read the predictions and choose the best one. Read them aloud to the class.

UNIT

21

Phrasal Verbs

Nervous Nellie Gives a Talk

Nelly is nervous about the talk she is going to give.

STEP ❶ Look at the pictures and describe the steps in Nellie's talk.

STEP ❷ Nelly has index cards to help her remember what to do. Read the first part of each index card. Find the second part of each card in the box, and read each complete card aloud.

sit down	calm down	take out
call up	ask for	stand up
put on		slow down

1. Take a deep breath and _____ .

2. _____ and introduce myself.

3. _____ my glasses.

4. _____ my notes.

5. Don't talk too fast. _____ .

6. _____ questions.

7. _____ and relax.

8. _____ all my friends and tell them it's over.

Phrasal Verbs

EXAMPLES	EXPLANATIONS

(a) **Turn on** the slide projector.	A phrasal verb is:
	
	     a verb + a particle
	     turn + *on*
	     sit + *down*
	     stand + *up*

(b) Plants grow.
    (grow = to increase in size)
 Children **grow up.**
    (grow up = to become an adult)
	The verb + particle together have a specific meaning.

EXERCISE 1

Look at Nelly's index cards from the Opening Task on page 326 and circle all the phrasal verbs.

1. Take a deep breath and (calm down.)
2. Stand up and introduce myself.
3. Put on my glasses.
4. Take out my notes.
5. Don't talk too fast. Slow down.
6. Ask for questions.
7. Sit down and relax.
8. Call up all my friends and tell them it's over!

Read each statement on the left to your partner. Your partner chooses a response from the right.

Statement

1. I don't want to cook tonight.
2. It's hot in here.
3. It's so quiet in here.
4. I can't read the map. The print's too small.
5. I can't do my homework with the TV on.
6. I'm bored.
7. My feet hurt.
8. I'm sleepy.
9. I'm really upset about our argument today.
10. I'm tired of sitting on this plane.

Response

a. Calm down.
b. Call up a friend.
c. Stand up for a few minutes.
d. Sit down for a while.
e. Lie down and take a nap.
f. Take off your jacket.
g. Put on your glasses.
h. Turn off the TV.
i. Let's eat out.
j. Turn on the radio.

FOCUS 2 ▷▷▷▷▷▷▷▷▷▷▷▷▷▷▷ **MEANING/USE**

Phrasal Verbs

EXAMPLES	EXPLANATIONS
(a) I **hung up** the picture.	Sometimes the meaning of a phrasal verb is clear from the verb + particle combination.
(b) I **ran into** Joe on the street the other day.	Sometimes it is difficult to guess the meaning of a phrasal verb. The meaning of *ran into* is not the combination of *ran* and *into*. *Run into* means "to meet someone by chance."
(c) Please **put out** your cigarette, Jake. **(d)** Please **extinguish** your cigarettes, ladies and gentlemen.	In informal English, phrasal verbs are more frequent than one-word verbs with the same meaning. In (c), you are talking to a friend. In (d), a flight attendant is speaking to passengers on an airplane.

Circle the phrasal verbs. Then match each phrasal verb with a one-word verb.

Sentences with phrasal verbs

One-word verb with same meaning

1. I called 911 Emergency. The firefighters will be here soon to (put out) the fire.
2. Don't just stand at the door. Come in.
3. Fill out the application.
4. We're going to practice some phrasal verbs. Henry, can you please hand out this exercise?
5. I left my book at school. I don't remember the homework for tonight. I'll call up Manny and ask him.
6. I can't talk to you now. Come back in fifteen minutes.
7. I can't concentrate! Would you please turn down the music!
8. I am freezing in this house. Please turn up the heat.
9. Please take off your wet shoes.
10. Hold on a minute. I'm not ready yet.

raise

remove

telephone

extinguish

enter

distribute

complete

wait

lower

return

Fill in the blanks with the phrasal verbs below.

| put away | turn on | pick up | throw away | turn off |

DIRECTIONS FOR LANGUAGE LAB ASSISTANTS

When you leave the language lab, there are several things you must do. First, (1) _____ all the trash from the floor. Then (2) _____ all the equipment—tape recorders, VCRs, etc. (3) _____ all the cassettes students used. (4) _____ any coffee cups or trash students left in the room. Finally, (5) _____ the alarm system before you lock the doors.

FOCUS 3

Separable and Inseparable Phrasal Verbs

Separable Phrasal Verbs

EXAMPLES	EXPLANATIONS
Verb Particle **(a)** The teacher **handed out** the exercise. **Verb** **Direct Object** **Particle** **(b)** The teacher **handed** the exercise **out.**	When the direct object is a noun, it can go: • after the particle (*out*) • between the verb (*handed*) and the particle (*out*)
(c) The teacher handed **it** out. NOT: The teacher handed out **it**.	When the direct object is a pronoun, it always goes between the verb and the particle.

Inseparable Phrasal Verbs

EXAMPLES	EXPLANATIONS
(d) I **ran into** an old friend on the street. **(e)** I **ran into** her on the street. NOT: I **ran** an old friend **into** on the street. NOT: I **ran** her **into** on the street.	The direct object—noun or pronoun—goes after the particle.

Sergeant Strict is giving orders to his new soldiers. Repeat the Sergeant's orders in a different way each time.

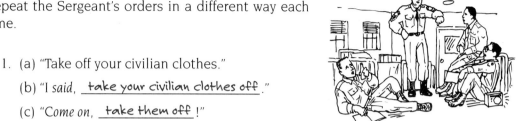

1. (a) "Take off your civilian clothes."

   (b) "I *said*, <u>take your civilian clothes off</u>."

   (c) "*Come on*, <u>take them off</u>!"

2. (a) "Hand out these uniforms."

   (b) "I said, _____."

   (c) "Come on, _____!"

3. (a) "Put on your new Army clothes."

   (b) "I said, _____."

   (c) "Come on, _____!"

4. (a) "Turn down that radio."

   (b) "I said, _____."

   (c) "Come on, _____!"

5. (a) "Put away your old clothes."

   (b) "I said, _____."

   (c) "Come on, _____!"

6. (a) "Throw out that junk food from home."

   (b) "I said, _____."

   (c) "Come on, _____!"

7. (a) "Clean up this mess."

   (b) "I said, _____."

   (c) "Come on, _____!"

8. (a) "Turn off the lights!"

   (b) "I said, _____."

   (c) "Come on, _____!"

Common Separable and Inseparable Phrasal Verbs

Separable Phrasal Verbs

SEPARABLE PHRASAL VERBS	MEANING	EXAMPLES
calm down	relax	**(a)** She is very upset about the accident. We can't **calm** her **down.**
call up	telephone	**(b)** I **called** my friend **up** the other night to ask about the homework.
cheer up	become happy, make someone happy	**(c)** My friend failed her final exam, so I brought her flowers to **cheer** her **up.**
clean up	clean	**(d)** **Clean** your room **up** before you watch TV!
figure out	solve, understand	**(e)** This puzzle is very confusing. I can't **figure** it **out.**
fill out	complete	**(f)** **Fill out** the application for a new license.
fill up	fill	**(g)** **Fill** it **up** with regular gas, please.
hand out	distribute	**(h)** The teacher **handed** the tests **out** to the the class.
hang up	place on a hanger or hook	**(i)** My husband never **hangs** his clothes **up**. **(j)** Please **hang up** the phone.
look up	search for in a reference book	**(k)** I didn't know his telephone number, so I **looked** it **up** in the phone book.

pick up	collect, lift	**(l)** In my neighborhood, they **pick up** the garbage every Tuesday.
		(m) I **picked** my pen **up** and started to write.
put away	put in its usual place	**(n)** My kids are neat! They always **put** their toys **away** .
put on	dress yourself	**(o)** It's really cold outside, so **put** a coat **on**.
put out	extinguish	**(p)** It took firefighters a few hours to **put** the fire **out**.
take off	remove	**(q)** **Take** your shoes **off** before you come into the house.
take out	put something outside	**(r)** Will you please **take** the garbage **out** ?
throw out/away	put in the garbage	**(s)** I have a lot of old things in the garage. I need to **throw** them **out**.
turn down	lower the volume	**(t)** It's 2:00 in the morning. **Turn** that stereo **down**!
turn off	stop the power	**(u)** There aren't any good programs on TV tonight. **Turn** it **off**.
turn on	start the power	**(v)** I always **turn on** the radio in the morning.
turn up	increase the volume	**(w)** When I hear my favorite song, I **turn** the volume **up**.
wake up	to open your eyes; to finish sleeping; to interrupt someone's sleep	**(x)** Be quiet! Don't **wake** the baby **up**.

Inseparable Phrasal Verbs

INSEPARABLE PHRASAL VERBS	MEANING	EXAMPLES
get in *get out of**	enter and leave a vehicle (car, taxi, truck)	**(y)** I **got in** my car and drove away. **(z)** My bag fell when I **got out of** the cab.
get on *get off*	enter and leave other forms of transportation (bus, plane, train)	**(aa)** I **got on** the train at 42nd Street. **(bb)** I **got off** the bus in front of the school.
go over	review	**(cc)** I **went over** my notes before the test.
run into	meet by chance	**(dd)** I **ran into** an old friend the other day.

*Sometimes phrasal verbs have three parts.

EXERCISE 6

Fill in the blanks with the phrasal verbs below. Use a pronoun in the second blank of each dialogue.

EXAMPLE: (clean up)

> **Mother:** Danny, don't forget to (a) __clean up__ the mess in your bedroom.
>
> **Danny:** Mom, I (b) __cleaned it up__ this morning.

pick up	cheer up	hand out	throw out	fill out

1. **Counselor:** You need to (a) _____ this application for college.

   Abdul: Can I (b) _____ at home?

2. **Susie:** Danny, I think it's time to (a) _____ all these old newspapers.

   Danny: I'm (b) _____ right now.

3. **Jackie:** Could you please (a) _____ that paper on the floor for me?

   Mark: I'll (b) _____ in a minute!

4. **Ms. Wagner:** Can you help me (a) _____ these exams, Wang?

   Wang: Sure, I'll (b) _____ right now.

5. **Mom:** Please try to (a) _____ your sister. She's in a bad mood.

   Bobbie: No one can (b) _____. She's always in a bad mood.

Sylvia is working late tonight. She's calling her husband, Abe, to see if he has done all the things on her list. Role-play the dialogue with a partner.

EXAMPLE: Sylvia: Did you pick up the children at school?

   Abe: Yes, dear. I picked them up.

1. pick up your shirts at the cleaners
2. clean up the kitchen
3. put away the clean laundry
4. take out the dog
5. throw out the old flowers in the vase
6. fill up the car with gas
7. pick up a pizza for dinner
8. turn on the movie for the children
9. call up Warren to invite him to dinner

Common Phrasal Verbs without Objects

Some phrasal verbs do not take an object.

PHRASAL VERBS WITHOUT OBJECTS	MEANING	EXAMPLES
break down	stop working	**(a)** My car **broke down** last night.
come back	return	**(b)** He left home and never **came back.**
come in	enter	**(c)** **Come in** and make yourself comfortable.
eat out	eat in a restaurant	**(d)** I hate to cook, so I often **eat out.**
grow up	become an adult	**(e)** I **grew up** in the United States.
show up	appear	**(f)** After two hours, he finally **showed up.**
sit down	sit	**(g)** I feel tired, so I think I'll **sit down** for a while.
stand up	stand	**(h)** In some countries, students **stand up** when the teacher enters the room.

EXERCISE 8

Fill in the blanks with a phrasal verb from the box.

stand up	sit down	break down	eat out
show up	come in	come back	grow up

What do you say when . . . ?

1. you are very late for an important date:

"Oh, I'm so sorry. Please forgive me, my car _____."

2. your friend's child runs away from home:

   "Don't worry, Elliot; I'm sure she'll _____ home very soon."

3. a teenager is sitting and an elderly man is standing on the bus:

   "_____ and give that man your seat."

4. your thirty-year-old friend is acting like a child:

   "Come on, Matt, _____. You're not a child anymore."

5. you are a car salesperson and you are trying to get people into your showroom:

   "Please _____, folks. We have many new models this year."

6. you and your roommate are hungry, but you're too tired to cook:

   "Let's _____."

7. your friend is crying about her date last night:

   Tammy: "What happened, Cheryl? Don't tell me your date didn't _____ last night?"

   Cheryl: "Oh, he did! That's why I'm crying!"

8. you are a receptionist in a very busy doctor's office and a patient is complaining about waiting so long:

   "Please _____, Mr. Brody. The doctor will be with you in a few minutes."

Put the pictures in the correct order. Then fill in each blank with a phrasal verb from the box below.

_____

_____

_____

_____

fill up	look up	break down
figure out	wake up	calm down
turn on	get out of	take out

It was a cold and rainy night. Forgetful Phil was on his way to visit his mother when his car suddenly (1) _____. He was angry and upset, but after a while, he (2) _____. It was dark, so Phil (3) _____ a flashlight. Then he took out his car manual. He tried to (4) _____, *What to do when your car breaks down in the middle of nowhere*, but he didn't find anything in the manual. Next, he (5) _____ the car and looked under the hood. He wasn't able to (6) _____ the problem. Then Phil began to understand. He asked himself, "Did I (7) _____ my tank with gas?" Near the car there was a house. He knocked on the door and shouted, but nobody answered. There were no other houses. There was no telephone. "What now??" Phil thought. Then, just as he turned around to go back to his car, another car crashed into the back of his car. Suddenly, the people in the house (8) _____ and (9) _____ the lights. Phil sat down on the ground and began to cry!

Activities

Work with a partner to create a story or dialogue about the situation below. Role-play the situation for the class. The phrasal verbs in the box will help you.

Situation: It is 11:00 P.M. You are sleeping very deeply. Suddenly, you hear some loud noise coming from the apartment downstairs. Your neighbor's stereo is very loud.

wake up	throw out	turn down	turn off
turn on	go back	calm down	call up

ACTIVITY 2

Work in a group or as a whole class. The first person begins a story. He or she says, "I woke up . . ." and completes the sentence. The second person repeats the first sentence and adds a second sentence using a phrasal verb. The third person repeats the first two sentences and then adds a third, and so on. Don't write anything down. Use your memory! Refer to the phrasal verbs from this unit.

EXAMPLE: Player #1: I woke up early.

Player #2: I woke up early, and turned off the alarm clock.

Player #3: I woke up early, turned off the alarm clock, and took off my pajamas.

ACTIVITY 3

STEP ❶ Work in a group. Put numbers 1 to 12 in a bag. Pick out a number from the bag. Read the sentence in the box that corresponds to your number and then do the action.

STEP ❷ After the group has done all the actions, write sentences about the things you did.

EXAMPLE: Mario put on Marcela's cap.

José turned off the light.

1. Put on a piece of a classmate's clothing or jewelry.	2. Turn off the light.	3. You spill a cup of hot coffee on yourself and on the floor. Clean it up.
4. Call up a friend and tell him or her you are sick.	5. Draw a picture of yourself on a piece of paper and hang it up on the wall.	6. Stand up. Put your hands on your head. Then sit down.
7. Cheer a classmate up.	8. Hand your telephone number out to all the people in the group.	9. Take something out of your pocket and throw it away.
10. Take off an article of clothing and put it on someone else.	11. Turn on something electrical (tape recorder, radio, light, etc.) and then turn it off.	12. Pretend you find a word whose meaning you don't know. Look it up in the dictionary.

ACTIVITY 4

Amy wants to buy a jacket. She goes to a store.

 STEP ❶ Listen to the conversation. Then look at the statements below. Check True or False.

	True	False
1. The store doesn't have any size ten jackets.	_____	_____
2. The jacket Amy tries on fits perfectly.	_____	_____
3. Amy thinks the jacket is too expensive.	_____	_____
4. Amy doesn't like the pink jacket she is wearing.	_____	_____
5. Amy will return to the store.	_____	_____

STEP ❷ Listen to the conversation again and complete the phrasal verbs you hear below:

take _____   put _____   throw _____   come _____   come _____

STEP ❸ Compare the phrasal verbs you found with those your partner found. Now make a dialogue on a similar topic with your partner. Use the five phrasal verbs in the dialogue and others from this unit.

STEP ❹ Role-play your dialogue in front of the class.

340   Unit 21

Comparison with Adjectives

Comparison Shopping for an Apartment

You are a college student and are looking for an apartment. You study during the day and have a part-time job at night.

FOR RENT

Studio Apartment. 200 square feet. Close to bus stop and market. Fully furnished. $500/month plus utilities.

FOR RENT

One-bedroom apartment. 900 square feet. Quiet. Lots of light. $800/month including utilities.

STEP ❶ Look at the apartment ads. Read the statements below about the studio apartment. Check (✓) Yes, No, or Maybe.

The studio apartment is		than the one bedroom apartment	YES	NO	MAYBE
	1. smaller				
	2. closer to the bus stop				
	3. farther away from the downtown area				
	4. more expensive				
	5. more spacious				
	6. noisier				
	7. safer				
	8. more convenient				
	9. sunnier				
	10. quieter				

STEP ❷ Which apartment is better? Give reasons for your choice.

I think the _____ is better because . . .

FOCUS 1 ▷▷▷▷▷▷▷▷▷▷▷▷▷▷▷▷▷▷▷▷▷▷▷▷ **FORM**

Comparative Form of Adjectives

Regular Comparatives

There are two regular comparative forms of adjectives in English.

1. For adjectives with one syllable or those ending in -*y*:

   X *is* _____ *er than* Y.

EXAMPLE	ADJECTIVE	COMPARATIVE	RULE
(a) This neighborhood is **safer than** that one.	*safe*	*safer than*	For adjectives ending in -*e*, add -*r*.
(b) The one-bedroom apartment is **bigger than** the studio.	*big*	*bigger than*	For adjectives that end in consonant-vowel-consonant, double the consonant, add -*er*.
(c) The studio is **noisier than** the one bedroom.	*noisy*	*noisier than*	For adjectives ending in -*y*, change the -*y* to *i*, add -*er*.
(d) The studio is **smaller than** the one-bedroom.	*small*	*smaller than*	For all other adjectives, add -*er*.

2. For adjectives with two or more syllables:

   X *is* (*more/less*) _____ *than* Y.

EXAMPLE	ADJECTIVE	COMPARATIVE	RULE
(e) The studio is **more economical than** the one-bedroom.	*economical*	*more economical than*	Use *more* or *less* before the adjective
(f) The studio is **less expensive than** the one-bedroom.	*expensive*	*less expensive than*	

Comparison with Adjectives   **343**

NOTES:

- Some adjectives with two syllables can take either -er or more/less. For example: quiet—quieter or more quiet.
- In formal English we say: Joe is taller than **I** (am).
  In informal English we sometimes say: Joe is taller than **me.**

Irregular Comparatives

EXAMPLES	EXPLANATIONS
(g) This neighborhood is **better than** that one.	The comparative forms of *good, bad,* and *far* are irregular.
(h) This year's winter was **worse than** last year's (winter).	*good—better*
(i) The one-bedroom is **farther** away from the bus stop **than** the studio is.	*bad—worse* *far—farther*
(j) This apartment is **much better than** that one.	Use *much* to make a comparison stronger.
(k) This apartment is **much larger than** the other one.	

EXERCISE 1

Write the comparative form of each adjective + *than* in parentheses.

EXAMPLE: A cat is (big) _bigger than_____ a mouse.

1. a. A tiger is (large) _____ a cat.

   b. It is (dangerous) _____ a cat.

2. a. Outgoing people are (nervous) _____ shy people.

   b. They are (comfortable) _____ in social situations.

3. a. The weather in Spain is (hot) _____ the weather in Sweden.

   b. The food in hot countries is (spicy) _____ the food in cold countries.

4. a. Dog lovers say cats are (intelligent) _____ dogs.

   b. Cat lovers think cats are (good) _____ dogs.

5. Today wasn't a very good day.

    a. We hope tomorrow will be (good) _____ today.

    b. We hope it will be (exciting) _____ today.

EXERCISE 2

Fill in the blanks with the comparative form of the adjective.

Jane: Kevin, I found these two apartment ads in the newspaper this morning. There's a studio and a one-bedroom. I think the one-bedroom sounds nice. What do you think?

Kevin: Well, the one-bedroom is definitely (1) (large) _____ than the studio, but the studio is (2) (cheap) _____. You know you only have a part-time job. How can you afford to pay $750 a month for rent?

Jane: I know the one-bedroom is (3) expensive _____, but I have so much furniture. The one-bedroom is (4) (big) _____ and I want to have guests visit and it will be much (5) (comfortable) _____. Besides, maybe someday I'll have a roommate, and I'll need a (6) (spacious) _____ apartment, Kevin. Right?

Kevin: Well, maybe, but you need to be realistic. The studio is in the center of town. You'll be (7) (close) _____ to transportation, stores, the library, and the college.

Jane: You're much (8) (practical) _____ than I am, Kevin. But the studio is directly over a video store, so it will be (9) (noisy) _____ than the one-bedroom. I will need peace and quiet so I can study.

Kevin: Listen—the studio is small, but it's much (10) (cozy) _____ than the one-bedroom and you'll spend much less time cleaning it!

Jane: True, but I think the one-bedroom will be much (11) (safe) _____ and (12) (good) _____ for me than the studio.

Kevin: It seems to me your mind is made up.

Jane: Yes, it is. By the way, Kevin, I'm going to see the one-bedroom later today. Can you come with me?

Kevin: Sure.

Write an advertisement for each product on the left. Compare it to the product on the right. Use the adjectives below.

EXAMPLE: _"Double Chocolate" cake tastes richer than "Chocolate Surprise."_

1. **Product:** Double Chocolate Cake Mix

   Compare with Chocolate Surprise Cake Mix.

   Adjectives: rich, creamy, delicious, sweet, thick, fattening

   _____

   _____

   _____

2. **Product:** Genie Laundry Detergent

   Compare with Bubbles Laundry Detergent

   Adjectives: strong, effective, expensive, fast-acting, gentle

   _____

   _____

   _____

3. **Product:** Save-a-Watt Space Heater

   Compare with Consumer Space Heater

   Adjectives: efficient, safe, reliable, small, economical, practical

   _____

   _____

   _____

Yoko wants to study English in the United States. She knows about an English program in Brattleboro, a small town in Vermont. She also knows about a program in Los Angeles, a big city in California. She needs to decide where she wants to live. Here is some information about the two places.

	Brattleboro, Vermont	**Los Angeles, California**
1. Rent for a one-bed apt.	$450 a month	$1,000 a month
2. Population	12,000	3 million
3. Weather	cold in winter	warm in winter
	hot in summer	hot in summer
4. Public Transportation	not good	good
5. Quality of Life		
a. the environment	clean	not so clean
b. the crime rate	low	high
c. lifestyle	relaxed	busy
d. the streets	quiet	noisy

Make comparative statements about Brattleboro and Los Angeles.

1. crime rate (low/high) _The crime rate is lower in Brattleboro than in Los Angeles._

2. (populated) _____

3. (cheap/expensive) _____

4. public transportation (good/bad) _____

5. winters (cold) _____

6. (dangerous/safe) _____

7. (clean/dirty) _____

8. (quiet/noisy) _____

9. (relaxed/busy) _____

10. In your opinion, which place is better for Yoko? Why?

_____

_____

FOCUS 2 >>>>>>>>>>>>>>>>>>>>>>>>> **FORM**

Questions with Comparative Adjectives

EXAMPLES

(a) Is the one-bedroom **more expensive than** the studio?

(b) Are studios **better than** apartments?

(c) Are studios **less practical than** one bedroom apartments?

(d) **Who** is **older,** you or your brother?

(e) **Which** is **more difficult,** English or Chinese?

(f) **Whose** apartment is **more comfortable,** yours or hers?

EXERCISE 5

Go back to the Opening Task on page 342 and ask a partner *yes/no* questions about the studio and the one-bedroom apartment.

EXAMPLE: economical

Is the studio more economical than the one-bedroom?

Yes, it is.

1. practical
2. far from the downtown area
3. small
4. cheap
5. sunny
6. comfortable
7. economical

8. roomy
9. quiet
10. convenient
11. close to the bus stop
12. pretty
13. large
14. good

EXERCISE 6

Interview your partner. Answer each other's questions.

EXAMPLE: Question: Is a theater ticket more expensive than a movie ticket?

Answer: Yes, it is. No, it isn't. OR I'm not sure.

1. people in the United States/friendly/people in other countries
2. English grammar/difficult/the grammar of your native language
3. a house/good/an apartment
4. a single person's life/exciting/a married person's life
5. reading/interesting/watching TV
6. electric heat/economical/gas heat
7. men/romantic/women
8. a Japanese watch/expensive/a Swiss watch
9. The American population/diverse/the population in your native country

EXERCISE 7

Ask a partner questions with *who*, *which*, or *whose* and the words in parentheses. Answer each other's questions.

EXAMPLE: (popular) Who is more popular, Madonna or Tina Turner?

(practical) Which is less practical, a cordless phone or a regular phone?

1. (intelligent) women or men?
2. (difficult) speaking English or writing English?
3. (hard) a man's work or a woman's work?
4. (bad) ironing or vacuuming?
5. (cheap) a public college or a private college?
6. (interesting) a taxi cab driver's job or a scientist's job?
7. (powerful) a four-cylinder car or a five-cylinder car?
8. (dangerous) a motorcycle or a car?
9. (sensitive) a man or a woman?
10. (good) Madonna's voice or Tina Turner's voice?
11. (delicious) Chinese food or Italian food?
12. (spicy) Indian food or Japanese food?
13. (American) jazz or salsa music?

FOCUS 3 ⟫⟫⟫⟫⟫⟫⟫⟫⟫⟫⟫⟫⟫⟫⟫⟫⟫ MEANING

Expressing Similarities and Differences with As . . . As

EXAMPLES	EXPLANATIONS
(a) Mark is **as tall as** Sam. **(b)** Tokyo is **as crowded as** Hong Kong.	To say two things are equal or the same, use *as* + adjective + *as*.
(c) Mark is**n't as tall as** Steve. (= Steve is taller than Mark.) **(d)** The studio is**n't as expensive as** the one-bedroom.	To say there is a difference between two things, use *not as* + adjective + *as*.

EXERCISE 8

Here is a dialogue between Tommy and his mother. Write the correct form of the comparative in the blanks. Use *-er, more than, less than,* and *as . . . as.*

Mother: Tommy, I don't want you to buy a motorcycle. Why don't you buy a car instead? A car is (1) ___more convenient than___ (convenient) a motorcycle and it's (2) _____ (practical), too.

Tommy: Maybe it's more practical, but a car isn't (3) _____ (economical) a motorcycle. I can get fifty miles to a gallon with a motorcycle! And a motorcycle's (4) _____ (cheap) a car.

Mother: Listen to me. You live in a big city. There are a lot of crazy people out there on the streets. A car is (5) _____ (safe) a motorcycle.

Tommy: Mom, I'm a good driver. I'm (6) _____ (good) you are. Besides that, it's (7) _____ (easy) to park a motorcycle in the city than it is to park a car.

Mother: Well, you're right about that. But I'm still your mother and you live in my house, so you will do as I say! When you are (8) _____ (old), you can do whatever you want.

Tommy: But all my friends are getting motorcycles, Mom. I won't look (9) _____ (cool) my friends.

Mother: I don't care, Tommy. Maybe their mothers aren't (10) _____ (nervous) I am, or (11) _____ (concerned) I am. My answer is no and that's final.

EXERCISE 9

Work with a partner and make *yes/no* questions with *as . . . as* about the countries you are from with the words below.

EXAMPLE: capital city/big

Is Quito as big as Santiago?

1. capital city/big
2. foreign cars in . . . /expensive
3. the school year in . . . /long
4. soccer in . . . /popular
5. your hometown/safe

6. teenagers in your country/ interested in rock music
7. beaches/crowded
8. foreign films/popular

FOCUS 4 ➤➤➤➤➤➤➤➤➤➤➤➤➤➤➤➤➤➤➤➤➤➤➤➤ USE

Making Polite Comparisons

EXAMPLES	EXPLANATIONS
(a) Hamid is **shorter than** Marco. **(b)** Hamid is **not as tall as** Marco.	Sentence (b) is more polite. To make a polite comparison, use *not as* + adjective + *as*.

You are "Blunt Betty." Read a statement from Column A. Your statements are very direct and a little impolite. Your partner, "Polite Polly," makes a statement with *not as* + adjective + *as* to make your statement more polite.

Column A	Column B
Blunt Betty	**Polite Polly**

1. Marco is fatter than Jonathan.   (thin)
   Marco is not as thin as Jonathan.
2. London is dirtier than Paris.   (clean)
3. Science class is more boring than math.   (interesting)
4. Your child is lazier than mine.   (energetic)
5. Your car is slower than ours.   (fast)
6. Detroit is more dangerous than Boston.   (safe)
7. This book is worse than that book.   (good)
8. Your apartment is smaller than ours.   (big)
9. Miguel's pronunciation is worse than Maria's.   (good)
10. American coffee is weaker than Turkish coffee.   (strong)
11. Your salary is lower than mine.   (high)

Use the categories below to write statements comparing yourself to a partner. Then report your information to the class.

EXAMPLE: My partner's older than I am. My partner's older than me.

I'm not as old as he is. I'm not as old as him.

	Me	My Partner
1. Age	19	24
2. Height		
3. Hair length		
4. Hair color		
5. Personality		
6. Other		

Correct the errors in the following sentences.

1. John is more tall than Mary.

2. Seoul is more safer than Los Angeles.

3. Paul is as intelligent than Robert.

4. Mary is not beautiful as Kim.

5. My test scores were more worse than Margaret's.

6. Lorraine's eyes are darker than me.

7. Jeff is more handsomer than Jack.

8. My parent's life was hard than mine.

9. Is New York exciting as Paris?

10. Is Lake Ontario cleaner that Lake Erie?

11. The Hudson River is polluted as the Volga River.

12. Mexico's capital city is more crowded than the United States.

Activities

How much do the following things cost in your country? Write the cost in United States dollars for each thing in your country. Ask a classmate the prices of the same things in his or her country. Add three items of your own. Present your comparisons to the class.

EXAMPLE: A gallon of gas is more expensive in Italy than in Mexico.

	Your Country	Your Classmate's Country
1. a gallon of gas		
2. a movie ticket		
3. bus fare		
4. a pair of jeans		
5. a cup of coffee		
6. rent for a one-bedroom apartment		
7. a newspaper		
8.		
9.		
10.		

ACTIVITY 2

Work in a group. Write six statements comparing cities, countries, or other places in the world. Make three statements that are true and three statements that are false. Read the statements to the class. The class guesses if they are true or false.

EXAMPLE: The United States is larger than the People's Republic of China. (False)

The Pacific Ocean is bigger than the Atlantic Ocean. (True)

ACTIVITY 3

STEP ❶ Look at the list of adjectives. Check *Very*, *Average*, or *Not Very* for each.

STEP ❷ Compare with a partner. Write a comparative sentence for each adjective.

STEP ❸ Then, tell the class about you and your partner.

EXAMPLE: I'm more talkative than my partner.

He's less practical than I am.

I'm as moody as he is.

	Very	Average	Not Very
1. talkative	_____	_____	_____
2. friendly	_____	_____	_____
3. shy	_____	_____	_____
4. neat	_____	_____	_____
5. practical	_____	_____	_____
6. optimistic	_____	_____	_____
7. moody	_____	_____	_____
8. lazy	_____	_____	_____
9. funny	_____	_____	_____
10. athletic	_____	_____	_____
11. jealous	_____	_____	_____
12. serious	_____	_____	_____
13. _____	_____	_____	_____
14. _____	_____	_____	_____
15. _____	_____	_____	_____

ACTIVITY 4

Work with a partner. Find a product or service you want to sell. Find a name for it. Then write a thirty-second radio commercial for the product or service. Present your commercials to the class.

ACTIVITY 5

STEP ❶ Compare life today with life fifty years ago. Read the first four sentences on the chart on the next page and then add six sentences of your own. Check Agree or Disagree under You. Then ask your partner and check Agree or Disagree.

	You		Your Partner	
	Agree	**Disagree**	**Agree**	**Disagree**
1. Life is more difficult.				
2. People are happier.				
3. Families are stronger.				
4. Children are more intelligent.				
5.				
6.				
7.				
8.				
9.				
10.				

STEP ❷ Compare your answers with your partner's. Then write six sentences that compare life today with life fifty years ago.

EXAMPLE: Today, children are more intelligent. They are more independent.

ACTIVITY 6

STEP ❶ Look at the three different apartment ads. Listen and say which apartment, A, B, or C, each person is talking about.

Ⓐ FOR RENT: Studio apartment. 200 square feet.
Close to bus stop and supermarket.
Fully furnished. $500/month plus utilities.

Ⓑ FOR RENT: One-bedroom apartment. 900 square feet.
Quiet. Lots of light. $800/month including utilities.

Ⓒ FOR RENT: Two-bedroom apartment. 1,500 square feet.
Close to subway. Quiet area. $1,000/month plus utilities.

STEP ❷ Which apartment is it? Work in a group. Each person gives two facts about one of the apartments and the others guess which apartment it is.

EXAMPLE: It's more expensive than the studio. It's closer to the subway.

Is it the _____?

Yes, it is. No, it isn't.

UNIT

23

Comparison with Adverbs

OPENING TASK

Comparing Men and Women

Check *Yes*, *No*, or *Maybe* for each question. Then talk about your answers with your classmates.

	Yes	No	Maybe
1. Do women work harder than men?			
2. Do men drive more safely than women?			
3. Do women communicate better than men?			
4. Do men dance more gracefully than women?			
5. Do women take care of children more patiently than men?			
6. Do men express their feelings more openly than women?			
7. Do women learn math more easily than men?			
8. Do men spend money more freely than women?			
9. Do women learn languages more easily than men?			
10. Do men think more clearly in emergencies than women?			

Comparative Forms of Adverbs

EXAMPLE	ADVERB/COMPARATIVE		RULE
(a) Women live **longer than** men.	*long*	*longer than*	For short adverbs, add *-er + than.*
(b) Do women drive **more safely than** men? **(c)** Do men drive **less carefully than** women?	*safely* *carefully*	*more/less safely than* *carefully than*	For adverbs with two or more syllables, use *more/less + adverb + than.*
(d) Eugene and Carol eat out much **more often than** Warren and Harriet.	*often*	*more/less often than*	With adverbs of frequency, use *more/less + adverb + than.*
(e) Do women cook **better than** men? **(f)** Do boys do **worse** in school than girls? **(g)** Can a man throw a ball **farther than** a woman?	*well* *badly* *far*	*better than* *worse than* *farther than*	With irregular adverbs, use the irregular form + *than.*

EXAMPLES	EXPLANATIONS
(h) Jason can climb higher than his brother (**can**). **(i)** She's better in school than I (**am**).	Sometimes, the auxiliary verb, for example *can, be,* or *will,* follows the subject after *than.*
(j) I type faster than my friend (**does**). **(k)** We speak Spanish better than they (**do**).	If there is no *be* or auxiliary verb, you can use *do.*
(l) I type faster than she (**does**). **(m)** I type faster than **her**.	In formal English, the subject pronoun follows *than.* In informal English, the object pronoun (*me, you, him, her, us, them*) follows *than.*

EXERCISE 1

Go back to the questions in the Opening Task on page 358 and underline the comparatives with adverbs.

EXAMPLE: Do women live <u>longer than</u> men?

EXERCISE 2

Write sentences comparing yourself with your partner. Use the verbs and adverbs in the chart.

Verb	Adverb	Comparisons
1. cry	easily	My partner cries more easily than I.
2. drive	carefully	
3. speak English	fluently	
4. exercise	regularly	
5. travel	often	
6. study	hard	
7. laugh	loudly	
8. participate in class	actively	
9. take exams	calmly	
10. read	fast	

FOCUS 2 >>>>>>>>>>>>>> FORM/MEANING

Expressing Similarities and Differences

EXAMPLES	EXPLANATIONS
(a) A woman can work **as hard as** a man. **(b)** A man can dance **as gracefully as** a woman.	To show similarities, use *as* + adverb + *as*.
(c) He does**n't** speak **as clearly as** I (do). **(d)** = I speak more clearly than he (does). **(e)** = He speaks less clearly than I (do).	To show differences, use *not as* + adverb + *as*.

EXERCISE 3

Sally Miller and Bill Benson are applying for a job as director of an art company. Decide who is better for the job. Make comparative statements about each person.

EXAMPLE: Sally works as hard as Bill.

Bill draws better than Sally./Sally doesn't draw as well as Bill.

Work Habits	Sally Miller	Bill Benson
1. works hard	X	X
2. draws well		X
3. thinks creatively	X	X
4. communicates openly	X	
5. plans carefully		X
6. works well with others	X	X
7. acts calmly in emergencies	X	
8. solves problems fairly		X
9. writes clearly	X	X
10. works fast		X

Comparison with Adverbs   **361**

Imagine you are the president of the art company. You want to compare Sally and Bill. Write some questions to ask about them.

EXAMPLE: Does Sally work as hard as Bill?

Does Bill draw better than Sally?

For each statement you read, your partner says how he or she is similar or different.

EXAMPLE: You say: I (can) cook well.

Your partner says: I can cook as well as you.

I can't cook as well as you.

I can cook better than you.

1. speak clearly
2. dance gracefully
3. sing sweetly
4. jump high
5. run far
6. add numbers quickly
7. meet new people easily
8. tell a joke well
9. study hard
10. learn English fast

Discuss these questions before you read.

1. Do you think boys and girls grow up differently?

   In what ways do they grow up differently?

2. Do you think boys and girls talk to each other differently?

3. In what ways do you think boys and girls play differently?

Now, read the following:

Boys and girls grow up in different worlds. Research studies show that boys and girls act very differently. For example, when boys and girls play, they don't play together. Some of their activities are similar, but their favorite games are different. Also, the language they use in games is different.

Boys usually play outside in large groups. The group has a leader. The leader gives orders. There are winners and losers in boys' games. Boys frequently brag about how good they are at something and argue about who is the best.

Girls, on the other hand, play in small groups or pairs. The most important thing for a girl is her best friend. Closeness is very important to girls. Girls like to sit together and talk. In their games, like jump rope, everyone gets a turn. In many of their activities, such as playing together with their dolls, there are no winners or losers. Girls don't brag about how good they are at something. They don't give orders. They usually make suggestions.

Does this text say the same things you said in your discussion? What information is the same? What information is different?

EXERCISE 7

With the information from the reading, check True or False for the statements below.

	True	False
1. Boys and girls play differently.		
2. Boys and girls usually play with each other.		
3. Girls act more aggressively than boys.		
4. Girls play more competitively than boys do.		
5. Boys brag about how good they are at something more frequently than girls.		
6. Girls talk to each other more intimately than boys do.		
7. Girls give suggestions more frequently than boys.		
8. Boys play more cooperatively than girls do.		

Write statements to compare boys and girls. Use *more/less/as . . . as*. Discuss your answers with the class.

1. build things creatively

   Boys build things more creatively than girls.

   Girls build things as creatively as boys (do).

2. score high on math tests

3. run fast

4. act aggressively

5. act independently

6. learn languages easily

7. solve problems peacefully

8. make friends quickly

9. study hard

10. express feelings openly

FOCUS 3 ➤➤➤➤➤➤➤➤➤➤➤➤➤ FORM/MEANING

Questions with *How*

EXAMPLES	EXPLANATIONS
(a) How old are you? **(b) How well** do you speak English?	An adjective (*old, tall*) or an adverb (*well, far*) is often used in a *how* question.
(c) How far is it from here to the park? It's about five blocks.	*How far* asks about distance.
(d) How long does it take to fly from New York to Beijing? It takes about twenty-four hours. **(e) How long does it take** you to prepare dinner? It takes me an hour.	*How long does it take* asks about time.

Ask a partner questions with *how*. Fill in your partner's answers on the right. Your partner asks you the same questions, and fills in your answers on the left.

EXAMPLE: 1. How far do you live from school?

2. How well can you cook?

	You	Your Partner
1. how far/live from school	5 miles	4 blocks
2. how well/cook	very well	very well
3. how fast/fall asleep at night		
4. how far/run		
5. how hard/study		
6. how fast/type		
7. how late/stay up at night		
8. how early/get up in the morning		
9. how well/know your classmates		
10. how often/speak to your best friend		

Compare yourself with your partner for each of the questions in Exercise 9.

1. I live farther away from school than my partner (does).

2. My partner cooks as well as I (do).

3. _____

4. _____

5. _____

6. _____

7. _____

8. _____

9. _____

10. _____

Fill in the chart. Say how much time it takes you to do each of the activities below. Then interview a partner. Write statements with the comparative form of adverbs.

EXAMPLE: It takes me longer to do my homework.

	You	Your Partner
1. do your homework	1 hour	45 minutes
2. get dressed in the morning		
3. get to school		
4. clean your room/apartment/house		
5. have breakfast		
6. take a shower		
7. cook dinner		
8. fall asleep at night		

Activities

ACTIVITY 1

Write sentences comparing two cities or places that you know.

EXAMPLE: The trains run more smoothly in Berlin than in New York.

1. trains/run smoothly

2. buses/run efficiently

3. people/work hard

4. taxi drivers/drive carelessly

5. traffic/move slowly

6. people/talk quickly

7. people/talk to foreigners politely

8. stores/stay open late

9. people/drive fast

10. families/take vacations frequently

Add two sentences of your own:

11. _____

12. _____

STEP ❶ Here is a list of adverbs and a list of actions. Write each adverb and each action on a card.

Adverbs	Actions
Slowly	Eat spaghetti
Sadly	Put on your clothes
Nervously	Make the bed
Angrily	Cook dinner
Fast	Type a letter
Carefully	Brush your teeth
Seriously	Comb your hair
Happily	Paint a picture
Loudly	Play tennis
Enthusiastically	Shake someone's hand
Shyly	Look at someone

STEP ❷ Mix up each group of cards separately. With a partner, take one adverb card and one action card.

STEP ❸ Both of you mime the same action and adverb. The class guesses the action and the adverb.

STEP ❹ The class compares your two performances.

   EXAMPLE: Angrily/Eat spaghetti

   Paola ate spaghetti more angrily than Maria.

Planning a Vacation

Here is a map of the southwestern United States. You and your friend want to take a three-week vacation to visit the national parks. Start from Denver, Colorado, and list the places you will visit in order. Then fill in the chart on the next page. Ask questions with *how far* and *how long does it take* to decide on the route you will take and the time you will need. Remember you will travel by car and the average speed is sixty-five miles per hour.

EXAMPLE: How far is it from Denver to the Grand Canyon?

It's 780 miles.

How long does it take to get from Denver to the Grand Canyon?

It takes about twelve hours by car.

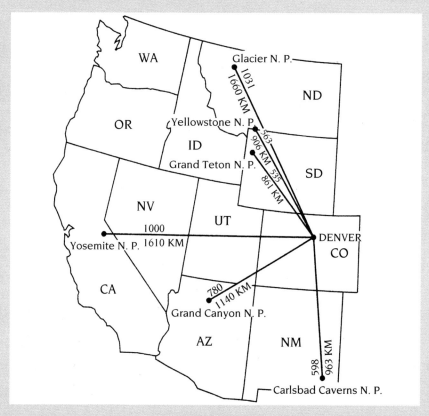

Depart from:	Denver, Colorado	Distance in miles/kilometers	Time
Stop 1			
2			
3			
4			
5			

ACTIVITY 4

Compare yourself with someone you know—a family member, a friend, your boyfriend/girlfriend, etc. Write ten sentences.

EXAMPLE: I dance better than my sister (does).

I can make friends more easily than she (does).

ACTIVITY 5

What does Richard like about London, England?

 STEP ❶ Listen to the tape and look at the list below. Check the things he thinks are good.

Richard likes . . .

1. _____ the people

2. _____ the hotel

3. _____ the buses

4. _____ the taxi drivers

5. _____ the subway

6. _____ English cooking

7. _____ the restaurants

STEP ❷ Listen again and say why Richard likes or dislikes the things.

STEP ❸ Tell the class about a place you visited. Use adverbs of comparison as much as possible.

Superlatives

General Knowledge Quiz

STEP ❶ Check the correct answer. Then compare your answers with your classmates'.

1. What is the largest ocean?
   a. Pacific   b. Atlantic   c. Indian

2. What's the most valuable painting in the world?
   a. Van Gogh's "Sunflowers"
   b. Leonardo da Vinci's "Mona Lisa"
   c. Rembrandt's "Self Portrait"

3. What's the most widely spoken language in the world?
   a. English   b. Spanish   c. Chinese

4. What's the hottest place in the world?
   a. Libya   b. Israel   c. Ethiopia

5. What's the tallest office building in the world?
   a. the Sears Tower, Chicago
   b. the World Trade Center, New York
   c. the Petronas Tower, Kuala Lumpur

6. What's the most crowded city in the world?
   a. Shanghai   b. Mexico City   c. Tokyo

7. What's the most expensive university in the United States?
   a. Harvard   b. Yale   c. M.I.T.

8. What's the wettest place in the world?
   a. Hawaii   b. India   c. Jamaica

9. What's the most nutritious fruit?
   a. banana   b. avocado   c. orange

10. What's the hardest gem?
    a. ruby   b. diamond   c. emerald

STEP ❷ Now write similar questions. Quiz your classmates.

11. _____

12. _____

13. _____

14. _____

15. _____

FOCUS I ➤➤➤➤➤➤➤➤➤➤➤➤➤➤➤➤➤➤➤ **MEANING**

Superlatives

EXAMPLES	EXPLANATIONS
(a) **The tallest** building in the world is the Petronas Tower. **(b)** **The least expensive** food on the menu is a hamburger. **(c)** Rosa writes **the most carefully** of all.	Superlatives compare one thing or person to all the others in a group.
(d) Dr. Diaz is the most respected teacher **at the school.** **(e)** M.I.T. is the most expensive university **in the United States.** **(f)** Etsuko performs the best **of all the dancers.**	Use prepositional phrases after superlatives to identify the group.

EXERCISE 1

Go back to the Opening Task on page 372. Underline all the superlative forms in the questions.

EXAMPLE: What is the <u>largest</u> ocean?

Regular and Irregular Superlative Forms

Regular Forms

EXAMPLES	ADJECTIVE/ ADVERB	SUPERLATIVE FORM	RULE
(a) The Sears Tower in Chicago is **the tallest** building in the United States.	*tall*	*the tallest*	One-syllable adjectives or adverbs: *the* + adjective/adverb + -*est*.
(b) My grandfather worked **the hardest** of his three brothers.	*hard*	*the hardest*	
(c) Jupiter is **the largest** planet.	*large*	*the largest*	Adjectives/ Adverbs ending in -*e*: add -*st*.
(d) I get up **the latest** in my family.	*late*	*the latest*	
(e) **The hottest** place in the world is Ethiopia.	*hot*	*the hottest*	One-syllable adjectives, ending in consonant-vowel-consonant: double the final consonant, add -*est*.
(f) **The easiest** subject for me is geography.	*easy*	*the easiest*	Two-syllable adjectives/adverbs ending in -*y*: change -*y* to -*i*: add -*est*.
(g) She arrived **the earliest.**	*early*	*the earliest*	
(h) **The most nutritious** fruit is the avocado.	*nutritious*	*the most nutritious*	Adjectives/ adverbs with two or more syllables: use *the* + *most*/ *least*.
(i) **The least expensive** food on the menu is a hamburger.	*expensive*	*the least expensive*	
(j) Of all his friends, he drives **the most carefully.**	*carefully*	*the most carefully*	
(k) She danced **the least gracefully** of all the students.	*gracefully*	*the least gracefully*	

Irregular Forms

EXAMPLES	ADJECTIVE	ADVERB	SUPERLATIVE
(l) That college has **the best** professors.	good	well	the best
(m) That was **the worst** movie I saw last year.	bad	badly	the worst
(n) He ran **the farthest.**	far	far	the farthest

EXERCISE 2

Here are some interesting facts from the *Guinness Book of World Records*. Write the superlative form of the adjective/adverb in parentheses in the blanks.

EXAMPLE: (cold) Antarctica is ___the coldest___ place on earth.

1. _____ (large) cucumber weighed sixty-six pounds.

2. _____ (popular) tourist attraction in the United States is Disney-world in Florida.

3. _____ (successful) pop group of all time is the Beatles.

4. _____ (heavy) baby at birth was a boy of twenty-two pounds eight ounces. He was born in Italy in 1955.

5. _____ (fat) person was a man in New York City. He weighed almost 1,200 pounds.

6. _____ (prolific) painter was Pablo Picasso. He produced about 13,500 paintings; 100,00 prints; 34,000 book illustrations; and 300 sculptures.

7. _____ (long) attack of hiccups lasted sixty-seven years.

8. _____ (big) omelet was made of 54,763 eggs with 531 pounds of cheese in Las Vegas, Nevada in 1986.

9. _____ (hot) city in the United States is Key West, Florida.

10. Mexico City is now the world's _____ (fast) growing city.

Fill in the name of a student in your class and the superlative form of each adverb.

Name   **Superlative**

1. __Juan__ does the homework the __most carefully__ (carefully).

2. _____ speaks English _____ (fluently).

3. _____ arrives in class _____ (early).

4. _____ guesses new words _____ (fast).

5. _____ raises his/her hand _____ (often).

6. _____ understands English _____ (well).

7. _____ communicates in English _____ (effectively).

8. _____ participates in class _____ (actively).

Add two statements of your own.

9. _____

10. _____

Information Gap. Work with a partner. One person looks at chart A, and the other person looks at Chart B on page E-16. Ask your partner questions to find out the missing information in your chart. Write the answers in the chart.

> **EXAMPLE:** **Student A:** What is the longest river in North America?
>
> **Student B:** The Mississippi.

CHART A

	North America	Central and South America	Asia	Europe	Africa	The World
long river		The Amazon		The Volga		The Nile
large country	Canada		The People's Republic of China		Sudan	
populated country		Brazil		Germany		The People's Republic of China
high mountain	Mt. McKinley		Mt. Everest		Mt. Kilimanjaro	
small country		Grenada		Vatican City		Vatican City

Play this Jeopardy game in two teams. Team 1 chooses a category and a dollar amount. One person in the class reads the questions under the CATEGORIES column on page 379 aloud. Team 1 has one minute to answer (choose an answer from the Answer Box). If the answer is correct, they "win" the money. If the answer is not correct, Team 2 answers the question to win the money. The team with the most money at the end wins.

EXAMPLE: Team 1: "Animals" for $20.

Reader: What's the most dangerous animal?

Team 1: Mosquitoes (can give you malaria)

$$$	Planets	Animals	Other
$10			
$20			
$30			
$40			
$50			

ANSWER BOX (Choose the answers to the questions from this box.)

Planets	Animals	Other
Pluto	mosquitoes	the Supreme Court
Mercury	the blue whale	the Sahara
Venus	giraffe	the winter solstice
Jupiter	cheetah	(first day of winter)
Mars	race horse	diamond
		Iraq

CATEGORIES

Planets

$10   What is the largest planet in the solar system?
$20   What is the fastest planet?
$30   What is the hottest planet?
$40   What is the farthest planet from the sun?
$50   What is the closest planet to the Earth?

Animals

$10   What is the tallest animal?
$20   What is the most dangerous animal?
$30   What is the fastest land animal?
$40   What is the most valuable animal?
$50   What is the largest and heaviest animal?

Other

$10   What is the hardest gem?
$20   What is the largest desert in the world?
$30   What is the highest court in the United States?
$40   What is the oldest country in the world?
$50   What is the shortest day of the year?

One Of The + Superlative + Plural Noun

EXAMPLES	EXPLANATION
(a) Bach was **one of the greatest composers** of all time.	*One of the* + superlative + plural noun is common with the superlative form. Example (a) means that there are several composers we think of as the greatest composers of all time. Bach is one of them.
(b) He is **one of the least popular** students in the school.	

EXERCISE 6

Fill in the blanks with *one of the* + superlative + plural noun. Use the words in parentheses.

That's <u>one of the most expensive cars</u> _____ you can buy.

1. (expensive car)

In my opinion, wrestling is _____

2. you can play. (exciting sport)

That was _____ of my life.

3. (proud moment)

---

4. That was _____ in the city.
(expensive hotel)

5. Drinking and driving is _____ you
can do. (bad thing)

6. The chocolate ice cream is _____
on the menu. (good dessert)

7. Dr Jones is _____ in the hospital.
(fine doctor)

8. Louis Armstrong was _____ in
America. (great jazz musicians)

9. This is _____ in the museum.
(beautiful sculpture)

10. Sergei Grinkov, the Olympic ice skater, died in 1995.
He was twenty-nine years old. This was
_____ in the history of ice
skating. (tragic death)

Make sentences with *one of the* + superlative + plural noun. Compare your answers with your classmates'.

EXAMPLE: 1. Prague is one of the most beautiful cities in the world.

1. a beautiful city in the world
2. an interesting place (in the city you are living in)
3. a good restaurant (in the city you are in)
4. a famous leader in the world today
5. a dangerous disease of our time
6. a serious problem in the world
7. a popular food (in the country you come from)
8. a funny show on television

Activities
ACTIVITY 1

Work in a group. Write five questions in the superlative form like the ones in the Opening Task on page 372. Then ask the class the questions.

EXAMPLES: What's the most expensive car in the world?

What is the largest island?

ACTIVITY 2

Write ten questions to ask another student in the class about his or her country or a country he or she knows. Use the superlative form of the words below or add your own.

EXAMPLES: What's the most crowded city in . . . ?

What's the most popular sport in your country?

What's the most unusual food in your city?

crowded city	popular sport	popular food
polluted city	dangerous sport	unusual food
beautiful city	expensive sport	cheap food
important holiday	hot month	important monument
cold month		

ACTIVITY 3

In groups, discuss the following statements. Say if you agree or disagree and why.

1. Money is the most important thing in life.

2. AIDS is the worst disease in the world today.

3. English is the most difficult language to learn.

4. Baseball is the most boring sport.

5. Democracy is the best form of government.

ACTIVITY 4

Interview a partner about his or her life experience. Use the adjectives below to write questions with superlatives. Tell the class about the most interesting things you learned about your partner.

EXAMPLE: What was the best experience you had this year?

What was the most embarrassing moment in your life?

Adjectives to describe experiences:

unusual	sad	exciting
embarrassing	interesting	frightening
happy	dangerous	beautiful
funny	good	bad

ACTIVITY 5

Write a paragraph on one of the topics below:

a. The most embarrassing moment in my life.

b. The most frightening moment in my life.

c. The funniest moment in my life.

STEP ❶ Listen to the quiz show. Circle the letter of the correct answer.

Quiz Choices:

1. a. North America   b. Asia   c. Africa

2. a. the elephant   b. the turtle   c. the bear

3. a. New York   b. Los Angeles   c. Chicago

4. a. Chinese   b. French   c. English

5. a. North America   b. Asia   c. Antarctica

6. a. The United States   b. China   c. Canada

7. a. Tokyo   b. Paris   c. Hong Kong

8. a. The Himalayas   b. The Andes   c. The Rockies

9. a. Spain   b. The United States   c. Italy

10. a. Islam/Muslim   b. Christian   c. Hindu

STEP ❷ Discuss your answers with your classmates.

UNIT

25

Factual Conditionals

If

That's Life

If you study hard, you get good grades.

Find a match for each statement on the left. Write the letter in the blank next to the number.

1. If you spend more money than you earn, _____
2. If you play with fire, _____
3. If you speak two languages, _____
4. If you don't wash your hands, _____
5. If you care about your health, _____
6. If you eat too much, _____

7. If you respect people, _____
8. If you read a lot, _____
9. If you work hard, _____
10. If you speak well, _____
11. If you study hard, _____

a. you get sick more often.

b. you don't smoke.

c. people respect you.

d. you have money problems.

e. you succeed.

f. you can communicate with more people.

g. people listen to you.

h. you get good grades.

i. you gain weight.

j. you get burned.

k. you learn a lot.

Now make two similar true statements of your own.

12. _____

13. _____

FOCUS 1 >>>>>>>>>>>>>>>>> **FORM/MEANING**

Expressing Facts

Factual conditionals tell about things that are always true and never change.

EXAMPLES		EXPLANATIONS
Clause 1 **(If Clause)**	**Clause 2** **(Main Clause)**	
(a) If you heat water to 212° (degrees) Fahrenheit,	it boils.	Use the simple present in both clauses.
(b) If you water a plant,	it grows.	
(c) When(ever) you mix black and white,	you get gray.	You can use *when* or *whenever* in place of *if*.

EXERCISE 1

Test your knowledge. Circle the correct clause on the right. Discuss your answers with a partner.

1. If you put oil and water together,
   a. the oil stays on top.
   b. they mix.

2. If the temperature outside drops below 32° (degrees) Fahrenheit,
   a. water freezes.
   b. ice melts.

3. If you stay in the sun a lot,
   a. your skin stays young and smooth.
   b. your skin looks old.

4. If you smoke,
   a. you have health problems.
   b. you stay in good health.

5. If you don't refrigerate milk,
   a. it stays fresh.
   b. it goes bad.

6. If you fly west,
   a. you gain time.
   b. you lose time.

7. If you fly east,
   a. you gain time.
   b. you lose time.

8. If your body temperature is 103° (degrees) Fahrenheit,
   a. you are well.
   b. you are sick.

Think of the definitions of the words in italics. Find the definitions on the right to complete each statement. Say your statements aloud.

1. If you live in a *democracy*, you
2. If you're *patient*, you don't
3. If you're a *night owl*, you
4. If you're a *teenager*, you
5. If you're a *member of the faculty*, you
6. If you're a *pediatrician*, you
7. If you're a *blue-collar worker*, you may
8. If you're *broke*, you

a. want to be independent.
b. go to bed late.
c. teach in a school or college.
d. lose your temper.
e. work in a factory.
f. don't have any money.
g. treat sick children.
h. vote.

FOCUS 2 ➤➤➤➤➤➤➤➤➤➤➤➤➤➤➤➤➤➤➤ **MEANING**

Expressing Habitual Relationships

EXAMPLES		EXPLANATIONS
Clause 1 **(If Clause)**	**Clause 2** **(Main Clause)**	
(a) If I **cook,**	my husband **washes** the dishes.	Factual conditionals express present or past habits. Use the same tense in both clauses.
(b) If I **lied,**	my mother **punished** me.	
(c) When(ever) it **snowed,**	we **stayed** home from school.	You can use *when* or *whenever* in place of *if*.

Make sentences with *if, when,* or *whenever* with the words below. Say your sentences aloud and compare your answers.

EXAMPLE: I drive to school/take

If I drive to school, it takes about twenty minutes.

1. I drive to school/take
2. I take the bus to school/take
3. you have elderly parents/worry
4. you live with a roommate/share
5. you buy things on credit/pay
6. you take a vacation every year/feel
7. you never take a vacation/feel
8. you don't own a car/use
9. someone sneezes/say
10. I don't want to cook/eat

In some cultures, people say, "If you go out with wet hair, you get sick." We call these kinds of statements "old wives' tales." They are not always true, but people believe them and repeat them. Read the following "old wives' tales" and decide in your group if they are true or not.

1. If you go out with wet hair, you catch a cold.
2. If your ears are ringing, someone is talking about you.
3. If you eat chicken soup, your cold gets better.
4. If you hold your breath, your hiccups go away.
5. If you eat spinach, you get big and strong.

Now add a few old wives' tales from your country and tell your group about them.

Complete the *if* clauses with a statement of your own.

EXAMPLE: If I feel very tired when I come home, <u>I take a nap for ten minutes</u> .

1. If I don't get my regular sleep, _____ .

2. If I get angry, _____ .

3. If I get a headache, _____ .

4. If I am late, _____ .

5. If I gain weight, _____ .

6. If I fail an exam, _____ .

7. If I have money to spend, _____ .

8. If I can't sleep at night, _____ .

9. If I eat too much, _____ .

10. If I get very worried, _____ .

Work with a partner. Ask each other questions about your childhood.

EXAMPLE: When you were a child, what happened if/when you . . . (and told a lie)

If I told a lie, my mother yelled at me.

1. told a lie

2. got sick

3. disobeyed your parents

4. did well in school

5. got a bad grade on your report card

6. came home very late

7. had a serious personal problem

8. fought with your brother or sister

Order of Clauses in Factual Conditionals

EXAMPLES	EXPLANATIONS
(a) If you study hard, you get good grades.	The *if* clause is usually first.
(b) How do you get an A in this class? You get an A **if you do all the work.**	When the *if* clause contains new information, the *if* clause can be second. When it is second, there is no comma between the two clauses.
(c) How do you get the color gray? You get gray **when(ever) you mix black and white.**	With *when* or *whenever*, you can also change the order of the clauses.

EXERCISE 7

Answer the questions below.

EXAMPLE: When do you feel nervous?

　　　　　I feel nervous if I have many things to do and little time.

　　　　　I feel nervous whenever I have a test.

1. When do you feel nervous?
2. When do you get a headache?
3. How do you catch a cold?
4. When do you have trouble sleeping?
5. When did your parents punish you?
6. When were your parents pleased with you?
7. When do you listen to music?
8. When do you get angry?
9. When do you feel happy?
10. How do you know if you're in love?

Activities

Psychologists say there are two personality types: A and B. "Type A" people worry, get nervous, and are under stress all the time. "Type B" people are calm and try to enjoy life.

STEP ❶ Which personality type are you? Complete the statements.

1. Whenever there is a change in my life, I . . .
2. If I have a test, I . . .
3. When I get stuck in traffic, I . . .
4. When I enter a room with people I don't know, I . . .
5. When another driver on the road makes a mistake, I . . .
6. If a friend hurts my feelings, I . . .
7. If I don't hear from my family and friends, I . . .
8. When I have a lot of things to do in one day, I . . .
9. When I don't succeed at something, I . . .
10. When someone criticizes me, I . . .

STEP ❷ Discuss your results in your group. Decide which students in the group are "Type A" personalities and which are "Type B." Explain why. Fill in the chart below.

Name	Type A Personality	Type B Personality
Stefan. If he has a test, he worries a lot.	✔	

Do you have any special problems or unusual habits? Write down any habits you have. Share your statements with your group. Try to find the person with the most unusual habits.

EXAMPLES: If I eat chocolate, I get a headache.

If I drink more than three cups of coffee a day, I can't sleep.

ACTIVITY 3

Think about your childhood. Make five sentences with *if* clauses about past habits in your childhood.

EXAMPLES: If my sister hit me, I hit her back.

If my mother yelled at me, I felt miserable.

ACTIVITY 4

STEP ❶ Compare habits in different countries. Write the name of a country and complete each *if/when(ever)* clause.

EXAMPLE: In the United States, when you have dinner in a restaurant, you leave a tip.

Country	If/When(ever) Clause 1	Clause 2
United States	you have dinner in a restaurant	Tip
	someone gives you a compliment	
	someone gives you a gift	
	you greet an old friend	
	a baby is born	
	someone sneezes	
	someone invites you to dinner	
	you want to refuse someone's invitation	

STEP ❷ Add two more habits to the list and make sentences about them.

Marcia and Eduardo are having a conversation about what they do if they can't sleep.

 STEP ❶ Listen to the conversation and then check the box if the statements below are true or false.

Read the statements. Check True or False.

	True	False
1. If Eduardo can't sleep, he takes a sleeping pill.		
2. If Marcia can't sleep, she drinks a glass of milk.		
3. If Eduardo can't sleep, he reads a boring book.		
4. If Eduardo drinks milk in the evening, he feels sick.		
5. If Marcia reads a boring book, she falls asleep.		

STEP ❷ What conditions make people have problems with sleep? Tell the class.

STEP ❸ Write three things you do if you can't sleep. Then share your ideas with your classmates. What is the thing people do most?

Appendices

FORMING VERB TENSES

Appendix 1A   *Be*: Present Tense

I	am	
He She It	is	from Japan.
We You They	are	
There	is	a student from Japan.
There	are	students from all over the world in this class.

Appendix 1B   *Be*: Past Tense

I He She It	was	happy.
We You They	were	
There	was	a party yesterday.
There	were	a lot of people there.

Appendix 1C   Simple Present

I You We They	work.
He She It	works.

Appendix 1D   Present Progressive

I	am	
He She It	is	working.
We You They	are	

Appendix 1E   Simple Past

I He She It We You They	worked	yesterday.

Appendix 1F   Future Tense with *Will*

I He She It We You They	will work	tomorrow.

Appendix 1G Future Tense with *Be Going To*

I	am	
He She It	is	going to work in a few minutes.
We You They	are	

Appendix 1H *Can/Might/May*

I He She It We You They	can might may	work.

Appendix 1I *Be Able To*

I	am	
He She It	is	able to dance.
We You They	are	

Appendix 2A   Plural Nouns

Nouns	Singular	Plural
Regular	book	books
	table	tables
Ends in vowel + *y*	toy	toys
Ends in vowel + *o*	radio	radios
Ends in consonant + *o*	potato	potatoes
	tomato	tomatoes
Ends in -*y*	city	cities
Ends in *f, fe*	thief	thieves
	wife	wives
(Except)	chief	chiefs
	chef	chefs
Ends in *ss, ch, sh, x,* and *z*	class	classes
	sandwich	sandwiches
	dish	dishes
	box	boxes
Irregular plural nouns	man	men
	woman	women
	child	children
	person	people
	foot	feet
	tooth	teeth
	mouse	mice
Plurals that stay the same	sheep	sheep
	deer	deer
	fish	fish
No singular form		scissors
		pants
		shorts
		pajamas
		glasses
		clothes

Appendix 2B   Simple Present: Third Person Singular

Rule	Example
1. Add -s to form the third person singular of most verbs.	My brother **sleeps** 8 hours a night.
2. Add -es to verbs ending in sh, ch, x, z, or ss.	She **watches** television every evening.
3. When the verb ends in a consonant + y, change the y to i and add -es.	He **hurries** to class every morning.
4. When the verb ends in a vowel + y, do not change the y. Add -s.	My sister **plays** the violin.
5. Irregular Forms: have go do	He **has** a good job. He **goes** to work every day. He **does** the laundry.

Appendix 2C   Present Progressive

Rule	Base	-ing
1. Add -ing to the base form of the verb.	talk study do agree	talking studying doing agreeing
2. If the verb ends in a single -e, drop the -e and add -ing.	drive	driving
3. If a one-syllable verb ends in a consonant, a vowel, and a consonant (c-v-c), double the last consonant and add -ing.	(c-v-c) s i t r u n	 sitting running
Do not double the consonant, if the verb ends in w, x, or y.	s h o w f i x p l a y	showing fixing playing
4. In two-syllable verbs that end in a consonant, a vowel, and a consonant (c-v-c), double the last consonant only if the last syllable is stressed.	beGIN LISten	beginning listening
5. If the verb ends in -ie, drop the -ie, add -y and -ing.	lie die	lying dying

Appendix 2D   Simple Past of Regular Verbs

1. Add -ed to most regular verbs.	start	started
2. If the verb ends in an -e, add -d.	like	liked
3. If the verb ends in a consonant + y, change the y to i and add -ed.	study	studied
4. If the verb ends in a vowel + y, don't change the y to i. Add -ed.	enjoy play	enjoyed played
5. If a one-syllable verb ends in a consonant, a vowel, and a consonant (c-v-c), double the last consonant and add -ed.	stop	stopped
Do not double the last consonant if it is w, x, or y.	show fix play	showed fixed played
6. If a two-syllable word ends in a consonant, a vowel, and a consonant (c-v-c), double the last consonant if the stress is on the last syllable.	ocCUR LISten	occurred listened

APPENDIX 3   PRONUNCIATION RULES

Appendix 3A   Regular Plural Nouns

/s/	/z/		/ɪz/
After voiceless sounds (f, k, p, t, th)	After voiced sounds (b, d, g, l, m, n, r, v, ng, and vowel sounds)		After s, z, sh, ch, ge/dge sounds. (This adds another syllable to the word.)
cuffs	jobs	pens	classes
books	beds	cars	exercises
maps	rugs	leaves	dishes
pots	schools	rings	sandwiches
months	rooms	days	colleges

Appendix 3B   Simple Present Tense: Third Person Singular

/s/	/z/	/ɪz/
After voiceless sounds (p, t, f, k)	After voiced final sounds (b, d, v, g, l, m, n, r, ng)	Verbs ending in sh, ch, x, z, ss. (This adds another syllable to the word.)
He sleeps. She works.	She drives a car. He prepares dinner.	He teaches English She rushes to class.

Appendix 3C   Simple Past Tense of Regular Verbs

/t/	/d/	/ɪd/
After voiceless sounds (s, k, p, f, sh, ch, x)	After voiced final sounds (b, g, l, m, n, r, v, x)	Verbs ending in t or d. (This adds another syllable to the word.)
He kissed her once. She asked a question.	We learned a song. They waved goodbye.	She painted a picture. The plane landed safely.

APPENDIX 4   TIME EXPRESSIONS

Appendix 4A   Simple Present

Adverbs of Frequency	Frequency Expressions		Time Expressions	
always	every	morning	in	1997
often		afternoon		October
frequently		night		the fall
usually		summer	on	Monday
sometimes		winter		Sundays
seldom		spring		January 1st
rarely		fall		the weekend
never		day		
		week	at	6:00
		year		noon
	all the time			night
	once a week			midnight
	twice a month			
	3 times a year			
	once in a while			

Appendix 4B   Present Progressive

now	this semester
right now	this evening
at the moment	this week
today	this year
these days	

Appendix 4C   Past

yesterday	last	ago	in/on/at
yesterday { morning, afternoon, evening	last { night, week, month, year, summer	{ an hour, two days, 6 months, a year } ago	in { 1988, June, the evening
			on { Sunday, December 1, weekends
			at { 6:00, night, midnight

Appendix 4D   Future

this	next	tomorrow	other	in/on/at
this { morning, afternoon, evening	next { week, month, year, Sunday, weekend, summer	tomorrow { morning, afternoon, evening, night	soon, later, a week from today, tonight, for 3 days, until 3:00	in { 15 minutes, a few days, 2 weeks, March, 2005
				on { Tuesday, May 21
				at { 4:00, midnight

APPENDIX 5   PRONOUNS

Appendix 5A   Subject Pronouns

Subject Pronouns		
I	am	
You	are	
He		
She	is	
It		happy.
We		
You	are	
They		

Appendix 5B   Object Pronouns

		Object Pronouns
		me.
		you
		him.
		her.
She	loves	it.
		us.
		you.
		them.

Appendix 5C   Demonstrative Pronouns

This That	is a list of subject pronouns.
These Those	are object pronouns.

Appendix 5D   Possessive Pronouns

This book is	mine.
	his.
	hers.
	*
	ours.
	yours.
	theirs.

*"It" does not have a possessive pronoun.

Appendix 5E   Reflexive Pronouns

I		myself.
		yourself.
We	love	ourselves.
You		yourselves.
They		themselves.
He		himself.
She	loves	herself.
It		itself.

Appendix 5F   Reciprocal Pronoun

Friends help each other.

Appendix 6A   Possessive Nouns

Bob's Thomas' Thomas's The teacher's The students' The children's Bob and Andrea's	house is big.

Appendix 6B   Possessive Determiners

My Your His Her Its Our Your Their	house is big.

Appendix 6C   Possessive Pronouns

The house is	mine. your. his. hers. * ours. yours theirs.

*"It" does not have a possessive pronoun.

Appendix 7A   Comparative Form (to compare two people, places, or things)

Betsy	is	older bigger busier later more punctual less talkative	than	Judy.
	plays the violin	faster more beautifully better		

Appendix 7B   Superlative Form (to compare one thing or person to all the others in a group)

Betsy	is	the oldest the biggest the busiest the most practical the least punctual	of all her sisters.
	plays the violin	the fastest the most beautifully the best	

Appendix 7C   A/As (to say that two people, places, or things are the same)

Betsy	is	as	old big busy practical punctual	as	Judy.
	plays the violin		fast beautifully well		

PAST-TENSE FORMS OF

COMMON IRREGULAR VERBS

Simple Form	Past-Tense Form	Past Participle	Simple Form	Past-Tense Form	Past Participle
be	was	were	leave	left	left
become	became	became	lend	lent	lent
begin	began	begun	let	let	let
bend	bent	bent	lose	lost	lost
bite	bit	bit	make	made	made
blow	blew	blown	meet	met	met
break	broke	broken	pay	paid	[aid
bring	brought	brought	put	put	put
build	built	built	quit	quit	quit
buy	bought	bought	read	read*	read
catch	caught	caught	ride	rode	ridden
choose	chose	chosen	ring	rang	rung
come	came	come	run	ran	run
cost	cost	cost	say	said	said
cut	cut	cut	see	saw	seen
dig	dug	dug	sell	sold	sold
do	did	done	send	sent	sent
draw	drew	drown	shake	shook	shaken
drink	drank	drunk	shoot	shot	shot
drive	drove	driven	shut	shut	shut
eat	ate	eaten	sing	sang	sung
fall	fell	fallen	sit	sat	sat
feed	fed	fed	sleep	slept	slept
feel	felt	felt	speak	spoke	spoken
fight	fought	fought	spend	spent	spent
find	found	found	stand	stood	stood
fly	flew	flown	steal	stole	stolen
forget	forgot	forgotten	swim	swam	swum
get	got	gotten	take	took	taken
give	gave	given	teach	taught	taught
go	went	gone	tear	tore	torn
grow	grew	grown	tell	told	told
hang	hung	hung	think	thought	thought
have	had	had	throw	threw	thrown
hear	heard	heard	understand	understood	understood
hide	hid	hidden	wake	woke	woken
hit	hit	hit	wear	wore	worn
hold	held	held	win	won	won
hurt	hurt	hurt	write	wrote	written
keep	kept	kept			
know	knew	known			
lead	led	led			

* Pronounce the base form: /rid/; pronounce the past-tense form: rɛd.

Answer Key
(for puzzles and problems only)

Answers to Opening Task (page 257)

1. Martin Luther King, Jr. wasn't African; he was African-American. He was a civil rights leader.
2. The Beatles were British. They weren't hairdressers; they were musicians.
3. Marilyn Monroe was American. She was an actress.
4. Indira Gandhi was Indian. She wasn't a rock singer; she was the Prime Minister of India.
5. Pierre and Marie Curie were French. They weren't fashion designers; they were scientists.
6. Mao was Chinese. He was a political leader in the People's Republic of China.
7. Jacqueline Kennedy Onassis wasn't Greek; she was American. She was the wife of John F. Kennedy, president of the United States, and later of Aristotle Onassis, who was a Greek millionaire.
8. George Washington, Thomas Jefferson, Abraham Lincoln and Theodore Roosevelt weren't Canadian, they were American. They were presidents. Their heads are on Mt. Rushmore in South Dakota.

Answer to Activity 1 (page 301)

The prisoner stood on a block of ice with the rope around his neck. When the ice melted, his feet didn't touch the ground, so he hanged himself.

Exercises
(second parts)

Exercise 6 (page 21)

Chart B

Name: Age:	Cindy 22	Shelley 27	Gloria 30
1. Height			
tall			
average height		✔	
short			
2. Weight			
thin	✔		
average weight			
overweight			✔
3. Personality			
shy		✔	
friendly			
quiet		✔	
talkative			
neat		✔	✔
messy			
funny			
serious		✔	✔
nervous			
calm		✔	

Answers to Exercise 6 (page 36)

MAP B

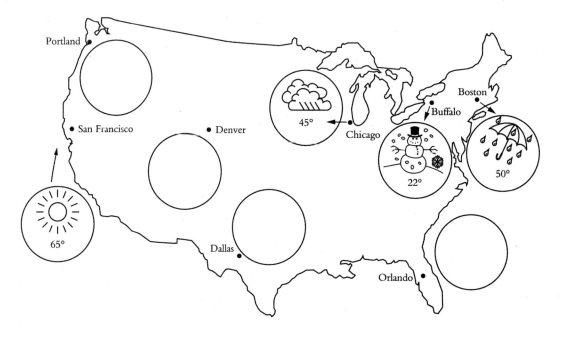

Exercise 10 (page 42)

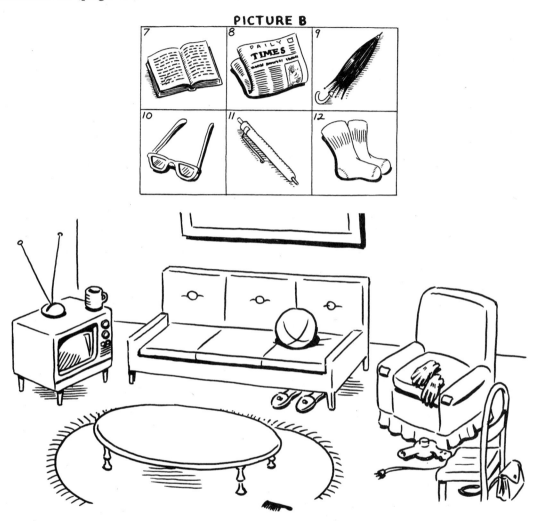

Exercise 2 (page 132)

Student B:

	Nahal		Sang-Woo	
	Yes	**No**	**Yes**	**No**
1. like to learn English			✔	
2. want to meet English-speaking people	✔			
3. feel nervous when speaking English			✔	
4. like to work in groups	✔			
5. need grammar rules to learn English			✔	
6. learn by speaking and listening to English	✔			
7. learn by reading and writing English			✔	
8. learn slowly, step by step		✔		
9. try new ways of learning				✔

Conclusion to Exercise 12 (page 286)

Answers to Exercise 15 (page 289)

Text B

1. Doina grew up in _____ (where).

2. She married a government official.

3. She had _____ in 1976 (what).

4. Doina was unhappy _____ (why).

5. She thought of ways to escape.

6. She taught her daughter _____ (what).

7. On October 9, 1988, she and her daughter swam across the Danube River to Serbia.

8. _____ caught them (who).

9. Doina and her daughter went to jail.

10. They tried to escape _____ (when).

11. Finally, they left Romania on foot in the middle of the night.

12. They flew to _____ in 1989 (where).

13. Doina went to school to learn English.

14. She wrote _____ (what) in her ESL class.

Activity 6 (page 292)

Only the Host looks at this game board.

GAME BOARD

$$$	Category 1 PEOPLE	Category 2 WH-QUESTIONS	Category 3 YES/NO QUESTIONS
$10	Ms. Ditto.	A VCR.	Yes, she did.
$20	Harry.	On the first day of classes.	Yes, he did.
$30	The Director.	In the language lab.	No, he didn't.
$40	Professor Brown.	Because he needed to pay for the ESL classes again this semester.	No, he didn't
$50	The students.	She noticed grammar mistakes in the note.	Yes, they did.

Exercise 4 (page 377)

CHART B

	North America	South America	Asia	Europe	Africa	The World
long river	The Mississippi		The Yangtze		The Nile	
large country		Brazil		France		The People's Republic of China
populated country	The United States		The People's Republic of China		Nigeria	
high mountain		Mt. Aconcagua		Mt. Elbrus		Mt. Everest
small country	Bermuda		Macao		the Seychelles	

Credits

Text Credits

Unit 8, Exercise 4: Cartoon by Sergio Aragones, from *Mad Magazine*. Reprinted by permission of Sergio Aragones.

Unit 18, Exercise 3: Cartoon by Sergio Aragones, from *Mad Magazine*. Reprinted by permission of Sergio Aragones.

Unit 18, Exercise 12, and Activity 2: Cartoon by Sergio Aragones, from *Mad Magazine*. Reprinted by permission of Sergio Aragones.

Photo Credits

Page 1: © Rob Crandall, The Image Works. Page 5: seated couple, © D. Young-Wolf, Photo Edit; student, © Michelle Bridwell, Photo Edit. Page 6: Argentinian students, © Michael Dwyer, Stock Boston; Nigerian men, © Beryl Goldberg. Page 29: Pyramids, The Bettmann Archive; Himalayan Mountains, Mark Antman, The Image Works; Fourth of July fireworks, © Archive Photos/Lambert; the Kremlin, © Bill Aaron, Photo Edit. Page 91: © Dana White, Photo Edit. Page 257: all photos, © Archive Photos. Page 258: all photos, © Archive Photos. Page 266: The Image Works. Page 303: © Archive Photos/Curry. Page 392: © Reuters/Jack Naegelen Archive Photos.

Index